P9-DXM-610

D0037873

DISCARD

SIX CONTEMPORARY BRITISH NOVELISTS

The six essays in this volume first appeared separately in the Columbia Essays on Modern Writers series published by Columbia University Press. This series of critical studies includes English, Continental, and other writers whose works are of contemporary artistic and intellectual significance. The editor of the series when these essays were written was William York Tindall. The current editor is George Stade. Advisory editors are Jacques Barzun, W. T. H. Jackson, and Joseph A. Mazzeo. The late Justin O'Brien was also an advisory editor. For this edition, the essays and the bibliographies have been updated.

SIX
CONTEMPORARY
BRITISH NOVELISTS

Edited with an Introduction

by

George Stade

Columbia University Press · New York

Library of Congress Cataloging in Publication Data
Main entry under title:

Six contemporary British novelists.

"First published as separate pamphlets for the series
of Columbia essays on modern writers."
Includes bibliographies.
CONTENTS: Lodge, D. Graham Greene.—Davis, R. G.
C. P. Snow.—Dodson, D. B. Malcolm Lowry. [etc.]
1. English fiction—20th century—History and
criticism—Addresses, essays, lectures.   I. Stade,
George.   II. Columbia essays on modern writers.
PR883.S53   823'.03   76-3598
ISBN 0-231-04054-7
Columbia University Press
New York   Guildford, Surrey
Copyright © 1964, 1965, 1966, 1968, 1970, 1976 Columbia
University Press
Printed in the United States of America

10 9 8 7 6 5 4 3

Contents

Introduction	GEORGE STADE	vii
Graham Greene	DAVID LODGE	1
C. P. Snow	ROBERT GORHAM DAVIS	57
Malcolm Lowry	DANIEL B. DODSON	115
William Golding	SAMUEL HYNES	165
Lawrence Durrell	JOHN UNTERECKER	219
Iris Murdoch	RUBIN RABINOVITZ	271
Selected Bibliographies		333
The Contributors		349
Index		351

Acknowledgments

Grateful acknowledgment is made to the following individuals and publishers: to William Heinemann Ltd., the Viking Press, Inc., and Graham Greene for permission to quote briefly from several of Mr. Greene's books; to City Lights Books for permission to reprint "Epitaph" from Malcolm Lowry's *Selected Poems* (copyright © 1962 by Margerie Lowry); to Faber & Faber, Coward-McCann, Harcourt, Brace & World, and William Golding for permission to quote from the novels of Mr. Golding; to Professor G. P. Wells, F.R.S., for permission to quote from H. G. Wells's *The Outline of History* (copyright 1920 by H. G. Wells); to William Golding and Frank Kermode for the BBC interview of August 28, 1959; to Arthur Crook and John Gross, the editors, for Samuel Hynes's discussion of William Golding's *The Spire, The Pyramid,* and *The Scorpion God,* first printed as reviews in the *Times Literary Supplement;* to Lawrence Durrell and E. P. Dutton and Co., Inc., publishers of most of Durrell's books in America, for their cooperation and assistance. The discussion in John Unterecker's essay of Durrell's *An Irish Faustus* is expanded from an article that first appeared in *Saturday Review* of March 21, 1964.

GEORGE STADE

Introduction

Six Contemporary British Novelists is a successor and companion to Six Modern British Novelists, published in 1974. Each of these volumes brings together six essays first published as separate pamphlets for the series of Columbia Essays on Modern Writers. In this new volume, as in the earlier one, the essays have been revised and the bibliographies brought up to date in response to new work by or about the novelists in question. The essays in the new volume, like those in the first, were each designed as an introduction that would at the same time make an original contribution to our understanding of a representative British novelist of this century. Evelyn Waugh, the youngest writer discussed in the first volume, was born in 1903; Graham Greene, the oldest writer discussed in this new volume, was born in 1904; the two volumes, then, introduce the first and second generations of British novelists to come of age during the modernist era.

From where we stand in the seventies our line of vision passes easily over the second generation to the first. From here, at least, the first difference seems to be one of size. So far as I can see, no British novelist born during this century has the stature of Conrad or Lawrence or

Joyce, or even of Forster or Woolf. A backward glance from the year 2000 may fall on a changed landscape, of course; the prominences we now look up to may well have been flattened by the critical winds of the interim. But that future glance, if sharp enough, will also note that the younger novelists seem to share our present estimate of their relations to their immediate predecessors. They write as though someone were looking down over their shoulders. The first generation of modernists wrote as though they were parricides or bastards or orphans, as though their literary pasts, at least, were no longer present, as though they were heirs only to their own succession. The second generation of modernists knows all too well whom or what they are heir to.

I mean, for example, that *Under the Volcano* (1947) is not only under the shadow of Popocatepetl. That novel, among other things, is at once an act of expropriation and of piety, an attempt to take in and take over not so much *Ulysses* as the modernist methods, moods, and themes that had received their classic expression in *Ulysses* (1922). These methods, moods, and themes seem a bit overripe in *Under the Volcano*, a little past their prime. And although that novel is a success in its own right, an immense and unique success, part of its success and part of its uniqueness lie in its having imitated the inimitable. *Under the Volcano* is unique among novels written by British writers of Malcolm Lowry's generation for being equal in ambitiousness to its great modernist progenitors as well as equal to its own ambitions. The ambitions of Graham Greene, William Golding, Lawrence Durrell, and Iris Murdoch are modest by comparison, and in any case different.

Among the numerous separate distinctions of their individual novels, these writers share the distinction of having adapted modernist techniques to one or another of the
forms of popular fiction. Although it is not just that, *The
Alexandria Quartet* is a kind of chronicle romance with
parallax, a soap opera in multiple perspectives, including
one that opens in on itself. In Graham Greene's thrillers
the buried motifs and blind alleys, the suspicious concords
and surprising collusions, add to the thrill, make the out-
come of the action look like the consequences of a secret
and sinister intent, like the slow return of the repressed.
In Iris Murdoch's novels the fantasies of female revenge
and of polymorphous and incestuous sex that are covert in
gothic romances become overt. The deadpan prose, the
radical juxtapositions, the dissolving scenes and discontin-
uous selves make explicit the obsessions that in the fictional worlds of Charlotte Brontë, Daphne Du Maurier,
and a host of imitators are only implicit. These techniques
not only reveal obsession—they are the formal equivalents
of its dynamics. William Golding writes modernist science
fiction.

In its relations to modernism, C. P. Snow's work is the
polar opposite of Malcolm Lowry's. C. P. Snow is to his
generation of British novelists what Arnold Bennett was to
his: an exemplary nonmodernist, a formal conservative
against whose familiarities of method the innovations of
his contemporaries stand out clear. Snow's contemporaries, when they think of him at all, must think of him as a
writer who begs the very questions they sought out techniques to pose. Except for a certain quality of insistence,
of defensiveness almost, Snow writes as though literary
modernism, a movement in the interrogative mood, had

never occurred. His novels do not adapt modernist technique to a form of popular fiction; they do not do anything to or with popular fiction; they are very close to being the thing itself.

The younger moderns, then, are not revolutionaries, except for those of them who carry on the permanent revolution to make it new; but even these make it new by variations of what their predecessors had already made aggressively new. The younger novelists are less challenging, more comfortable, less likely to overpower, more likely to accommodate, less likely to be solemn about Art, more willing to be popular. We read the two bodies of work in different frames of mind, with different kinds of attention, and get different kinds of rewards. I would not myself like to do without either of them.

There are, of course, other ways of talking about writers than by relating them to their predecessors, ways better able to bring out the writers' individualities—but that is the accomplished task of the six essays before you.

DAVID LODGE

Graham Greene

A buzzard flaps across a dusty Mexican square and settles
heavily on a tin roof . . . in Brighton the lights go out
above the black struts of the Palace Pier and the dark shifting water . . . in Saigon old wrinkled women in black
trousers squat gossiping on the landing outside the *urinoir*
. . . over Clapham Common solitary walkers move with
bowed heads through the slanting rain . . . in West Africa
the laterite roads turn a fragile pink at sundown, then are
swallowed by darkness.

These are some characteristic scenes from a country of
the mind known internationally as Greeneland. No one interested in modern literature has failed to explore it; but
the explorers have brought back conflicting reports. The
reception and reputation of Graham Greene's fiction is, indeed, a subject in itself. Briefly, he enjoys the admiration
of reviewers, fellow novelists, and "general readers," who
praise particularly his "craftsmanship," his ability to "tell
a story"; and of some critics with a vested interest in
Christian or specifically Catholic literature. But in the
mainstream of Anglo-American literary criticism his repu-

tation does not ride so high. The bibliography of Greene studies grows longer and longer, but the proportion of unfriendly and depreciative criticism is enough to force Greene's admirers into a characteristically defensive stance.

It is difficult not to see behind a good deal of the hostile comment on Greene a certain academic suspicion of the popularly successful writer. But there is evidence that Greene himself is far from complacent about the kind of praise he has received. Frank Kermode has pointed out that the sardonic fable of the jeweler, maker of ingenious jeweled eggs, in *A Burnt-Out Case* (1961) fits Greene himself as well as the character of Querry, the famous Catholic architect, to whom it is applied in the novel:

Everyone said he was a master technician, but he was highly praised too for the seriousness of his subject-matter because on the top of each egg there was a gold cross set with chips of precious stones in honour of the King.

The popular image of Greene as a master technician with a crucifix hidden behind his back (or up his sleeve) obviously will not do. But his work does not fit into the categories that orthodox literary criticism has evolved in its appraisal of serious modern fiction. While the mass media of entertainment have figured as the villains in most contemporary cultural discussion, Greene has not only enjoyed popular success as a writer of thrillers and stories (like *The Third Man*) designed for the movies, but has drawn extensively on their conventions in his most ambitious work. In a period when the most influential school of criticism in England has proclaimed the duty of the novelist to be "on the side of life," Greene has spoken eloquently on the side of death. Belonging by language and nationality to a tradition in the novel based essentially on the values of secularized Protestantism, Greene has adopted the alien dogmatic system of Roman Catholicism, and put it at the very center of his mature work. Eschewing the "poetic" verbal texture, the indifference to "story," and the authorial impersonality of most of the accredited modern masters of fiction, Greene has cultivated the virtues and disciplines of prose, favored involved and exciting plots, and reasserted the right of the novelist to comment on his characters and their actions.

The result of all this, one can't help thinking, is that Greene has represented for many critics a temptation of a kind to which criticism of the novel is always susceptible: the temptation to abstract from fiction the author's version of reality, measuring this against a supposedly normative version, rather than assessing the persuasiveness with which the novelist realizes his version. "We must grant to the artist his subject, his idea, his *donnée:* our criticism is applied only to what he makes of it," said Henry James (a novelist, incidentally, for whom Greene has enormous admiration). But many critics have not been prepared to grant Greene so much: in their view Greene's technical skill is not legitimate rhetoric, but a kind of trickery.

Part of the trouble, no doubt, is that Greene's *données* are often based on Catholic dogma and belief, on such assumptions as that there is such a thing as "mortal" sin, that Christ is "really and truly" present in the Eucharist, that miracles can occur in the twentieth century. The fictional endorsement of such ideas in the context of a pluralist and largely secular culture presents very real artistic problems. In seeking to convey to his non-Catholic audience a technical and emotional understanding of Catholic experience, the Catholic novelist risks arousing in this audience whatever extraliterary objections and suspicions it entertains about the Catholic Church as an active, proselytizing institution; while on his own part he has to grapple with the problem of retaining his artistic integrity while belonging to a Church which has never accepted the individual's right to pursue intellectual and artistic truth in absolute freedom.

George Orwell argued in *Inside the Whale* (1940) that any kind of ideological orthodoxy was inimical to the production of good fiction. "How many Roman Catholics have been good novelists?" he asked. "Even the handful one could name have been bad Catholics." Not a few of Greene's critics have implied that his conversion to Roman Catholicism was his undoing as a writer. Yet Greene's religious convictions were late in rising to the surface of his fiction, and they did so in precisely those novels that are, by general agreement, his best. This evidence does not, however, completely falsify Orwell's opinion. In an exchange of letters with Elizabeth Bowen and V. S. Pritchett (*Why Do I Write?* [1948]) Greene admitted that loyalty to his own imagination involved him in a certain "disloyalty" to his Church. By this he meant that in pursuing his artistic aims he could not consult the counsels of religious prudence or the interests of ecclesiastical propaganda. The result has been that Greene's novels have offended Catholics at least as much as non-Catholics. *The Power and the Glory* (1940), for instance, provoked a condemnation from the Holy Office itself. The passing of time and, one hopes, the deepening of understanding have made the novel acceptable to Greene's coreligionists; but in the meantime he has found new ways of demonstrating his "disloyalty."

It is obvious that no writer subscribing to the Catholic faith could prevent it, even if he wished to, from invading his most deeply felt creative work. But Catholicism as a public system of laws and dogmas is far from being an adequate key to Greene's fiction. There is a good deal of evidence, internal and external, that in Greene's fiction Catholicism is not a body of belief requiring exposition and demanding categorical assent or dissent, but a system of concepts, a source of situations, and a reservoir of symbols with which he can order and dramatize certain intuitions about the nature of human experience—intuitions which were gained prior to and independently of his formal adoption of the Catholic faith. Regarded in this light, Greene's Catholicism may be seen not as a crippling burden on his artistic freedom, but as a positive artistic asset.

Graham Greene was born in 1904, the son of C. H. Greene, the headmaster of an English public (*i.e.*, private) school, Berkhamstead, which he himself attended as a pupil before entering Balliol College, Oxford. Greene read history but, like many Oxford undergraduates, he wrote poetry, publishing a "slim volume," *Babbling April*, in 1925. In the same year he graduated from Oxford, and after a number of false starts, began a career in journalism, working first for the Nottingham *Journal*. It was in this industrial Midland city that Greene, an Anglican by upbringing, was received into the Catholic Church, in 1926. He moved to London to work as a sub-editor on the London *Times*, a post he resigned after the publication of his first novel, *The Man Within* (1929). Since that time Greene has been a free-lance writer, except for brief spells of journalistic work in the thirties, and service with the British government during World War II.

Greene has not yet published an autobiography, but he has made some interesting autobiographical revelations in his essays, prefaces, travel books, and other miscellaneous writings. Some of these revelations are so obviously dropped in the critic's path as clues to the fiction that, knowing Greene's reputation as an accomplished hoaxer and practical joker, one hestitates to pick them up. But the temptation to do so is irresistible. Of particular interest is the information about Greene's childhood and youth, for he frequently insists on the lasting effect of early experience on adult life.

"There is always a moment in childhood," comments the authorial voice of *The Power and the Glory*, "when the door opens and lets the future in." For Greene himself, we learn in his Mexican travel book *The Lawless Roads* (1939), the door was a real door, a door that crops up here and there in his fiction, the green baize door that separated his family's quarters, smelling of "books and fruit and eau de cologne," from the corridors and dormitories of Berkhamstead school; and what it let in for the young Greene was nothing less than evil.

In the land of . . . stone stairs and cracked bells ringing early, one was aware of fear and hate, a kind of lawlessness—appalling cruelties could be practised without a second thought; one met for the first time characters, adult and adolescent, who bore about them the genuine quality of evil . . . And so faith came to one— shapelessly, without dogma, a presence above a croquet lawn, something associated with violence, cruelty, evil across the way. One began to believe in heaven because one believed in hell, but for a long while it was only hell one could picture with a certain intimacy.

In the youthful Greene's gloomy intimations of immortality, it is easy to see the origin of that Manichaean or Jansenist coloring which critics have detected in the religious perspective of his fiction, in his vision of a fallen world for which the chances of redemption seem slender and difficult. Greene seems to confirm this analysis in the title essay of *The Lost Childhood,* where he describes the effect of reading Marjorie Bowen's historical novel *The Viper of Milan* at the age of fourteen: "she had given me my pattern—religion might later explain it to me in other terms, but the pattern was already there—perfect evil walking the world where perfect good can never walk again . . ."

It may be doubted whether Greene has altogether done himself a service by these fascinating confessions. It is true that they echo or foreshadow views to be found in the fiction, but they do so more crudely and extravagantly; and they have perhaps given too much encouragement to critics anxious to apply to Greene his own observation (in an essay on Walter de la Mare) that "every creative writer worth our consideration . . . is a victim: a man given over to an obsession." Greene, like most writers—and perhaps most men—has more than one obsession, and in his fiction generally has them well under control.

One of these obsessions—the impact of childhood experience—has already been mentioned. Another is certainly death. A prey to boredom, melancholy, and disgust from an early age, Greene has evidently found death an alluring prospect or one whose imminence can revive the will to live. In his remarkable essay "The Revolver in the Corner Cupboard" he describes various suicidal experiments he made in youth. Years later, sick and lost in Liberia, he discovered in himself "a thing I thought I had never possessed: a love of life." In the Introduction to a new edition of *It's a Battlefield* he writes, "as one approaches death one lives ahead; perhaps it is a hurry to be gone." Many of Greene's characters seem to be in a hurry to be gone. With the unimportant exception of *Loser Takes All* (1955), all Greene's novels and entertainments involve the death—usually violent, sometimes suicidal—of one or more of the chief characters. If "hurry" is a misnomer it is because these characters have religious misgivings about the afterlife, or, like Fowler in *The Quiet American* (1955), they find that "though my reason wanted death, I was afraid like a virgin of the act." The last image reminds one of another Greeneian obsession: the association of death with the "little death" of sexual love.

Then there is the obsession with treachery and betrayal—the "Judas complex" which Greene has detected in Henry James, but which is far more evident in his own work. To betrayal we may add other moral and emotional abstractions that haunt Greene's imaginative writing: trust and distrust, justice and injustice, pity, responsibility, innocence, jealousy. Beyond this there is Greene's fascination with squalor and failure, with what he has himself called "seediness." Then there is his obsession with the theme of pursuit, of the relationship between hunter and hunted. Already we have reviewed too many items to be talking in terms of "obsession," but the list is far from complete. There is his obsession with dreams: John Atkins counted sixty-three dreams in Greene's fiction up to and including *The Quiet American*. (I agree with Atkins, incidentally, in finding them, for the most part, oddly unconvincing.) There is his obsession with dentistry and dental decay. There is his obsession with a certain kind of waiflike heroine. There is his obsession, particularly evident in the short stories, with resurrection and animated corpses. There is his obsession with his own name, which Philip Stratford has documented in a witty and ingenious article, "Unlocking the Potting Shed." Stratford investigated a number of books and stories by and about other Greenes or Greens, and found several highly plausible sources for Graham Greene's own work. Though the article is not entirely serious, it is a useful caution against interpreting Greene too rigidly in terms of personal trauma and psychological obsession, and encourages us to put more emphasis on the creative, inventive, and rhetorical side of his work. That, at least, will be the aim of the remainder of this essay.

In his travel book *Journey Without Maps* (1936) Greene described Liberia as a country "saved from melodrama by its irony," and the same might be said of his own fiction, particularly the earlier work. It is melodramatic insofar as moral choice is dramatized by extreme circumstances, often arising out of crime, war, revolution, and espionage, and the narrative aims to excite and engage very basic emotions: horror, compassion, fear, admiration. The irony resides in the fact that in Greene's stories the conventions of melodrama are handled with a sophisticated and very personal sense of values so as to displace the usual melodramatic distribution of sympathy and antipathy. We are led to identify, not with the honest and brave, but with the criminal and cowardly; not with the rich and beautiful, but with the poor and ugly; and there is rarely an unequivocally happy ending. In Greene's own words:

"The little duke is dead and betrayed and forgotten: we cannot recognize the villain and we suspect the hero and the world is a small cramped place." (*The Ministry of Fear*, 1943)

Sometimes the irony is not sufficiently subtle and controlled to transform the melodramatic stereotypes. That would seem to be the trouble with Greene's first novel, *The Man Within*, though the hero is, to be sure, an antihero. Set in a vaguely defined historical past—eighteenth- or nineteenth-century England—this novel centers on the plight of a young man called Andrews, who has betrayed to the authorities a gang of smugglers (previously led by his father, now by a man called Carlyon) of which he himself has been a member. The betrayal is an act of perverse self-assertion by Andrews, who has always felt himself to be despised and neglected. Carlyon and three others escape, and are pursued by the law, while they in turn, intent on revenge, pursue Andrews across the bleak, befogged Sussex Downs. Andrews takes refuge in the cottage of a solitary young girl, Elizabeth. Failing to impress her in the role of desperate and unscrupulous outlaw, Andrews is himself impressed by Elizabeth's courage and self-possession, and becomes more keenly aware than ever of "the man within me that's angry with me" (the phrase is Sir Thomas Browne's). Elizabeth seeks to redeem Andrews from his self-disgust by encouraging him to testify against the smugglers at the local assizes. This he does, but not before he has been unfaithful to Elizabeth with Lucy, the seductive mistress of counsel for the prosecution. In the denouement Elizabeth dies protecting Andrews from Carlyon's men, and Andrews atones for all by surrendering himself as her murderer.

Some of Greene's most characteristic themes and devices appear in his first book: betrayal (" 'He's a sort of Judas,' [Carlyon] said softly"), pursuit ("He saw himself friendless and alone, chased by harsh enemies through an uninterested world"), and the yearning for death ("He felt no fear of death, but a terror of life, of going on soiling himself and repenting and soiling himself again"). Though immature, *The Man Within* is by no means a bad novel. There are some exciting scenes that already bear the Greene imprint—notably one where Andrews stands motionless in the middle of a road obscured by fog while his would-be murderers pass within a few feet searching for him. But the vaguely sketched, rather dreamlike setting of the story lacks the authenticating particularity of Greene's later work, and gives him too much room for a rather self-indulgent romanticism in the presentation of his hero. Elizabeth and Lucy, the sexual extensions of Andrews's inner dualism, are crude stereotypes of pure and carnal love, untouched by saving irony.

Similar, but more damaging criticisms can be leveled at Greene's second and third novels, *The Name of Action* (1930), which describes a young Englishman's rather gratuitous involvement in a Ruritanian revolution, and *Rumour at Nightfall* (1931), which is set against the background of the Carlist wars in Spain. Greene has excluded these two novels from the Uniform Edition of his works, and there seems no justification for resurrecting them in a study as short as the present one.

The literary and financial failure of these two books occasioned a serious crisis in Greene's career, from which he recovered with his first "entertainment," *Stamboul Train* (1932). Greene later wrote of it: "One had never really taken the book seriously, it had been written hurriedly because one had desperately needed the money." Yet there are strong indications that for Greene the novelist it was *Stamboul Train* that opened a door and let the future in. Greene followed it up with two "novels" whose literary pretensions are more serious; but what is successful in them derives from *Stamboul Train* rather than from *The Man Within*. Correspondingly, it is in the early entertainments rather than in the early novels that we may observe most clearly the genesis of Greene's mature art.

Stamboul Train follows the fortunes of a number of travelers on the Orient Express, which runs from Ostend to Istanbul. The main characters are Dr. Czinner, a disappointed Communist revolutionary; Myatt, a Jewish merchant; and Coral Musker, a young dancer, who in her combination of courage and vulnerability and her minimal expectations of happiness foreshadows many future Greene heroines. In her brief liaison with Myatt there is, characteristically, more pathos than pleasure: "helpless and sick under the dim unsteady lamp of the corridor, her body shaken by the speed of the train, she woke a painful pity." There are a number of minor characters: a murderer on the run, a lesbian journalist, a clergyman of the muscular Christianity school, a best-selling novelist, and some dim English tourists. The structural device that weaves these diverse strands together, involving the characters wittingly or unwittingly in each other's destinies, is the journey itself. Time and place are marked by the progress of the train between the various stations on its route, which supply the titles of the five parts of the novel.

The railroad train is one of the few products of the industrial revolution to have acquired a certain mythic quality; and in its headlong rush across Europe the Orient Express provides just the right combination, for Greene's purposes, of the familiar and the unfamiliar. Greene has admired this combination in the work of John Buchan, entertainer of an earlier era, quoting from Buchan's *The Power House* a line that might well stand as an epigraph to any of his own entertainments: "Now I saw how thin was the protection of civilization." In *Stamboul Train* the protection is as thin as the walls and windows of the train. Once she leaves its safety Coral is helplessly involved in the callous trial and condemnation of Czinner, and separated from Myatt. She is rescued only to fall into the clutches of the lesbian, Mabel Warren.

Greene's next entertainment, *A Gun for Sale* (1936), is particularly interesting as being a kind of secular rehearsal for *Brighton Rock* (1938), his first overtly Catholic novel. Both novels explore, through their warped, murderous "heroes," a paradox that is crucial in Greene's work, a paradox most forcefully put by T. S. Eliot in his essay on Baudelaire, which Greene has quoted in his own essays:

So far as we are human, what we do must be either evil or good; so far as we do evil or good we are human; and it is better, in a paradoxical way, to do evil, than to do nothing: at least we exist. It is true to say that the glory of man is his capacity for salvation; it is also true to say that his glory is his capacity for damnation. The worst that can be said for most of our malefactors, from statesmen to thieves, is that they are not men enough to be damned.

If in theological terms this view leads to the celebration of the sinner as one perversely aware of supernatural values, in secular terms it leads to the celebration of the

criminal, who becomes the symbolic scapegoat, victim and
scourge—the existential hero in fact—of a society characterized by moral anarchy. So it is with Raven, the hare-
lipped killer of A Gun for Sale. At the beginning of the
novel we see him commit the brutal murder of a rather
saintly European politician, yet by the end we have come
to identify and almost to sympathize with him. Raven is
paid for the assassination with stolen notes, and the action
of the novel describes his flight from the English police on
this account while he himself seeks revenge on those who
have double-crossed him—a group of wealthy armament
manufacturers who stand to profit by a European war. Raven's violence is thus an extension of a much larger public
violence ("There's always been a war for me," he says)
and his guilt is diminished by juxtaposition with those
who kill with clean hands. The conventions of the thriller
are precariously maintained—Raven is shot down at last,
and the heroine Anne is reunited with her policeman-
fiancé—but not before Raven, rather in the style of a Jaco-
bean revenger, has purged society of corruption in high
places.

In A Gun for Sale Greene calls attention to the theme
of treachery and betrayal more insistently than ever before. At the outset of the story the only value Raven
cherishes is a belief in honor among thieves, and it is his
disillusionment on this score that awakens in his twisted
mind (itself partly excused by traumatic childhood experience) the first glimmerings of moral awareness. His sense
of grievance colors his interpretation of Christmas, the sea-
son that forms a sad, ironic background to the story. Raven
looks at a crib in a shop window, "staring at the swaddled
child with a horrified tenderness, 'the little bastard,' be-

cause he was educated and knew what the child was in
for, the damned Jews and the double-crossing Judas and
only one man to draw a knife on his side when the soldiers
came for him in the garden"—a passage anticipating
Greene's startling and unconventional use of religious allusion in later fiction.

The reiteration of the betrayal motif in *A Gun for Sale*
exemplifies a characteristic feature of Greene's fiction, in
which the properties of realism—the sharp visual images
presented through cinematic devices of montage and
close-up, the catalogues of significant particulars, the keen
rendering of sensation, the touches of local color laid on
with so skilled a hand—seem to cluster around the nucleus
of some ambiguous moral concept which is "the heart of
the matter" and which is represented by some word or
words recurring as insistently as a drum beat. One is reminded of the narrator of *Under Western Eyes* (by Joseph
Conrad, a writer Greene abandoned in 1932 because "his
influence on me was too great"), who speaks of the necessity of finding "some key word . . . a word that could
stand at the back of all the words covering the page, a
word which, if not truth itself, may perchance hold truth
enough to help the moral discovery which should be the
object of every tale."

The key word of *The Confidential Agent* (1939), for instance, is *trust,* or its negative forms *distrust* and *mistrust:*
even the "trust-system" for buying newspapers contributes significantly to the plot. This, the third of Greene's
entertainments, describes the mission of D., a confidential
agent representing a foreign government (which is pretty
obviously the Republican side in the Spanish Civil War)
who is sent to England to negotiate a coal contract. Pacing

the deck of the cross-channel steamer as it nears Dover, D. thinks:

You could trust nobody but yourself, and sometimes you were uncertain whether you could trust yourself. *They* [*i.e.*, his own government] didn't trust you . . . He wasn't certain that he wasn't watched at this moment. He wasn't certain that it wasn't right for him to be watched . . . And the watcher—was he watched? He was haunted by the vision of an endless distrust.

In the subsequent action D.'s mission, and his life, are constantly threatened by the intervention of his own side as well as that of his political enemies. He is caught up in a web of intrigue and violence, plausibly unraveled against the background of an outwardly calm and reassuring England. The irony of the title is clear: D. is a confidential agent in whom no one has confidence, and who can have confidence in no one.

All three entertainments discussed above concern political crisis of one kind or another, and depict Europe as a place of tyranny, violence, and unrest. In this respect Greene's early fiction clearly belongs to the thirties. It presents a vivid picture of that period of economic depression and the threat of war, a picture made up of people anxiously watching news flashes, people demonstrating, people looking for jobs, people turning over secondhand clothes, jerry-built housing estates, TO LET and FOR SALE signs, desolate slag heaps, the pervasive evidence of decline and despair. The writers of the thirties characteristically confronted these circumstances by committing themselves to Marxist political solutions, and by adopting a more open, robust, and popular literary style than that of the "aesthetic" twenties. Greene was a Party member for

only four weeks in early youth, but the sympathies in his
fiction go out to the underprivileged and the characters
who are ideologically on the left. His rejection, after a few
unsatisfactory experiments, of the "stream of consciousness" technique, and his development of a fictional mode
that was serious without being highbrow, using devices of
journalism and the cinema, shot through with the sense of
social and political crisis, were in accord with the literary
program of Auden, Isherwood, and their associates.

Greene, however, avoided the cruder kind of political
simplifications that characterize much of the writing of the
thirties: Czinner is a flawed character, and D. is by no
means convinced of his side's ideology. Greene's whole
fictional world seems ripe for dissolution rather than revolution. This may be accounted for by reference to his Catholicism, and his own innate pessimism. Increasingly
there flows into his work the current of antihumanism that
runs so strongly through most Christian and specifically
Catholic writing from the Decadence onward; so that by
1939 we find Greene (in *The Lawless Roads*) declaiming
against "Progress, Human Dignity, great empty Victorian
concepts that life denies at every turn." Greene, however,
never moved toward the political right, though for his generation of intellectuals this was the logical consequence of
conversion to Catholicism.

In Greene's best writing, in fact, there is always a
fruitful tension between two systems of value. As he
neatly puts it in *Journey Without Maps:* "I find myself
always torn between two beliefs: the belief that life should
be better than it is and the belief that when it appears better it is really worse." In his mature fiction this dialectic is
deepened by being placed in a Christian and hence "eter-

nal" perspective; but in his earlier work we are conscious of a secular despair stifling creative achievement.

This seems particularly true of the "novel" *It's a Battlefield* (1934), in which Greene is also laboring under Conrad's excessive influence. This novel has its key word—*justice*—but does not get much further than the discrediting of all ideas of justice as it follows, through a cross section of metropolitan London, the repercussions of a Communist bus driver's conviction for the murder of a policeman. The possibility of divine justice is not introduced; and we are left with the depressing spectacle of rootless, unhappy, or culpably complacent individuals coexisting without communicating, impotent contenders on a befogged battlefield.

Greene's next novel, *England Made Me* (1935), is much more successful. Set mainly in Stockholm, it concerns a number of characters associated with a Swedish millionaire tycoon (modeled on Kreuger, the match king), particularly his mistress Kate Farrant and her ne'er-do-well brother Anthony. Kate persuades Krogh to give Anthony a job, but there is no *rapport* between these two "hollow men": the tycoon whose colossal financial power has cut him off from human values, and the social failure sheltering behind a bogus Harrow tie. When Anthony threatens to expose the crooked basis of Krogh's empire, he is murdered by Krogh's faithful henchman, Hall. Minty, the genuine Harrow article, but even more down-at-heel, provides another, jaundiced perspective on events.

England Made Me is the most carefully wrought of Greene's novels of the thirties, but its success seems to represent a kind of dead end for his particular talent. The characters are drawn with brilliant observation, but the brilliance is all on the surface: Greene's attempts to penetrate their minds through interior monologue are not happy. The characters seem trapped, deprived of free will and of the capacity to develop, by the very finality and authority with which Greene categorizes them. The analysis, which they illustrate, of the disorder of society as a whole is thus drawn inevitably to a defeatist conclusion. Several critics have pointed out that Greene's view of human destiny has always tended to the deterministic, and his characterization to caricature. But in his "religious" novels the determinism is checked by the mysteries of Christianity, and the caricature becomes a generally legitimate and highly effective means of dramatizing the interplay of the divine and the human.

Explaining, in *Journey Without Maps* (1936), why he made the first long journey of his life to so unpromising a place as Liberia, Greene writes: "There seemed to be a seediness about the place you couldn't get to the same extent elsewhere, and seediness has a very deep appeal: even the seediness of civilization." Greene draws a daunting picture of the boredom, fear, disgust, and physical discomfort he experienced in the uncharted depths of Liberia, but it all weighed more heavily in the balance for him than "the smart, the new, the chic, the cerebral." Throughout the book Africa is contrasted with England by means of a kind of cultural synecdoche very common in Greene's writing:

It isn't a gain to have turned the witch or the masked secret dancer, the sense of supernatural evil, into the small human viciousness of the distinguished military grey head in Kensington Gardens with the soft lips and the eyes which dwelt with dull lustre on girls and boys of a certain age.

Too honest to be an exciting travel book, and too confused to be a satisfying spiritual journal, *Journey Without Maps* is nevertheless a curiously fascinating work, and one that helps to explain his next, *Brighton Rock* (1938), in which "the sense of supernatural evil" and "the seediness of civilization" are imaginatively fused.

Briefly, *Brighton Rock* describes the decline and fall of Pinkie Brown, a teen-age criminal who has inherited the leadership of a gang of racecourse hoodlums operating from the popular seaside resort of Brighton. At the outset of the novel they murder the associate of a rival gang, making one small slip which is observed by a young waitress, Rose. In order to secure his own safety, Pinkie befriends the girl and marries her in a registry office. Since they are both Catholics this means they are living in sin—a source of perverse satisfaction to Pinkie, who despises and revolts from sexuality. Meanwhile Ida Arnold, a big, cheerful, irrepressible Cockney, who made a chance contact with the murdered man just before he was killed, undertakes her own private investigation of the crime. Harried by Ida, by his distrust of Rose, and by the machinations of the rival gang, Pinkie is driven to committing another murder and unsuccessfully conniving at a third. But the net closes in inexorably, and he seeks to escape it by the most diabolical act of all: disposing of Rose by luring her into a faked suicide pact with himself. In the end it is Pinkie who dies when, blinded by his own vitriol, he dashes over a cliff.

Such a synopsis, suggestive merely of a violent and sensational crime story, scarcely conveys an idea of the extraordinary displacement of conventional values and sympathies which Greene effects in *Brighton Rock*. In this novel he explores the Eliot-Baudelaire paradox in its most extreme form. Pinkie is self-consciously man enough to be damned, yet Greene persuades us to respect him more than Ida Arnold, who with her cheerful humanism and sense of fair play, represents secular values in the novel. He does this partly by stressing the loyalty and devotion of Rose to Pinkie. Rose, Greene's most successful "waif" character, is as good as Pinkie is evil; but as Ida discovers, good and evil have more in common with each other than with the code of "right and wrong" that is always on her own lips:

Good and evil lived in the same country, came together like old friends, feeling the same completion, touching hands beside the iron bedstead. "You want to do what's Right, Rose?" she implored.

Like Charles Péguy, the French Catholic writer (often mentioned by Greene) who challenged the idea of eternal punishment by deliberately remaining in a state of mortal sin, Rose "had chosen her side; if they damned him, they'd got to damn her too." In the end she resists the temptation to damn herself by suicide, or rather she succumbs to what François Mauriac has called "the good temptation to which many men succumb in the end"— God. Pinkie resists the good temptation, which, like Francis Thompson's Hound of Heaven, presents to his tormented mind the aspect of some incomprehensible disaster:

An enormous emotion beat on him; it was like something trying to get in, the pressure of gigantic wings against the glass. *Dona nobis pacem.* He withstood it, with all the bitter force of the school bench, the cement playground, the St. Pancras waiting

room, Dallow's and Judy's secret lust, and the cold, unhappy
moment on the pier. If the glass broke, the beast—whatever it
was—got in, God knows what it would do. He had a sense of
huge havoc—the confession, the penance and the sacrament—an
awful distraction, and he drove blind into the rain.

As at the climax of *A Gun for Sale*, a certain pity and understanding is solicited for the criminal hero by recapitu-
lating his appalling social background. But there is more of
the tragic and less of the pathetic spirit about Pinkie. With
a desperation reminiscent of Macbeth, he asks himself,
"Had he got to massacre a world?"; and his lawyer Dre-
witt is given to quoting *Hamlet, Othello,* and *Dr. Faustus.*

But the paradox on which *Brighton Rock* is based cannot be sustained to its logical conclusion. It is plainly better to do nothing than to damn yourself. In other novels
Greene acknowledges this by holding out the hope of
mercy for his sinners, but hardly in *Brighton Rock.* The
priest at the end of the novel seeks to console Rose by
suggesting there was some love, and hence some good in
Pinkie. But we leave her walking toward "the worst horror
of all"—the phonograph record on which, unknown to her,
Pinkie had recorded: "God damn you, you little bitch, why
can't you go home and let me be?"

The effort of sustaining this bleakly pessimistic vision
leads Greene into some falsities (as when Pinkie improbably intones *"Credo in unum Satanum"*) but on the whole
the novel holds us appalled and fascinated in its coil. Its
popularity may be accounted for by reference to Greene's
utterly authentic evocation of Brighton and what it stands
for in British "folk" culture, and to the fact that on a very
superficial level it can be read as an entertainment (which
it was called in some editions). On a deeper level of liter-

ary appreciation, however, one has to acknowledge the force of the book's demonic rhetoric: the pervasive poison imagery (Pinkie's veins run with poison, and even the sea is "poison-bottle green"), the perverse sexual imagery ("a prick of sexual desire disturbed him like a sickness"), the bizarre emblems of cruelty (Pinkie dismembering a fly, murmuring, "She loves me, she loves me not . . ."), the sensational religious allusion ("She was good, but he'd got her like you got God in the Eucharist—in the guts").

In *Brighton Rock*, indeed, Greene may be said to have finally discovered his personal style, his artistic *métier*, though the excitement of the discovery leads him into a certain extravagance. I have already remarked on the way he shapes a vividly particularized narrative around a thematic abstraction. The same kind of effect is to be observed in microcosm in his use of language, his employment of synecdoche, oxymoron, metaphor, simile, and other tropes in which the abstract and the concrete are brought into arresting conjunction, often enforced by alliteration: "the music drifting landward, grief in the guts"; "she felt responsibility move in her breasts"; "Camaraderie, good nature, cheeriness fell like shutters before a plate-glass window"; "A dim desire for annihilation stretched in him, the vast superiority of vacancy." As Richard Hoggart has observed, Greene sometimes reverses the normal figurative relationship of abstract to concrete. Thus, the priest in *The Power and the Glory* "drank the brandy down like damnation." Greene might say with Mauriac, "I am a metaphysician who works in the concrete."

It was in an essay on the French novelist that Greene took the opportunity to question the modern prejudice against authorial comment in fiction. Greene reasserted "the traditional and essential right of a novelist to comment, to express his views," which he associated particularly with the "religious sense" lost to English fiction in its post-Jamesian phase. Authorial comment is certainly an important element in Greene's own fiction, though he is enough of a "modern" to employ it more subtly and more unobtrusively than a Victorian novelist. His method is usually to develop his commentary out of the thoughts and situation of one of his characters, so that we are scarcely aware of the transition, and accept the comment almost as an articulation of the character's consciousness, though at the same time we feel the force of the superior expressiveness and deeper perspective which the authorial voice commands.

In *The Lawless Roads*, the record of a journey through Mexico in 1938, when the Catholic Church was subject to persecution in some states, Greene frequently alludes to the growing cult of the martyred priest, Father Pro, who died heroically, praying for his enemies; but it is entirely characteristic that his imagination was fired by the casual mention of a much less impressive priest:

I asked about the priest in Chiapas who had fled. "Oh," he said, "he was just what we call a whiskey priest." He had taken one of his sons to be baptized but the priest was drunk and would insist on naming him Brigitta. He was little loss, poor man . . . but who can judge what terror and hardship and isolation may have excused him in the eyes of God?

The Power and the Glory (1940) is an imaginative exploration of that final question.

The story is very simple, and divides into four sections. In the first we are introduced to the whiskey priest, trying to escape from the state in which he is the last representative of the Church, and to a number of other characters, Mexican and European, who become associated with him. In the second part, he returns to his native village, where he has an illegitimate daughter (Brigitta) and narrowly escapes detection by the Lieutenant of Police, who is looking for him. Later he turns up in the town looking for wine with which to celebrate Mass, and is ironically arrested for violating the antiliquor laws. In the third part, having been released, unrecognized, from prison, he is on the point of escaping to a safe state when he is called back to minister to a dying gangster—a call he obeys though he knows it is a trap. He is executed, and the effect of his death on the other characters is studied in the fourth part.

The structural devices developed in the entertainments are therefore still in evidence: the story of a chase thrown across a vividly authentic background, drawing in a number of characters who dramatize the theme by their involvement or indifference. But the eschatological perspective that struggles against the conventions of the thriller in *Brighton Rock* is all-pervasive here. Only the whiskey priest's belief in his sacramental powers saves him from utter despair:

Now that he no longer despaired, it didn't mean of course that he wasn't damned—it was simply that after a time the mystery became too great, a damned man putting God into the mouths of men.

It is the priest's wavering, undignified but persistent loyalty to his vocation that makes him a genuine martyr, even though he has to be carried to the place of execution, his legs buckling under the influence of fear and alcohol.

In this novel Greene challenges conventional ideas of sanctity and of the priesthood. The picaresque progress of the whiskey priest is deliberately contrasted with the conventional saint's life that a Mexican mother reads to her son and daughters; but it is the former that has the breath of life—and more in common with the passion of Christ. The relationship between the priest and the half-caste who betrays him, for instance, parallels the story of Christ and Judas; and the climax of the brilliant scene in which the *Jefe* and his cousin greedily consume the priest's precious wine recalls the death of Christ on the cross. (Trying to explain his tears the priest says that when he is drunk he sees " 'all the hope of the world draining away. . . .' Lightning filled the windows like a white sheet and thunder crashed suddenly overhead.") The sentimentality of the hagiographical account alienates the little Mexican boy, and throws him temporarily into allegiance to the atheistic Lieutenant of Police; but the death of the whiskey priest restores the boy's loyalty to his faith.

It is this boy who welcomes the new priest who arrives at the end of the novel to fill the vacuum left by the death of the whiskey priest. We are told that "the boy had already swung the door open and put his lips to his hand before the other could give himself a name." The new priest thus shares the anonymity of the whiskey priest, which underlines the fact that his priestly ministry transcends his personal imperfections. This is also stressed by the fact that he is the last frail source of religious consolation in a place otherwise characterized by a desolating sense of abandonment. In his Mexican travel book Greene wrote of Villahermosa (the "port" of *The Power and the Glory*): "One felt one was drawing near to the centre of something—if it was only of darkness and abandonment," and "abandon" is a word that recurs significantly throughout the novel. Padre José, for instance, figures the earth rolling "heavily in space under its fog like a burning and abandoned ship," and Mr. Tench, the dentist, reflects, when his ether cylinder fails to arrive, that "a little additional pain was hardly noticeable in the huge abandonment." The priest's personal sense of abandonment is, however, associated with his shedding of the conventional attitudes of his station in life, a stage in his self-discovery. After his night in the prison (that brilliantly evoked microcosm of the Greeneian world, "overcrowded with lust and crime and unhappy love") the priest "had passed into a region of abandonment—almost as if he had died there with the old man's head on his shoulder and now wandered in a kind of limbo because he wasn't good or bad enough . . ."

With deliberate irony, enforcing the novel's thesis, the Lieutenant of Police appears, in every respect except faith, much more like an ideal priest. He is chaste, honest, ascetic, and dedicated. His room is "like a monastic cell" and "there was something of a priest in his intent observant walk—a theologian going back over the errors of the past to destroy them again." His zeal in hunting down the whiskey priest is purely ideological, and he twice acts with real generosity toward his victim. "I have nothing against you, you understand, as a man," he says to the priest, who replies, "Of course not. It's God you're against." When the priest is shot the Lieutenant's feelings echo the words of the former when his wine is consumed:

"He felt without a purpose, as if life had drained out of the world."

As the above remarks may suggest, *The Power and the Glory* is a highly schematic novel, which perhaps explains why, although it is the most widely respected of his books, and his personal favorite among them, it stands up to repeated reading less well than some of the later works. But I have not had sufficient space to do justice to those aspects of the book which largely conceal its simplifications and carry it to the success of a tour de force: the gallery of vividly drawn minor characters, and Greene's remarkable skill in evoking the physical and metaphysical atmosphere of his Mexico.

Published inauspiciously at the beginning of World War II, *The Power and the Glory* had to wait for the reputation it deserved until interest was revived by the international success of *The Heart of the Matter* (1948). In the meantime Greene published an entertainment, *The Ministry of Fear* (1943), a rather uneven work which applies the devices of the prewar thrillers to the circumstances of the London blitz and the activities of fascist spies, with an effect that sometimes comes near self-parody. The book also looks forward, however. The background of wartime London and the comic exploitation of a private detection agency were to reappear in *The End of the Affair*. More significantly, the organization of *The Ministry of Fear* around the concept of pity (the hero has murdered his incurably ill wife out of pity) makes it a kind of rehearsal for *The Heart of the Matter*. The entertainment was written during Greene's service for the Foreign Office in Freetown, Sierra Leone, during the war—the time and place of the novel's action.

I intend to short-circuit the theological debate, which the novel provoked in some quarters, about whether the hero is damned or not. The novel leaves us in little doubt that the answer should be in the negative, and a theological approach to the novel is limiting. Scobie's case is that of a man with an overdeveloped sense of pity and responsibility (both words recur in the novel with about the same frequency) and neither quality is a prerogative of Catholics. The effect of Scobie's Catholicism is to enlarge and intensify the implications of a situation that *could* have been treated in purely secular terms (though not, so powerfully, by Greene). Scobie's distress at the spectacle of innocent suffering is a familiar human trait, but his belief in a benevolent God gives an extra turn of the screw to his anguish and bewilderment. The plot of the novel turns on one of the most hackneyed situations in literature—adultery; but Scobie's Catholicism means that the moral issues of adultery are present, for all their complexity, in terms that are precise and inexorable, while at the same time it introduces into the "eternal triangle" a fourth character whose claims to love and loyalty have to be considered. In this way, a story of essentially ordinary people acquires some of the moral and metaphysical dimensions of high tragedy.

We are first introduced to Henry Scobie as the Assistant Commissioner of Police in a British West African Colony, married to a rather unlovable wife, Louise, and childless since the death of a daughter. He is at the right age for promotion, but although Scobie is an honest and efficient policeman (Greene establishes this with great skill and economy) he lacks the qualities of a successful careerist. In the small, spitefully intimate colonial society, Louise feels the slight keenly, and vents her spleen on the long-suffering Scobie. He promises her a holiday in South Africa, though this involves him in an imprudent debt to a Syrian merchant, Yussef. Greene comments (his use of comment is both bold and wonderfully assured in this novel):

He would still have made the promise even if he could have foreseen all that would come of it. He had always been prepared to accept the responsibility for his actions, and he had been half aware too, from the time he made his terrible private vow that she would be happy, how far *this* action might carry him. Despair is the price one pays for setting oneself an impossible aim. It is, one is told, the unforgivable sin, but it is one the corrupt or evil man never practices. He always has hope. He never reaches the freezing-point of knowing absolute failure. Only the man of good-will carries always in his heart this capacity for damnation.

The Eliot-Baudelaire paradox is given a new, and perhaps more interesting twist. Scobie's "capacity for damnation" has already been hinted at by his conduct during a routine inspection of a Portuguese cargo boat, when he discovers a contraband letter. Scobie resists the captain's attempts to bribe him, but succumbs to his appeals for pity. Shortly afterward, Scobie has to report on the suicide of a young district commissioner. The episode foreshadows Scobie's own end, and establishes the doctrinal framework within which he makes his desperate decision.

By the time Louise leaves, therefore, the stage is set for Scobie's tragedy, the fall of a good man. He has to assist in the reception of a number of survivors from a ship torpedoed in the Atlantic. Most of them are in bad shape, and some die. The group includes two children and a young woman widowed by the sinking. The manifestation

of meaningless and undeserved suffering makes enormous
demands on Scobie's sense of pity and responsibility.

It was as if he had shed one responsibility [*i.e.*, Louise] only
to take on another. This was a responsibility he shared with all
human beings, but there was no comfort in that, for it sometimes
seemed to him that he was the only one who recognized it.
    Outside the rest-house he stopped again. The lights inside
would have given an extraordinary impression of peace if one
hadn't known, just as the stars on the clear night gave also an impression of remoteness, security, freedom. If one knew, he wondered, the facts, would one have to feel pity even for the planets?
if one reached what they called the heart of the matter?

Both passages, while they do credit to Scobie's humanity,
indicate that he is guilty of a kind of emotional egoism, a
compulsion to take the whole load of cosmic suffering on
his own shoulders. This leads him, as he watches beside
the little girl who is in agony, to make a generous but rash
vow: "Father . . . give her peace. Take away my peace for
ever, but give her peace." The prayer is answered, am-
biguously, by the little girl's death.

    It is perhaps because the young widow, Helen, with
her schoolgirl idiom and her stamp album salvaged from
the sinking ship, is more like a child than a woman that
Scobie succumbs so easily to her claims on his protec-
tiveness. They become lovers. Scobie is not spared an immediate awareness of the impossible situation he has
created for himself, as we learn in a passage notable for its
delicate religious allusion:

He had sworn to preserve Louise's happiness, and now he had
accepted another and contradictory responsibility. He felt tired
by all the lies he would some time have to tell: he felt the

wounds of those victims who had not yet bled. Lying back on the pillow he stared sleeplessly out towards the grey early morning tide. Somewhere on the face of those obscure waters moved the sense of yet another wrong and another victim, not Louise, not Helen. Away in the town the cocks began to crow for the false dawn.

Scobie's efforts to keep secret his liaison with Helen wreak havoc with his professional integrity: he is blackmailed by Yussef into assisting the latter's diamond smuggling, and even connives, half willingly, in the murder of his boy Ali, who is reporting on him to a British security agent, Wilson. Ironically, Scobie survives the investigation and is rewarded by the belated promise of promotion. But with the return of Louise the possibilities of any human happiness are closed to him.

It is at this point that Scobie's Catholicism becomes crucially important, for even if he can, by deception, keep both Louise and Helen relatively happy, it is only at the expense of "another wrong, another victim." Addressing God, Scobie says, "I've preferred to give you pain rather than give pain to Helen or my wife because I can't observe your suffering. I can only imagine it." But when, in order to convince Louise of his fidelity, he is driven to make a sacrilegious communion, Scobie's imagination is very vivid: "the punch-drunk head of God reeling sideways . . . his damnation being prepared like a meal at the altar . . . God was lodged in his body and his body was corrupting outwards from that seed." Such images, in which the doctrines of Catholicism are brought startlingly—even shockingly—to life, indicate that Scobie's sense of pity and responsibility has acquired a new dimension, a new depth of perception. His decision to commit suicide, rather than

choose between injuring Louise, Helen, or God, is in a
perverse way an act of generosity, of sacrifice, illustrating
Péguy's apothegm, which furnishes the epigraph to the
novel: "The sinner is at the heart of Christianity . . . No-
one is as competent in the matter of Christianity as the sinner. No-one, unless it is the saint."

Greene was to push this idea a stage further in his
next novel, *The End of the Affair* (1951), which has a similar kind of epigraph from Léon Bloy: "Man has places in
his heart which do not yet exist, and into them enters suffering, in order that they may have existence." By this
stage in his career Greene's work shows the influence of
the French Catholic literary tradition very clearly. Beginning with Huysmans, and continuing in such writers as
Bloy, Péguy, Bernanos, and Mauriac, this tradition reveals
its Decadent origins in its fascination with evil, its rejection of optimistic materialism, its stylistic tendency to epi-
gram (weaving Pascalian *pensées* into the fabric of narrative), and its interest in extreme religious situations: vows,
conversions, challenges to God, miracles, and the idea of
"mystical substitution" (when an individual takes upon
himself the suffering and guilt of others). With the exception of Mauriac, however, there is no evidence that
Greene greatly admires the literature produced by this
tradition. He draws on it for ideas, but domesticates these
in fiction that owes much more to his native literary tradition. Indeed, one is conscious of how much that is finely
realized in *The Heart of the Matter* one overlooks by concentrating on Scobie and his dilemma: the superb realization of time and place, of the petty, exhausting tensions in
colonial society, of racial conflicts and contrasts, of the
work men do. The minor characters are kept in their place

but in their different ways they are as memorable as Scobie: Harris keeping the public-school spirit alive with his
cockroach hunts; Wilson, the poet and lover doomed to absurdity; the smooth, ambivalent Yussef; even Robinson the
bank manager, brooding over books on diseases of the
urinary tract.

Although Scobie believes that "we [Catholics] know
all the answers," this certainly makes life more, not less,
difficult for him. In all Greene's work there is a powerful
tension between the imperatives of religious orthodoxy
and the human impulses (rendered with deep sympathy
and understanding) that run counter to them. In *The End
of the Affair* Greene presents this conflict in the character
of a woman to whom religious faith comes unbidden but
irresistibly, wrenching her from the one relationship she
values in life; and further dramatizes it by using as narrator her lover, a novelist and an agnostic.

When Sarah Miles abruptly broke off her affair with
Maurice Bendrix, shortly after he had narrowly escaped
death in a wartime bomb explosion, Bendrix assumed the
rivalry of another lover. Two years later he meets her husband, Henry, who is, belatedly it seems to Bendrix, suspicious of his wife's behavior. Still deeply jealous, Bendrix
arranges to have Sarah investigated by a private detective,
Parkis, and is put in possession of her journal. From this
he learns that Sarah had been convinced that he had been
killed by the bomb, and had prayed to a God in whom she
did not really believe, promising to give up Bendrix in return for his life. Since that time, convinced that her prayer
was answered, she has resisted the severe temptation to
return to him, and has moved, despite herself, toward positive belief in God through the Catholic faith. Thus enlight-

ened, Bendrix begs her to return to him, but she refuses, and dies shortly afterward. Bendrix is bitterly resentful of the destructive effect of religion on their happiness; but he is disturbed by the aura of sanctity that surrounded Sarah at the end of her life, by information which establishes that Sarah, unknown to herself, had been a baptized Catholic, and by certain phenomena that have the appearance of miracles performed through her intercession.

Such a summary scarcely indicates the complexity of the novel's structure and time scheme. Sarah's journal of her dramatic conversion is embedded in Bendrix's account, which itself reflects his progress from disbelief to a kind of exhausted defiance of God. On one level, *The End of the Affair* is an enormously complicated—and deeply absorbing—detective story, in which a divine culprit is pursued by a godless detective. It is also the story of an "eternal triangle" in a highly significant sense: Bendrix's rival for Sarah's love is not another man, not Henry, but God. There can be no end to this "affair." Moreover, God is not only divine culprit and divine lover, but divine novelist, as Frank Kermode was the first to point out. Bendrix, the professional novelist, comes to see himself as a character in a plot more ingenious than any human imagination could contrive:

We are inextricably bound to the plot, and wearily God forces us, here and there, according to his intention, characters without poetry, without free will, whose only importance is that somewhere, at some time, we help to furnish the scene in which a living character moves and speaks, providing perhaps the saints with the opportunities for their free will.

There is no mistaking, of course, which human novelist God most resembles.

The End of the Affair illustrates Greene's use of key words more strikingly than any other novel: it rings with the repetition of *love* and *hate*. For the statistical record, these words or forms of them recur about three hundred and one hundred times respectively in this short novel. The effect is not monotonous because Greene is continually exploring new dimensions and interrelationships of love, hate, and the mixture of love and hate that is jealousy. Both Bendrix and Sarah become aware that love and hate are equally strong evidence that the defenses around simple selfhood are down. Toward the end of his narrative Bendrix writes:

If I hate her so much as I sometimes do, how can I love her? Can one really hate and love? Or is it only myself that I really hate? . . . I took her journal and . . . read, "Oh, God, if I could really hate you, what would that mean?" And I thought, hating Sarah is only loving Sarah, and hating myself is only loving myself. I'm not worth hating. . . . Nothing, not even Sarah, is worth our hatred, if You exist, except You.

Of equal importance with the play on love and hate is the correspondence established between human (*i.e.*, sexual) love and divine love. Bendrix interprets a fragment stolen from Sarah's wastepaper basket—"I know I am only beginning to love, but already I want to abandon everything, everybody but you"—as part of a love letter, though it is in fact part of a prayer. "Reading her letter to my unknown successor would have hurt less if I hadn't known how capable she was of abandonment," comments Bendrix. The irony of his misunderstanding, however, is not total, for Sarah's love of God proceeds from her capacity for carnal love. This connection is subtly employed to make credible Sarah's orientation to Catholicism, with all its literalist dogmas and materialistic trappings. When Sarah first entered a Catholic Church she "hated the statues, the crucifix, all the emphasis on the human body"; she seeks a God that is "vague, amorphous, cosmic . . . like a powerful vapour moving among the chairs and walls." But the recollection of Bendrix's body makes her wish for its resurrection and the resurrection of her own.

And of course on the altar there was a body too—such a familiar body, more familiar than Maurice's, that it had never struck me before as a body with all the parts of a body, even the parts the loin-cloth concealed. . . . I looked at that material body on that material cross and I wondered, how could the world have nailed a vapour there?

With *The End of the Affair* Greene seems to have finally rid himself of Manichaeism. In other respects, too, the novel represents his art at its most mature; but at the time of publication it was difficult to say who were most scandalized—non-Catholic readers at the introduction of miracles into realistic fiction, or Catholics at the attribution of miracles to a woman like Sarah. There was, therefore, a general sigh of relief when in his next novel Greene turned away from explicitly Catholic subject matter. Yet *The Quiet American* (1951) is far from being a purely secular novel. Set against the background of the French war in Indochina, it is concerned overtly with political and ideological conflict. But the conflict is dramatized and analyzed in terms that are consistent with Greene's earlier theological perspective; and the agnostic narrator, Fowler, is left in the end, like Bendrix, troubled and dissatisfied with any purely human explanation of experience.

The elected stance of Fowler, the British journalist covering the war in Indochina, is one of complete detachment. "The human condition being what it was, let them fight, let them love, let them murder. I would not be involved." Thus, when Fowler begins to feel irritation with Pyle, a young American working ostensibly with a medical mission in Saigon, his reasons are at first personal: a general dislike of Americans "with their private stores of coca-cola and their portable hospitals and their not-quite-latest guns," and a resentment of Pyle's attempts to woo his oriental mistress Phuong away from him. But when Pyle proves responsible for a bomb outrage, Fowler decides that his enthusiasm for the idea of a Third Force breaking the deadlock between Colonialism and Communism is not merely foolish but dangerous. In consequence, Fowler becomes "involved" to the point of conniving, half willingly, at the murder of Pyle by the Communists.

Fowler's judgment of Pyle's character is formulated in terms of "innocence." The menace of Pyle's kind of innocence is expressed in a beautifully molded image, its force cunningly held back until the last moment:

Innocence always calls mutely for protection, when we would be so much wiser to guard ourselves against it: innocence is like a dumb leper who has lost his bell, wandering the world, meaning no harm.

This judgment is consistent with Greene's suggestions, in earlier novels, that the recognition of evil, in oneself and in others, is a necessary part of any proper understanding of life. "I wish sometimes you had a few bad motives," says Fowler to Pyle. "You might understand a little more about human beings. And that applies to your country, too,

Pyle." Fowler himself, however, by his act of involvement
burdens himself with a sense of guilt for which his cynicism provides no relief. His guilt and uneasiness destroy
the happiness he would otherwise have enjoyed when his
wife agrees to divorce him, allowing him to marry Phuong.
The last words of the novel are:

Everything had gone right with me since [Pyle] had died, but
how I wished there existed someone to whom I could say that I
was sorry.

Greene impresses one as being a "professional" writer
in the best sense of the word. While working on *The Quiet
American* he made four trips to Indochina, staying there
twelve months in all, and this careful preparation is evident in the complete authority with which he establishes
the novel's setting. We never doubt that Fowler is a reliable reporter of the Southeast Asian scene, of the war, and
of the conflicts and interests behind it; while certain repeated motifs—the old trousered women squatting on the
landing, Phuong's dexterity with an opium pipe—give
the whole picture the characteristic mood and coloring of
Greeneland.

The novel has acquired a certain notoriety as an expression of venomous anti-Americanism. While it is true
that Greene has never been enraptured by the public face
of American civilization, in contrasting American innocence and European experience he is following a long
line of American writers; and if he comes down hard on
the Americans, it is on behalf of the Asians, not of the European colonialists. On one level the novel certainly
suggests that American intervention in Southeast Asia is
both impolitic and unjustifiable; but in the light of sub-

sequent events this seems a prophetic rather than a prejudiced judgment.

In the chronology of Greene's work, *The Quiet American* is flanked by two plays, *The Living Room* (1953) and *The Potting Shed* (1957), in which the author's interest in religious themes is still much in evidence. The first of these ends with the suicide of the heroine, provoked by the irreconcilable claims of her lover (non-Catholic, middle-aged, and unhappily married) and her faith, as forbiddingly represented by her two aged aunts and a crippled priest, their brother. In *The Potting Shed* the son of a once famous rationalist discovers after his father's death that at the age of fourteen he (the son) committed suicide and recovered life by an apparent miracle, obtained by his uncle, a Catholic priest, who sacrificed his faith to this end in a vow. The parallels with *The Heart of the Matter* and *The End of the Affair* are obvious; but, denuded of Greene's narrative resources, the dramatic plots creak somewhat. The conventions of the realistic "well-made play" which he adopts impose an improbable and unseemly hurry on the characters in their spiritual and emotional development, and the dialogue is liable to seem either too flat or too solemnly epigrammatic. There are some fine things in both plays (such as the ritual closing of rooms by which the old aunts in *The Living Room* deny both life and death); and they are certainly superior to the average product of the commercial theater. But, even when the far more successful comedy, *The Complaisant Lover* (1959) is taken into account, it does not seem likely that Greene will add a significant chapter to the history of British drama.

Greene's excursion into the theater is in one way characteristic of the latter part of his career. During this time his work seems to be directed by a restless search for new themes or new modes of exploring familiar themes; and beneath it all one detects a certain impatience with the categories with which critics have sought to define his literary identity. The dedication to *Loser Takes All* (1955), a slight comic novella about gambling, contains a wry allusion to "some of my Catholic critics"; and in this and his next entertainment, *Our Man in Havana* (1958), Greene takes a light-hearted view of marital and sexual behavior that is, by Catholic standards, highly irregular. "Catholic critics" consoled by the uncompromising supernaturalism of *The Potting Shed* must have been disconcerted by *The Complaisant Lover*, in which the adulterous situation so productive of misery in Greene's previous work is resolved by the bland acceptance of a *ménage à trois*. In these years, Greene is giving his humorous vein, subdued though wholly delightful in such characters as Harris and Parkis, its full chance. *Our Man in Havana* is an extravagant burlesque of the British Secret Service—and also, incidentally, of the apparatus of Greene's early entertainments.

These and other new developments in Greene's work—such as his renewed interest in the short story, a form in which he has never excelled—naturally provoked a number of questions in the minds of his audience. Had he worked out the vein of Catholic inspiration for his work? If so, what would replace it? Would he, in fact, produce any more novels of real consequence? *A Burnt-Out Case* (1961) intensified the debate without settling it.

But it does suggest that Greene had been asking himself the same questions, and had decided to objectify them in an imaginative form.

I referred, at the beginning of this essay, to the parallel that can be drawn between the hero of this novel and his creator: between Querry, the Catholic architect who comes to a remote leprosarium in the Belgian Congo, no longer believing in religion or love or art, in flight from *Time*-style celebrity and from official adoption by his Church; and Greene, the Catholic novelist, known for his unconventional travels, his melancholia and pessimism, his dislike of publicity, and his controversial standing among coreligionists. It is worth taking note, however, of Greene's words in the Dedication: "This is not a *roman à clef*, but an attempt to give dramatic expression to various types of belief, half-belief and non-belief." The most important feature of Querry, as his name suggests, is that he is a mystery. In his fascinating Congo journal, *In Search of a Character* (1961), Greene describes his decision to restrain the authorial voice from penetrating the thoughts of any character in the novel: "This makes for the mood of mystery which I want to catch." One might suggest, therefore, that insofar as Greene is using himself as a lay figure for the character of Querry, it is not in a confessional way, but by drawing back and regarding his own public image and what others make of it. *In Search of a Character* is full of such reflections.

Given, as the subject for a novel, the discrepancies between the real character of a famous man and the character others ascribe to him, the ironies inherent in the situation will be intensified if he has virtually no character at all—if he is in the painful process of shedding his identity and

finding a new one. This is precisely Querry's situation. Dr.
Colin correctly diagnoses Querry as a "burnt-out case,"
like one of "the lepers who lose everything that can be
eaten away before they are cured." But even the perceptive doctor had at first suspected Querry of being a lepro-
phile; and others are not so ready to abandon their
theories.

Rycker, the odious *colon,* is the first to discover that
Querry is *the* Querry, and takes it upon himself to pro-
claim the architect a new Schweitzer. This suggestion is
eagerly endorsed by Father Thomas, an insecure priest
who finds the rather hearty and humdrum community life
at the leprosarium lacking in spirituality. Parkinson, the
syndicated journalist, contributes his own theory that
Querry is atoning for a lurid past. Something like a cult
begins to grow around the exasperated Querry. The
ironies are extremely well managed. Querry's denials of
missionary zeal are put down to humility, and his protesta-
tions of disbelief are attributed to the mystical symptom of
"aridity." In the end, of course, Querry's admirers cannot
tolerate his refusal to play the roles they require. Rycker,
wounded by Querry's rebuffs, flies into a jealous rage
when Querry imprudently takes pity on the man's pathetic
young wife; and Parkinson, also stung by Querry's scorn,
passes Rycker false but circumstantial evidence of adultery. When the scandal reaches the leprosarium, Father
Thomas is the first to believe it.

Meanwhile the ambiguous concept of the "cure" of
the burnt-out case has been taking on a more positive
aspect. Querry begins to find a way of life at the leprosarium, and to talk "as a hungry man eats"—particularly
with Dr. Colin. Colin is easily the most sympathetic non-

believer in Greene's work. Unlike the Lieutenant in *The Power and the Glory*, whom he remotely resembles in his austere devotion to duty, Colin does not see his humane vocation as opposed to the religious vocation. "Sometimes I think that the search for suffering and the remembrance of suffering are the only means we have to put ourselves in touch with the whole human condition," he says. "With suffering we become part of the Christian myth." Religious faith has often been associated with suffering in Greene's work, but never before with the relief and conquest of suffering. Yet Colin proceeds, with the obvious approval of the author, to develop an essentially optimistic theory of human development, in which evolutionary progress is identified with the spirit of Christian love. Greene has acknowledged the influence of Teilhard de Chardin's *The Phenomenon of Man* on *A Burnt-Out Case;* and it says much for the openness of his mind and imagination that he responded enthusiastically, at a fairly late stage of his career, to a philosophical argument which in some ways runs against the grain of his most characteristic fiction. In *A Burnt-Out Case* "the belief that life should be better than it is" seems to be slowly winning over "the belief that when it appears better it is really worse."

But the issue is left in some doubt: Querry retains his mystery to the last. He has reached the point of recognizing suffering, and hence identity, in himself; of "fingering" his lack of faith, in Marie Rycker's words, "like a sore you want to get rid of." But his self-discovery is interrupted by a bullet from the demented Rycker. Querry dies murmuring, "This is absurd or . . . " "This" presumably refers not only to his tragifarcical death, but to his whole life, in which the public appearances of success and fulfillment have been hollow and deceptive. Either this life and death are "absurd"—*i.e.*, meaningless—or (we may tentatively complete the thought) they acquire meaning only in some transcendent pattern: the pattern offered by religion, or the less orthodox pattern expounded by Dr. Colin.

The idea, deriving from existentialist thought, of human life as "absurd" is a familiar one in contemporary literature, where its effect has been to break down traditional genre categories and to displace potentially tragic materials toward disquieting forms of comedy. Greene's latest novel is significantly entitled *The Comedians* (1966), and is pitched, in tone, somewhere between *The Quiet American* and *Our Man in Havana,* mingling laughter with pity and fear.

Brown, the rootless, cosmopolitan, middle-aged narrator, meets on board a ship bound for Haiti a rather dubious "Major" Jones with claims to an adventurous and heroic war record, and an American called Smith who once ran obscurely for the American Presidency on a vegetarian ticket. The absurd convergence of these three overworked names establishes the note of a story in which the characters are mostly denied the luxury of dignity as they contend with the vicissitudes of life. The vicissitudes are supplied in ample measure by Haiti, "the shabby land of terror," in which the action is largely set, an impoverished and desperate country languishing under the tyranny of a ruthless dictator and his secret police, the "Tontons Macoutes," whose inscrutable malice is chillingly symbolized by the black sunglasses they wear night and day. Brown is returning to Haiti to look after the hotel he has failed to sell, and to pick up the threads of a rather joyless love affair with Martha, wife of a South American ambassador

and daughter of a German war criminal. Smith and his
wife are hoping to set up a vegetarian center in Haiti.
Jones's mission is more obscure, but proves to be some
kind of financial swindle involving government funds.
Brown's association with Smith and Jones, and his discovery in his swimming pool of the corpse of the Secretary for
Social Welfare, Dr. Philipot, who has cut his throat to
avoid arrest, draws him into the dangerous world of political intrigue. More from personal than ideological motives
Brown collaborates with a group of pathetically ineffective
guerrillas led by Philipot's nephew, and at the end of the
story narrowly escapes to Santo Domingo, where he adds
to an already varied career the profession of undertaker.

　　Like the Liberia of *Journey Without Maps*, Haiti gives
the lie to liberal optimism. Thus, the experience of a
Negro police state is a cruel blow to the civil-rights ideal-
ism of the Smiths. Greene, however, has lost his old zest
for attacking Pelagians. The Smiths are in many ways admirable characters, and the narrator explicitly denies that
he finds them comic. For in this novel the words *comedy*
and *comedian* are used in a traditional, theatrical sense,
denoting the improvisation of roles and the wearing of
masks. The theme of the book seems to be that in an era in
which cruelty and injustice in the public life have grown
to uncontrollable proportions (and it is emphasized that
Haiti is representative, not abnormal in this respect) the
private pursuit of happiness is inevitably attended by absurd incongruities and indecorums that compel the individual into the resigned adoption of a "comic" role. The
alternative is some kind of irrational commitment—to
force, to vegetarianism, to voodoo—which is validated by
defeat, and ultimately by death. Thus, Brown comments

on the Negro lover of his mother, when he commits suicide after her death: "perhaps he was no *comédien* after
all. Death is a proof of sincerity." In these terms Jones is
the arch-comedian. His role is the most outrageous deception of all; yet he has the gift of amusing people and winning their affection. And when Brown, out of misplaced
jealousy, forces him to make good his boasts and take over
the leadership of Philipot's guerrillas, he has the courage
to go through with his performance to the point of dying
for it.

Early in his narrative, Brown (a lapsed Catholic) remarks:

When I was a boy I had faith in the Christian God. Life under his
shadow was a very serious affair; I saw Him incarnated in every
tragedy. He belonged to the *lacrimae rerum* like a gigantic figure
looming through a Scottish mist. Now that I approached the end
of life it was only my sense of humour that enabled me sometimes to believe in Him. Life was a comedy, not the tragedy for
which I had been prepared, and it seemed to me that we were all
. . . driven by an authoritative practical joker towards the extreme point of comedy.

Without interpreting this passage as a personal confession
we may perhaps see it as some kind of gloss on Greene's
progress from fiction based on a "tragic" conflict between
human and divine values, to fiction conceived in terms of
comedy and irony in which the possibility of religious
faith has all but retreated out of sight in the anarchic confusion of human behavior. In Bendrix a secular and cynical
view of life is still powerfully challenged by the divine
order, but in Fowler, Querry, and Brown the challenge is
progressively weaker, and more oblique. There is evi-

dence, here, of a greater capacity for imaginative development than Greene is usually given credit for. But the permeation of his later work with negative and skeptical attitudes, characteristically filtered through the consciousness of a laconic, disillusioned narrator, has resulted in some loss of intensity. Fowler, Querry, and Brown are all created with Greene's accustomed skill, and the actions in which they are involved never fail to interest; but they do not possess the imagination and linger in the memory as do Pinkie, or Scobie, or the whiskey priest.

"Patronizingly in the end he would place me probably a little above Maugham," Bendrix the novelist sourly predicts of his critic, Waterbury, thus cautioning critics intent on "placing" Greene himself. Let it merely be suggested that among his own generation of British novelists it is difficult to find his equal; and that he has produced a number of novels that seem certain to live, by the force with which they embody a highly individual, genuinely challenging view of life. Finally, there is something disarming about an eminent author who has twice won *New Statesman* competitions by parodying himself. "Fame falls like a dead hand on an author's shoulders," Greene has written; but few have borne its weight with more self-possession than he.

Since the above account was written, Graham Greene has published two more novels, *Travels with My Aunt* (1970) and *The Honorary Consul* (1973) and a new volume of stories, *May We Borrow Your Husband? and Other Comedies of the Sexual Life* (1967), which were incorporated in *Collected Short Stories* (1972). In 1969 the *Collected Essays* were published, including many previously uncollected pieces. In 1971 Greene published a short autobiography, *A Sort of Life*, in the course of which he referred to an unpublished biography of Lord Rochester which he had written in the early 1930s. This has since been published as *Lord Rochester's Monkey* (1974).

Like the novels, the autobiography has its key word, *failure*, which is introduced in the very first paragraph: "I have preferred to finish this essay with the years of failure which followed the acceptance of my first novel." In fact the book literally ends with the description of a conversation some twenty years later between the mature, successful Greene and an old friend living a life of contented obscurity in the Far East. But the theme is the same: "For a writer, I argued, success is always temporary, success is only delayed failure." In a commercial sense, of course, nothing Graham Greene writes can "fail"—which perhaps explains why he constantly reminds himself of the possibility of artistic failure.

A Sort of Life is a muted, discreetly selective memoir, which confirms and fills out the sketches of Greene's early life already provided in his essays and travel books, without making any startling new revelations. In any case, the more we learn about his life, the less it seems to explain the peculiar character and power of his imagination. The description, for example, of his emotions as a pupil in the school where his father was headmaster ("I was a foreigner and a suspect, quite literally a hunted creature") foreshadows obviously enough his obsession with the figure of the hunted outcast, but there is nothing in the *facts* of his school life, as given, which explains the intensity of that emotion, or the remarkable way in which it was later tapped to create extreme and exotic figures like Pinkie and

the whiskey priest. One might almost say that it is only by
a feat of style that Greene throws across the low contours
of a generally comfortable, protected, unremarkable
bourgeois upbringing in the Home Counties the somber
lighting that makes it a plausible source for his imaginative work. This is not to deny the reality of his adolescent
misery, which is sufficiently attested by his frequent flirta-
tions with suicide, but to suggest that the misery, and the
imaginative vision, were generated from within rather
than derived from external circumstances. This made
Greene an essentially romantic writer, but what he had
painfully to learn (as he recognises in *A Sort of Life*) was
that the romantic impulse needed to be disciplined by the
reality principle, connected in narrative with "external circumstances." From *Stamboul Train* onward these have
been characteristically the circumstances of contemporary
politics.

Greene has embedded further reflection on this theme
in his most recent novel. One of the subsidiary characters
in *The Honorary Consul*, set in contemporary Argentina, is
a novelist called Jorge Julio Saavedra, who writes in "a
heavily loaded melancholy style, full of the spirit of *machismo*." He insists that "A novelist today who wishes to
represent tyranny should not describe the activities of
General Stroesner in Paraguay—that is journalism, not literature. Tiberius is a better example for the poet." *The
Honorary Consul* is itself concerned with political opposition to General Stroesner's regime, and its half-English,
half-Paraguayan hero Dr. Edward Plarr presumably speaks
for Greene in finding Saavedra's work romantically self-
indulgent and false to reality. "Your fisherman is timeless," he says irritably of one of Saavedra's characters,

"because he never existed." Yet Greene remains a *roman-tic* realist, and arguably it is the Saavedra within him that drives his literary imagination. Though Greene learned to tighten up and pare down the "heavily loaded melancholy style" of his own early work, the phrase is still not entirely inapplicable to his mature prose; and despite the telling criticism of the Latin American cult of *machismo* in *The Honorary Consul*, it is surely true that, in however ironic and negative a fashion, Greene himself sees conduct in very much these terms. The heroines of his fiction, as I remarked earlier, tend to be waifs, at once innocent and available, submissive to the demands of heroes who observe symptoms of tenderness in themselves with alarm, as a kind of fatal weakness (the relationship between Plarr and the childlike ex-prostitute Clara in this latest novel is typical). And of course Greene, in life as well as art, has always been fascinated by situations of extreme physical danger that test personal courage. Perhaps one reason why he has written no major novel set in England since *The End of the Affair* (where the Blitz provided the necessary climate of risk) is that his kind of realism can no longer get a purchase on our kind of reality: the latter is too dull, too bland, too suburban.

One way of reading *Travels with My Aunt* is as an act of self-definition and self-justification along these lines, for its hero is a man who in late middle age decides to exchange the safe limitations of life in a London suburb for the risks and surprises of Greeneland. In the past the novelist has expressed some irritation with this coinage, claiming that Greeneland is simply the world of suffering and oppression which we are too smugly provincial to recognize; but he permitted the blurb-writer for *Travels* to

use the word, and the book itself carries an implied acknowledgment that Greeneland is a region as much made
as found. The novel is, indeed, on one level an elaborate
exercise in self-parody.

The narrator Henry Pulling (the suggestion of self-
abuse in the name humorously signifies the absence of
eros from his life) is a retired banker leading a life of dull
respectability in a London suburb when, at his mother's
funeral, he meets his Aunt Augusta for the first time since
he was a child. Despite her advanced years, Aunt Augusta
is vivacious, dominating, and to her conventional nephew
at once fascinating and disconcerting. First she startles
him with the information that the mother he has just cre-
mated was not his real mother. Then she sweeps him off
on a series of missions that are either whimsically sentimental or illegal—gold and currency smuggling. Out of the
constant stream of anecdote with which she entertains
him, Henry gradually infers that Aunt Augusta has been a
high-class prostitute for most of her life, that she has had
liaisons with all kinds of dubious characters in several different countries and (some time after the reader) that she
is his mother.

The travels in Part I of the book (almost two-thirds of
its length) constitute a kind of tour of Greeneland. Thus
Aunt Augusta and Henry first visit Brighton, then take the
Orient Express (now sadly bereft of its prewar glamour,
lacking even a restaurant car) to Istanbul. Like the hero's
mother in *The Comedians*, Aunt Augusta has a Negro
lover, and he comes from Freetown, the setting of *The
Heart of the Matter*. At Milan station Aunt Augusta is
reunited with her son by an Italian confidence trickster

called Visconti, the name of the villain in Marjorie Bowen's *The Viper of Milan* which so affected Greene in adolescence. Not all these literary jokes are self-referring: in the Istanbul episode there are allusions to Ian Fleming's *To Russia with Love* and to Kingsley Amis, an admirer, and on one occasion imitator, of the James Bond books. A detective sergeant in the British police is given the name of the present Warden of All Souls' College, Oxford. And so on.

The structure of the novel is uncharacteristically loose—a string of episodes and tall stories—until Part II, when a series of implausible coincidences, parodying the "well-made novel," ties most of the characters together. This section is set in what was then new territory for Greene: South America. Aunt Augusta has been reunited with her lover Visconti in the sinister, freebooting republic of Paraguay, and Henry is summoned to join them. Unknowingly he brings with him a Leonardo sketch looted by Visconti in World War II which is to provide the capital for a smuggling enterprise in Paraguay. When he discovers how he has been used, Henry does not protest but throws in his lot with the aged, irrepressible pair. On the river journey up from Buenos Aires he has already made the existential decision to renounce suburbia and respectability. "It was as though I had escaped from an open prison, had been snatched away, provided with a rope ladder and an open car, into my aunt's world, the world of the unexpected character and the unforeseen event." More than once in the novel Aunt Augusta is identified with the creative artist, specifically the novelist. Both, we are given to understand, are likely to be by turns generous and cruel, passionate and ironic; they may be amoral but they are life-giving, and their stories are not to be tested by the vulgar standard of empirical truthfulness.

Travels with My Aunt had all the signs of a valedictory work, but it was not long before Greene produced another novel, also set in South America, but this time a tightly constructed book of completely serious intent. The story, concerning the kidnapping of a diplomat by Paraguayan revolutionaries, bears the characteristic hallmarks of topicality, suspense, and irony. These terrorists, led by the Marxist renegade priest Father Leo Rivas, are pathetic rather than terrifying. They kidnap the wrong man—the insignificant British honorary consul instead of the American ambassador—and are too humane, or too human, to extricate themselves from the resulting muddle. Greene's sympathies, as usual, are with the failures—and his compassion embraces the guerrillas' victim, Charley Fortnum, also a kind of failure, living on the prestige and perks of his honorary consulship, an acoholic and a cuckold. Plarr, a character very much in the line of Greene's postwar heroes—dry, laconic, skeptical, world-weary (it is a surprise to learn that he is only in his early thirties)—is doubly involved in these events: as the son of a political prisoner in Paraguay he is drawn reluctantly into collusion with the revolutionaries, and as the cuckolder of the unsuspecting Fortnum he feels a chivalrous obligation to protect his life. There is a typically existential moment for Plarr when he is summoned by the kidnappers: "The small patch of marble floor on which he stood seemed like the edge of an abyss; he could not move one step in either direction without falling deeper into the darkness of involvement or guilt." But Plarr's choice of political involvement does not free him from sexual guilt, which goads him finally into sacrificing his life.

In the long final sequence in which Plarr and the terrorists and their hostage are cooped up in a hut waiting for their, and the authorities', ultimata to expire, the intense pressure of their situation compels them into personal introspection and metaphysical debate. The leitmotif here is paternity. "Father" is the last word Plarr hears. He and Fortnum are haunted by their dead fathers. Plarr is the father of the child in Clara's womb, which Fortnum fondly believes to be his. The leader of the terrorists is called "Father" by the woman he regards as his wife. And arching over all these ambiguous father figures is the question of the Father: does He exist, and if so, what is His nature?

Here, through the mouth of Father Rivas, Greene develops the Teilhardian ideas first explored in *A Burnt-Out Case,* but with a bold Manichaean twist: "The God I believe in suffers as we suffer while He struggles against Himself—against His evil side. . . . God is joined to us in a sort of blood transfusion. His good blood is in ours and our tainted blood runs through His." Such startling theological speculations are counterpointed by Charley Fortnum's sentimental humanism. Dialectically fascinating, these conversations are however dramatically unconvincing, so that the novel's tension slackens just when it should be at its most taut. This is unfortunate, for the climax is prepared for with consummate skill and much of the local color and minor characterisation in the earlier part of the novel is up to the author's highest standard. One cannot help feeling, as one feels to some extent in all Greene's later fiction, that his growing skepticism and relativism concerning morals and metaphysics, however

much to his credit as a reflective human being, is to some
extent at odds with the fictional form he has perfected: the
well-made novel in which the paradoxes of theme are ultimately resolved as ingeniously as the complications of
plot. No longer willing to exercise the prerogative of authorial commentary, Greene now prefers to pursue his thematic interests in dialogue between his characters that
risks seeming both overexplicit and inconclusive. The epigraph to *The Honorary Consul*, from Thomas Hardy, expresses accurately enough his present view of the world:
"All things merge into one another—good into evil, generosity into justice, religion into politics . . ." but his most
successful work was based on the clash of antithetical
ideas rather than this hazy, ambiguous flow of one idea
into another. In conclusion, however, it would be churlish
not to recognize, and salute, Graham Greene's continuing
creativity, and capacity for surprising us with the vivid
evocation of neglected corners of the world.

ROBERT GORHAM DAVIS

C. P. Snow

Since his influential Rede Lecture, "The Two Cultures,"
in 1958, it has seemed deceptively easy to place Charles
Percy Snow—both as novelist and man of ideas. In that
lecture and any number of public appearances, he has
done the placing for us. We think that we know, through
Snow himself, precisely where he stands and what he
wants.

The most powerful revolutionary force in the world
today, his lecture told us, is science—science lifted to a
new level by Einstein, Rutherford, Kapitza, Bohr, and
Dirac. Its heroic age was the 1920s; the center of activity
was Cambridge, where Snow himself, then a research student, heard these men describe their discoveries as they
were making them.

Science is essentially progressive, Snow argues, and
so are the political views of most of its creators. They
possess the means—and the desire—to end want and disease in every corner of the world. They see no necessary
barriers to collaboration with their colleagues in the Communist countries. Ultimately, of course, scientists have to

face as individuals the facts of the human condition, face loneliness and death. Their interest in literature, unfortunately, tends to be minimal.

Literary men, on the other hand, according to Snow, have little or no knowledge of the new science, and their social attitudes are often contemptible. A physicist of distinction said to him: "Yeats, Pound, Wyndham Lewis, nine out of ten of those who have dominated literary sensibility in our time—weren't they not only politically silly, but politically wicked? Didn't the influence of all they represented bring Auschwitz that much nearer?" Snow could not

defend the indefensible . . . The honest answer was that there is, in fact, a connection which literary persons were culpably slow to see, between some kinds of early twentieth-century art and the most imbecile expressions of anti-social feeling. That was one reason, among many, why some of us turned our backs on the art, and tried to hack out a new or different way for ourselves.

A scientist by training, a writer by vocation, Snow offers himself as a unique living bridge between the two cultures. But his capacities and experience extend further than this. If we are to speak of "cultures" in the plural, there is no need to be limited to two. Administrators in the universities, in business, and government belong neither to science nor the arts, and may be considered to constitute a culture of their own. "One of the most bizarre features of any industrial society in our time," Snow wrote in *Science and Government*, "is that the cardinal choices have to be made by a handful of men . . . who cannot have a first-hand knowledge of what these choices depend upon or what their results may be." Nonscientific administrators now decide how science is to be organized and used.

During the thirties, as fellow and tutor at Christ's College, Cambridge, Snow saw university administration at first hand. From 1939 on, he really walked the corridors of power. He recruited scientists for the war effort and helped to decide how they were to be distributed among the competing, understaffed war agencies. After the war he was a director of the English Electric Company. When the Labor Party came to power in October, 1964, with Harold Wilson as Prime Minister, Snow was appointed Parliamentary Secretary, the second-ranking post, in the new Ministry of Technology, and was made a baron, Lord Snow of Leicester, so that he could represent the ministry in the House of Lords. All through his rapid climb, Snow never forgot that he grew up in a poor family and that his first serious education was of his own winning in a provincial, red brick, technical evening school. His background and sense of class differences bring him into natural sympathy with younger social-minded postwar writers like Amis and Osborne.

Not since Disraeli has a popular, political-minded novelist been so intimately involved with the actual exercise of power. Not since H. G. Wells has a popular, social-minded novelist known so much at first hand about science. For nearly twenty years before 1958, Snow had been in an ideal position to carry out in his fiction the program defined in "The Two Cultures." By bringing together two kinds of imagination which he had himself experienced, he could enable scientists and literary men to appreciate each other, and the lay public to appreciate both. He could dramatize for his readers the struggle to-

ward those social goods which he condemned the major
writers of his century for betraying.

But if we—by act of will—forget temporarily about
"The Two Cultures" and read carefully through Snow's
fiction to see what actually occurs there, we find it almost
totally inconsistent with what we had been led to expect.

In all of C. P. Snow's novels taken together there is
less concrete evidence of how the scientific mind works
and how its methods and discoveries differ from those of
the literary man or philosopher or theologian than we
could find in almost any article in any issue of *Nature* or
Scientific American. There is simply no comparison, in
this respect, between his work and that of Aldous Huxley
or of H. G. Wells himself.

This is not because of any intrinsic difficulties that
make the new science incommunicable. While Snow's
later novels were being written, the educated public was
already fascinated by living cells and the role of the giant
molecules in life processes. The attempts to "break" the
genetic codes carried by DNA had obvious appeal to the
Wellsian type of imagination. But such matters are not
touched upon in any of Snow's serious fiction, even
though Arthur Miles in *The Search* had seen the coming
importance of the protein molecules and had decided to
devote his future work to determining their structure. Nor,
except for one early, anonymous, and now unobtainable
effort, is Snow a writer of science fiction.

There are similar discrepancies in his treatment of
politics. Snow's reference in "The Two Cultures" to "nine
out of ten" of the writers as wickedly reactionary is extremely misleading. In the thirties, writers were very active internationally in the fight against war and Fascism.

The statement by Snow—or the scientist he quotes—
makes sense only if "literary sensibility" is given a very
restricted and poetic meaning. Most major novelists and
playwrights—and at least the younger poets—were
engaged politically, on what Snow and his alter ego Lewis
Eliot would surely regard as the right side. If we think of
Mann, Silone, Barbusse, Bernanos, Aragon, Hemingway,
Steinbeck, O'Casey, Spender, Dreiser, Dos Passos, Sartre,
and Camus, we realize that the literary "culture" was
quite as responsible as the scientific, and as progressive
politically. In fact, in the West generally, writers were far
more energetic and conspicuous than scientists in supporting the Spanish loyalists and working for a united front
against Fascism.

"Strangers and Brothers" is a long series of interrelated novels all told in the first person by Lewis Eliot.
In his personal friendships and partisanships, Snow's narrator is curiously indifferent to politics. "The Two Cultures" posited a connection between advanced literary
sensibility and wicked political attitudes. Snow never possessed such sensibility and so could not repudiate it. But
in his novels there is a remarkable tolerance for those
whose views brought "Auschwitz that much nearer." The
man whom Lewis Eliot loves, Roy Calvert, is, during the
years in which they are closest, an active pro-Nazi who
tries to convert Lewis. In *The Masters* the candidate
whom Lewis works to elect, a man named Jago, is ultimately defeated because of his reactionary political views.
His opponents decide that they cannot afford to have such
a man at the head of a college when everything for which a
college should stand is being threatened by the spread of
Hitlerism. Though Lewis Eliot describes himself as a left-

liberal, Jago's views do not seem to disturb him in the slightest, and he supports Jago staunchly to the end. Other supporters are Roy Calvert and a Tory named Arthur Brown.

There is no reason, of course, why a character should not take a different political position from his creator, even when he is the sole reporter of all that occurs. But Lewis Eliot's relation to Snow is puzzling. Year by year, event by event, their careers are parallel, and in his general reflections on life Eliot seems to be speaking for his creator.

But why is he named Lewis Eliot? Snow, as we shall see, takes names seriously and plays on them freely. His spokesman's name links those of two of the villains mentioned most conspicuously in "The Two Cultures": Wyndham Lewis and T. S. Eliot. And yet the narrative method, which lets Lewis Eliot do all the talking and describing, without subjecting him to the kind of test that would permit us to judge his self-judgments, makes it difficult to see exactly how he is more or less than Snow's spokesman or other self.

Though less bouncy and ideological and restlessly introspective, Snow's autobiographic narrative mode in *The Search* and the Lewis Eliot series is essentially that of H. G. Wells in novels like *The New Machiavelli* and *Tono Bungay*. When H. G. Wells sent Henry James a copy of *The New Machiavelli*, James replied with high praise, but lamented "the bad service you have done your cause by riding so hard again that accurst autobiographical form." The novelist, James said, cannot present an authentic vision unless a particular detachment operates, a detachment "terribly wanting in autobiography brought, as the horrible phrase is, up to date."

Since this detachment is wanting in Snow's work and since all events are colored by the autobiographic narrator's moods and interpretations, the reader has to make his own judgments, trusting that the narrator's reports are at least factually reliable.

The action consists largely of talk among small groups of people. This talk is directed toward practical or emotional ends; rarely are literary, scientific, or political ideas developed for their own sake. In Snow's novels people seldom write letters, and they telephone chiefly to arrange face-to-face meetings. At these meetings something unexpected is usually revealed—often reluctantly, hesitantly, as a result of close questioning—which makes it necessary to plan at once a meeting with somebody else. If Lewis is not present, the participants arrange to see him immediately, tell him what occurred, and get his advice. Even if it is two o'clock in the morning, it is better to see Lewis Eliot then than wait until next day. We always have a meeting to look forward to, at the same time that we are absorbing the implications of one that has just occurred. The novels consist of a series of short dramatic chapters, each marking a stage in the careful step-by-step development of some issue or affair.

In recent years perhaps the most influential academic critic in England has been F. R. Leavis. In 1962 Leavis devoted his farewell lecture at Cambridge, where he had taught for many decades, to a savage personal attack on Snow. This caused even more furor than Snow's "The Two Cultures" lecture. In one of his cruder gibes, Leavis reported a rumor that Snow's novels were written by an electronic computer named Charlie to which Snow simply fed chapter titles. An enthusiast for D. H. Lawrence,

Leavis said that Snow had no talent as a novelist whatsoever, and no sense of what a novel can or should be.

This is unfair. Stylistically, imaginatively, and mimetically, Snow's resources as a novelist are limited, but he husbands them carefully and employs them with conscious skill. Some of Snow's repetitions, it is true, lend themselves to parody, but by his sneer Leavis can legitimately call attention chiefly to the very traditional mode in which Snow writes. Some years ago, criticizing Henry James, Leavis found James's main weakness as novelist the result of an upbringing which kept him, for all his interest in civilization, from developing "any sense of society as a system of functions and responsibilities." This is what Snow's fiction is about.

The novelist whom Snow most resembles is Anthony Trollope. Trollope's Barsetshire novels—that series of six, beginning with *The Warden* in 1857—has many of the same ingredients as the "Strangers and Brothers" series, dramatized in the same way. Complex institutions—governmental and clerical—are staffed by the worldly, the selfish, the conscientious, the refractory, battling for principles, place, and power. Strong-minded ladies intervene in matters that should not be their concern. Official bodies examine cases whose moral complexities are almost impossible to untangle. Trollope's social range is wide, from noble lords, often of dubious morality, to ambitious young clerics from poor families. There are, as in Snow, dramatic confrontations in a series of chapters with such titles as "Mrs. Proudie Wrestles and Gets a Fall" and "The Bishops Sit Down to Breakfast." Snow's chapter titles are deliberately prosy and unenterprising. His first serious novel, *The Search*, includes "The Institute Is

Talked About" and "They Discuss a Change." The forty-
five chapter titles of *Last Things*, published thirty-six years
later, are undramatic to the point of self-parody. Typical
are "Discussion of Someone Absent" and "Domestic Evening, Without Incident."

The "Strangers and Brothers" sequence, with Lewis
Eliot as its persisting "I" character, was planned as early
as 1935. Beginning with *Strangers and Brothers* in 1940,
and ending with *Last Things* in 1970, it stretched finally to
eleven volumes. All that we know of its characters and
events is what Lewis Eliot knows and chooses to tell. The
ideas developed are principally Eliot's ideas. The ideas of
others are expressed either in quoted conversation—never
at very great length or in very great detail—or as Eliot interprets them for us. Obviously Snow draws heavily, if
discreetly, on his own experiences. Where external events
in Eliot's life differ from those in Snow's we can tell fairly
well from the public record. Where their ideas and inner
life differ is not evident. As technician of the novel, Snow
wants his fiction to seem transparently to reflect reality
and his reflections on it. He has no interest in experi-
menting with the "inauthentic" narrator or even in one
distinctively distanced from himself.

As in Trollope's Barsetshire series, the same characters appear in novel after novel playing now major roles,
now minor ones. The great originator of such a scheme—
sometimes called *roman fleuve*—was of course Balzac, in
his *Human Comedy*. Though individual novels in a *roman
fleuve* are self-sufficient in the sense that the reader is
always given enough information to make sense of what is
occurring, the interest is deeper and richer if he has read
some or all of those that precede. Since Snow's were not

published in an order corresponding to the chronological order of the events that they describe, we are free to group them according to their principal themes.

In *Time of Hope* (1949) and *Homecoming* (1956) Lewis Eliot tells his own story up through a period in which his second marriage has been tested and proved sound. In *Strangers and Brothers* (1940), *The Light and the Dark* (1947), *The New Men* (1954) and *The Conscience of the Rich* (1958), Eliot describes the flawed lives of the four men to whom he felt closest: George Passant, Roy Calvert, his brother Martin, and Charles March. *The Masters* (1951) and *The Affair* (1960), the two most concentrated dramatically of the novels, tell how the fellows of a college at Cambridge handle two controversial cases sixteen years apart. These two novels resemble the others in the series, however, because of the characters of the principals in the two cases.

Corridors of Power (1964) immediately anticipated Snow's period of greatest fame and official power, in the Ministry of Technology and as member of the House of Lords. Of all his novels, *Corridors of Power* deals most directly with how governmental decisions are made at the highest levels of authority.

In *The Sleep of Reason* (1968) and *Last Things* (1970), both of which describe his agonizing eye operations, Lewis Eliot, though still famous and still active as a writer, has given up official responsibilities. His writing as such is never discussed. His curiosity and receptivity to confidences are as lively as ever, but directed more now to the problems of a younger generation—many of them the children of his friends and associates—whom we and he have seen growing up, falling in love with each other, and entering careers.

Three serious social novels stand formally apart from the "Strangers and Brothers" series, though they deal with similar scenes and characters. One, *The Search* (1934), preceded it; two, *The Malcontents* (1972) and *In Their Wisdom* (1974), followed. It is natural to begin a discussion of Snow's fiction with *The Search*, since this is a kind of trial autobiographical run. It uses a hero slightly different from Lewis Eliot (at least his name is different), but draws on the fund of experience which was to be used again for the early volumes of "Strangers and Brothers."

When *The Search* was republished twenty-four years later, in 1958, the year of "The Two Cultures" lecture, Snow wrote that he was encouraged to reissue the work because so many scientists remembered it as showing what science looked like from inside. I. I. Rabi, Nobel Prize physicist, calls it "the one novel which I knew which was really about scientists living as scientists." The introduction ends with a plea for the kind of education that will bring science and other aspects of culture into creative union.

As so often happens with works of imaginative truth, *The Search* as a novel seems to be saying something quite different and much less "constructive." The hero not only fails at science and decides that he has no true vocation for it, but in a silent act of complicity decides not to expose a friend who has violated the most basic scientific ethics.

We first see the narrator, Arthur Miles, as an eleven-year-old boy with an ineffectual, vaguely speculative father. They try to put together a telescope. When the father fumbles the placing of the lens, Arthur pretends, to save his father's feelings, that he can see more than he really does. The "personal thing," he realizes years later, counts more with him than honesty. Nevertheless, he determines to know, to learn, instead of merely wondering, like his father. Despite all sorts of discouragement, Arthur wins science scholarships and makes his way through King's College.

After taking a first in the examinations, young Miles plans his career with considerable shrewdness. Beginning in a known area in crystallography, where results are fairly certain, he will then move slowly into an unexplored area, that of the structure of the protein, where great things can be accomplished. Before his limitations, especially in mathematics, become evident, Arthur hopes to make enough of a mark so that he can organize and direct research carried out by others.

"I shan't mind giving up working with my own hands," he tells Audrey, the girl who loves him.

"It's a waste of time when I can get people to do it better. But—I want to run the work. That's the important thing."

She frowned: "You'll like the power?"

"I think I shall," I said. I burst out: "Of course I shall, but it's not all."

After long frustrating research at Cambridge, Arthur sees a very pretty pattern emerging. In a final check of his X rays, he notices in the next-to-last one some black dots that ruin the whole scheme. He thinks, "If I had not taken this photograph, what would have happened?" He would have published his results and gone ahead. If a later researcher discovered something wrong it would have been attributed to honest error. "I suppose, for a moment, I wanted to destroy the photograph." A counterimpulse rules this out, but Arthur now understands the psychology of fraud. Frauds occur very frequently in Snow's novels. "After that afternoon, I could not help being tolerant toward them."

Later, with dramatic cabled help from a friend in Germany, he makes a genuine though modest discovery, and has a glimpse, at least, of the almost mystic joy of revelation. A friend of his, a moody young genius named Constantine, brings Arthur in as a nonvoting member of a committee planning a National Institute for Biophysical Research, with the hope that Arthur will become its director. Arthur works skillfully toward compromise among the five rather stubborn committeemen in a series of meetings less fully developed and dramatized than those in *The Masters* and *The Affair*. "I found points as I went on to meet each of their interests." But he leaves his research largely to his assistant.

Just at the crucial moment a rumor spreads that a recent paper of Arthur's will "not hold water." He spends frantic hours reviewing all the research, and comes finally upon a fact supplied by the assistant which "was wrong. Which he could not know was wrong, because there was a small technical point involved. Which I had looked over twenty times, but passed because of his assurance. Which if I had inspected it with a moment's care would have shouted itself as wrong. Upon that flaw, the whole structure rested."

Arthur loses the directorship, and then loses Audrey too. She is a restless girl, unable to settle down to anything, the line of uncertainty deepening in her forehead.

Clearly she would have married Arthur if he had asked her. He returns from a period of research in Germany to find that she is going to marry his old friend Sheriff, a rather fraudulent charmer. Arthur and Audrey spend a last night of troubled physical love together, in one of Snow's most moving chapters. It is titled, interestingly enough, "Homecoming."

Arthur discovers that he has also lost his devotion to science, and wonders how genuine it had ever been. Scientific truths, though truths, are too limited. The "human" interest has become stronger.

Arthur marries a sexually inhibited woman of means, a political-minded woman, and himself writes a political invective called *The Gadarene Swine*. Preparing to leave science, and concerned about Audrey's fate, Miles tries to get Sheriff well established by giving him records of uncompleted researches. When Miles comes across Sheriff's published results in an American periodical, he sees at once that the conclusions have been faked. Arthur decides to say nothing. "And so, after the years of struggle, the personal things had won, I thought."

Scientific ethics mean less than a rather dubious personal commitment. *The Search* shows why Snow became a novelist. In his writings, men are frequently judged—and judged severely—so far as specific professional qualifications for a specific responsibility are concerned. But apart from such *ad hoc* or functional judgments, his narrators seem able to accept their friends completely for what they are. Even when they hold "wicked" political views or commit fraud, the basic feeling is unaffected. This is a proper novelist's kind of sympathy, and is why Snow's novels are so readable.

The Search is an interesting novel so long as it is not regarded as an imaginative introduction to science or as a bridge between the two cultures. As a matter of fact, in most of Snow's novels, what really moves men is not the two cultures—art and science—but the need for women and the need for success. Sometimes these are in harmony, more often at war.

In *The Search* science comes off badly. Of the four consequential experiments, two are botched and one is faked. None is explained. We have to take on faith what lay behind the one moment of joy in discovery, and even this is put in doubt by Arthur's later reflections. We have no idea what the disconcerting little dots meant in the X ray, or what "small technical point" the research assistant so disastrously overlooked.

Of *The Gadarene Swine* we learn even less. But it clearly stands for the two books Snow himself had written and published immediately before *The Search:* a detective story, *Death under Sail* (1932) and a science fantasy, *New Lives for Old* (1933), about rejuvenation and a war between Fascism and Communism.

Arthur Miles says of *The Gadarene Swine:* "I knew it to be fairly good, but quite a number of young men could have done it as well, and several considerably better." Neither in form or theme are Snow's own earliest publications in any way distinctive. He began by practicing the two forms of writing—the detective mystery and science fiction—most read by those who care nothing about the novel as art or truth. He learned how to handle conventional forms simply for diversion, before it occurred to him that he might use these forms to say something serious.

The murdered man in *Death under Sail* is a Harley

Street cancer specialist; one of the suspects is a brilliant young doctor whose researches the specialist financed and whose ideas he appropriated, a familiar Snow motif. The young scientist-doctor is extremely able analytically and administratively, but in emotional matters a fifteen-year-old. He could "run a society, because that's really an absolutely inhuman pastime . . . but he could never run a love affair."

Though he now knew writing was his vocation, Snow did not produce his second serious novel, *Strangers and Brothers*, the first of the Lewis Eliot series, until 1940, six years after *The Search* and a year after he had thrown himself into recruiting scientists for the war effort. The first of the two autobiographical accounts of Lewis Eliot's own life, *Time of Hope*, did not appear until 1949, fifteen years after *The Search*. Though far more richly and evocatively told, Lewis Eliot's life is in outline much like Arthur Miles's.

The very first chapter is a "homecoming." After a happy picnic in a lush river setting in June, 1914, the nine-year-old Lewis is filled with panic as he returns to the incompletely understood tensions of his home. Once again the father is an ineffectual man, facing bankruptcy, quite unable to contend emotionally with his strong-minded wife and sister.

The boy's mother is romantic, superstitious, hopeful that some lucky gamble may change her fate.

On those afternoons, as we sat in the dark, the fire casting a flickering glow upon the ceiling, my mother talked to me about the hopes of her youth, her family, her snobbish ambitions, her feeling for my father, her need that I should rectify all that had gone wrong in her life.

Snow's novels return again and again—often as the only physical description—to effects of light, to fires glowing in ancient college rooms, to water shining under a night sky at a moment of lovemaking, to a single window illuminated in the darkness when someone lies gravely ill, to candles reflected in silver platters or bottles of wine or polished tables, to ornate chandeliers under which important decisions are being made.

As a result of the séances before the fire, Lewis accepts his mother's ambitions but rejects as an impossible burden the love she offers. For a long while thereafter he can only love—and is impelled to love—someone who does not love him. This unhappy need interferes with his career, keeps him from realizing the ambitions his mother inspired. Almost willfully he recreates her experience, her double frustration, on a higher level and in different form.

Inspired by George Passant's evening lectures at the local college, Lewis decides to become a lawyer. Though George arranges to have him articled to his own firm of solicitors, Lewis, on inadequate means, risks enrolling in one of the Inns of Court and preparing to be a barrister. George's anger teaches Lewis that even friends like to help on their own terms. Much later his brother Martin finds this true of Lewis also, and asks what selfishness lies beneath all Lewis's helpfulness to others.

Lewis has met Sheila Knight, a handsome, troubled girl whom none of his friends like. He falls almost instantly in love with her, as Arthur Miles had with Audrey. Sheila makes difficulties as Audrey had not. When she does finally give herself to Lewis, she says, "I don't love you, but I trust you. Get me out of this." "This" is the intolerable prison of her incapacity to love or even be at ease

except with waifs and misfits. Her well-to-do parents understand Sheila even less than Lewis does. The portrait of
her father, a shrewd, indirect, theatrical, hypochondriac
clergyman, is one of the best of Snow's humorous, sympathetic pictures of emphatic old men.

Sheila often disappears or makes Lewis deliberately
jealous. He breaks with her to concentrate on his work.
Passing his examinations, he is taken as pupil into Herbert
Getliffe's firm. Getliffe is a sly, muddled, successful lawyer who appropriates the researches of brilliant young as-
sistants whom he shamelessly underpays. But with the
help of his former fellow student Charles March, whose
wealthy Jewish family has powerful connections, Lewis
gradually establishes himself. A grinding effort of will is
required, for Lewis suffers from a frightening illness of un-
determined origin. He admires March and is fascinated by
the world he moves in, a world more fully described in
The Conscience of the Rich. He is determined someday to
be "as sure of myself, as much able to move by instinct
among the sources of information and power."

With torment over Sheila added to illness, life becomes unbearable. Lewis cannot forget her, and finally
seeks her out. "I had sent her away, and now I was crawl-
ing back." It is surrender, unconditional surrender. He
sees this "with absolute lucidity" and yet it is totally inconsistent with what he has always wanted of life. "I was
ardent and sanguine and certain of happiness. It would
have seemed incredible to hear that, in the deepest recess
of my nature, I was my own prisoner." Different as Sheila
is from the vulgar Mildred, this suggests the disastrous attachment in Maugham's *Of Human Bondage.*

When Lewis returns home after a difficult convalescence in France, Sheila tells him that at last she has found someone whom she can love, though she knows the man's weaknesses. We remember how Arthur Miles returned from Germany to learn that Audrey would marry the charming prevaricator Sheriff. Lewis asks Sheila what she expects of him. "See that I don't lose him."

It is a heartfelt plea, but Lewis does exactly the opposite. He puts all his lawyer's experience into scaring her lover away.

She is shattered, but finally returns to Lewis. She can no longer go it alone. Their marriage is as unhappy as what preceded it. Despite his asserted self-knowledge, Lewis is not able to act tenderly, creatively, or even acceptingly. He is full of self-pity, and appalled that his professional life is so unreal to Sheila—she cannot even pretend interest in it—and that she is so ill at ease with his friends. During the trial of George Passant for embezzlement, Lewis is so impressed by George's courage, his belief that a future is still open to him, that he decides to act as boldly. "My ambition was as imperative now as in the days when George first helped me. . . . If I died with it unfulfilled, I should die unreconciled . . . my ambition was part of my flesh and bone." He comes home from the trial to tell Sheila that he cannot bear their marriage any longer.

She takes the news stoically. This time, she tells him, there will be no return. "I have done you enough harm." But when he walks in the garden, in the moist, lime-scented air, waiting for her to finish packing, and sees the light shining from her window, he knows that he cannot let her go. "I was about to sentence myself for life." Once again "the personal things" have seemed to triumph, to prove themselves stronger than conventional ambition or the need for power. Lewis blames poor Sheila, though he had always been the pursuer. Bound to her though he is, Lewis cannot accept Sheila as he accepts the men he is fond of, and so we cannot see in her what it is he loves, sexually and otherwise. In what she says and does Sheila is often appealing and pathetic; Lewis is often contemptible. But the autobiographical method makes it difficult to know what Snow really thinks of him, or how Lewis's behavior toward Sheila is related to the almost universally admired behavior which he describes himself as exhibiting through the rest of the series.

When Lewis's autobiography is continued in *Homecoming,* published seven years later, in 1956, we learn how brief the self-imposed life sentence turns out to be.

It is now 1938, five years after the reconciliation that ended *Time of Hope.* Lewis has modified his ambitions because of the difficulties of his marriage. Five days a week he lives comfortably as fellow and lecturer on law in a Cambridge college. Two days he spends in London with Sheila and as legal consultant to a high-powered manufacturer named Lufkin.

It is hard on Sheila, who tries desperately to fill her loneliness. Lewis's homecomings are attended with the same kind of anxiety he recalled from childhood at the beginning of *Time of Hope.* He is encouraged when Sheila uses her independent income to back a courtly, unscrupulous, once-distinguished literary man in a publishing venture. She is even able to put some of her secret thoughts on paper with a book in mind. But the publisher, one of the more complex and interesting of the many self-defeating characters in Snow's novels, hates to seek patronage

and circulates malicious stories about Sheila and Lewis.
When Lewis confronts him, he seems relieved and
promptly returns Sheila's money. But for Sheila the exposure is too great, the wound too deep. A few months
later, while Lewis is off having dinner with a friend, she
commits suicide.

Charles March, now a doctor, tries to be helpful, but
there are terrible scenes with Sheila's parents. Lewis, himself, feels an unbearable need to speak to Sheila which, in
his total lack of religious faith, he knows never can be satisfied. A quarter of the way through, the novel seems to
come to an end.

Two years later, in 1939, when Lewis is working in a
war ministry, he meets Margaret Davidson, daughter of a
prominent art critic, and falls almost at once into a spontaneous, apparently happy love affair. She discovers, however, that Lewis had not told her of Sheila's suicide, and
wonders how free emotionally he really is.

"With anyone who wants you altogether" [Margaret tells him]
"you are cruel. Because one never knows when you're going to
be secretive, when you're going to withdraw. With most people
you're good, but in the end you'll break the heart of anyone who
loves you."

They begin drifting apart. Suddenly, without warning, she
reveals that she is going to marry a capable young doctor.
She does so and has a child. For over two years, Lewis
knows nothing of her life. But once he has worked out in
his mind what was wrong with his attitude toward
Margaret, he sets out to win her back, deliberately, pa-
tiently, step by step. At a clandestine meeting at a restau-

rant, Margaret sits smiling in the aura of a table lamp, "her face open and softened, as though breathing in the present moment. When I first met her, I had been enraptured by her capacity for immediate joy, and so I was now." We remember that once Sheila pressed Lewis to tell her what, if anything, he really believed in and what he would sacrifice for his beliefs. They had been talking of one of George Passant's employers who gave up all his possessions to become an itinerant preacher. Defensively Lewis tossed the question back to Sheila. She said, curiously enough, that she believed "in joy."

Lewis arranges Margaret's divorce, though people close to both Lewis and Margaret think he is wrong to do so. He persists, they are married, have a child, and seem happy. He must, however, pay a price. Their child falls ill with an infection of the brain. When Charles March makes a wrong diagnosis, for apparently excusable technical reasons, Margaret's first husband, with more recent advanced training, is called in, and the child is saved, with much spiritual purgation for all concerned. Despite his interest in science, Snow fails to explain exactly what the clinical situation is, or the reasons for Charles's mistake.

On the way back from the hospital Lewis notices a scent of lime blossom beneath the smell of hot grass and traffic fumes.

We were in sight of home. A light was shining in one room: the others stood black, eyeless, in the leaden light. It was a homecoming such as, for years, I thought I was not to know. Often in my childhood, I had felt dread as I came near home. It had been worse when I went, as a young man, toward the Chelsea house. Now, walking with Margaret, that dread had gone.

They live happily ever after. In later novels, Margaret is entirely the admiring, reassuring, understanding companion. There is never a hint of any serious conflict between them or in their feelings about each other. The nature of their sexual life is left discreetly unrecorded.

In the four novels devoted to each of the four men closest to him, Lewis mentions his own concerns only obliquely, presenting himself entirely as friend or brother. "Not by virtue but simply by temperament, I was bound by chains to anyone who had ever really touched my life; once they had taken hold of me, they had taken hold for good." In each novel Lewis gives himself up single-mindedly, in a Jamesian way, to playing the role of observer, intermediary, and confidant in another man's life. Because of this, we tend to forget, when Lewis is concentrating on George Passant, say, or Roy Calvert, how deeply involved he may be at the same time with Martin Eliot or Charles March or with Sheila or Margaret. In the interests of dramatic simplicity, Snow sacrifices the complex interweaving of themes and relations that the general design of his series—inspired, he suggests, by Proust—ought to encourage.

Strangers and Brothers, the first and weakest of these four portraits, is about George Passant. Lewis always thinks of George as built along the lines of a great man, but no evidence supports this. The novel begins with a chapter characteristically titled "Firelight on a Silver Cigarette Case." The case, esoterically designed, has been given to Jack Cotery, a member of George's group (or coterie) by fifteen-year-old Roy Calvert, who has a crush on him. Roy's father, Jack's employer, is ready to ease Jack out of his job and cut off his firm-sponsored scholarship. Though it may get him into trouble professionally in the town, George fights the matter vigorously in a school committee, with Lewis Eliot—of course—serving temporarily as secretary. As usual in Snow's novels, a not fully satisfactory compromise results.

In the course of the next five years, George becomes involved with Jack in various side activities. They take over an advertising weekly, acquired earlier by the former member of George's law firm who has become a religious fanatic. They buy the farm where George and his disciples meet weekends, and turn it into a hostel, intended to be the first of a chain. After borrowing money privately—from women mostly—for these enterprises, they run into real trouble when some of those from whom they borrowed prosecute them for misrepresentation.

Since this is a small city, a serious scandal is in the making. Sexual relations within the group have become complicated. George, who is a man of strong passions, had always sought release by picking up girls on the street in Nottingham, or going to low dives there. More and more, after the group acquires the farm, he makes love fairly promiscuously with girls whom he takes there for weekends.

The trial raises questions of honest understanding of one's own motives similar to those confronting Arthur Miles in *The Search*. George tends to push from his mind uncomfortable facts, as Arthur Miles was tempted to do when his beautiful research results were threatened. Jack Cotery blithely makes use of falsehood, as Sheriff had done.

At the trial, Herbert Getliffe saves Jack and George from an unfavorable verdict, but not from scandal. At the last moment the religious wanderer turns up to confess that it was he who gave a wrong impression of the weekly paper's circulation figures because he was so eager to be free of it. Sympathizing with the jury's condemnation of the sexual life at the farm, Getliffe still manages to make it seem symptomatic of the war-caused disorientation of the twenties.

George Passant is furious at this defense. It denies his dignity as a man, his existential freedom. After a generous sampling of his vapid diary entries the reader can hardly take George Passant as seriously as Lewis and the author seem to. This is the tumultuous late twenties and early thirties, but George's allegedly powerful analytic mind is unengaged by the books, ideologies, and political events abroad which preoccupied practically all the ardent young of that period. Nor is he tested in the hurly-burly of left-wing politics.

Though he had marked time professionally in the nine years before the trial, George finds his justification in the existence of the group. The final, painful, unanswered question of the novel is whether he has not been deceiving himself about the motives and character of his influence. Is his persisting courage and self-confidence after the trial possible only because his self-accounting is flawed? Once again the narrative method makes it hard to judge. Does Snow admire the mind behind these diaries as much as Lewis Eliot seems to, or is he giving us the portrait of a sentimental, self-protective fornicator moving into middle age?

Lewis Eliot's profoundest friendship is with Roy Calvert. In 1933, after he begins living most of the week at the

Cambridge college where Roy, now twenty-four, is a research student in Middle Eastern languages, they see each other once or twice a day on terms of warm intimacy. Roy's tenderness, raillery, and grace charm nearly everyone, but especially women. He is close to Lady Muriel, wife of the gravely ill master of the college; to Joan, her daughter; and to their amusing, snobbish relatives Lord and Lady Bocastle. Lewis is drawn into these circles too, where the conversation is worldly, witty, and sharp-edged, as it had not been in the series before.

Roy is nearly as desperate within himself as Sheila, but he is far more articulate in explaining his problem and more varied and theatrical in seeking relief from it. He has an absolute conviction of isolation from God. "It's much more real than anything one can see or touch—that God and His world exist. And everyone can enter and find their rest. Except me. I'm infinitely far away for ever."

Roy's deep spiritual malaise finds expression in provocative academic behavior; in trips to Germany because of fascination with Nazism; and in a series of affairs sufficiently numerous and conspicuous to affect his chance of a fellowship. When, for instance, an old scholar who does not deserve it is being honored at a grand testimonial meeting, Roy devastatingly and with pretended innocence speaks of the scholar's long-dead young collaborator from whose unpublished literary remains and without acknowledgment the scholar almost certainly wrote his one substantial book.

Roy goes frequently to Germany, lives there in a nether world like that described in Isherwood's *Mr. Norris Changes Trains*. Roy and Lewis's disagreement about Nazism has no effect on their friendship, even though Roy tries deliberately to convert Lewis. Roy's sense of the inadequacies of the Communist and left-liberal view of life is precisely what caused the politically "wicked" views of the modern writers whom Snow attacks in "The Two Cultures." Lewis Eliot—and Snow—can sympathize with this in Roy, and yet not understand its far profounder expression in Yeats, in Pound, in Eliot, in Lawrence.

Eliot's reason for loving Roy is more convincing than his love for Margaret or Sheila. We have more detailed awareness of Roy's physical presence in a room, his manner, his appearance. The conversational exchanges are richer. Of a walk near the college Lewis says fervently:

We talked on, so attuned that each word resounded in the other's heart. And at the same moment that I felt closer to him than I had ever done, I was seized and shaken by the most passionate sense of his nature, his life, his fate. It was a sense which shook me with resentment, fear and pity, with horror and unassuageable anxiety, with wonder, illumination and love. I accepted his nature with absolute gratitude . . . to know him was one of the two greatest gifts in my life.

He is quite frank about the quality of this feeling. He says of Roy that "with his first-hand knowledge of life, he knew that any profound friendship must contain a little of the magic of love. And he was always as physically spontaneous as an Italian."

Through most of the novel Roy is involved in a triangular relationship with Joan and a hardheaded, pretty, socially insecure girl named Rosalind. Young, untried, awkward, passionate, Joan gives herself totally in love for Roy until he breaks abruptly with her. In the chapter about Joan called "A Young Woman in Love," the heightened prose suggests abandonment of the usual narrative indirection in favor of something close to omniscience. During Roy and Joan's love affair, Rosalind rather surprisingly becomes engaged to a clergyman protégé of Roy's. After the outbreak of the war, even more surprisingly, Roy marries her. They have a child, and it makes him happy enough to regret the suicidal wish that led him to pull wires to get into a bomber brigade.

Before Roy's inevitable death in combat, he and Lewis go on a strange melodramatic trip to Spain and across occupied France to Switzerland to make contact with former friends of Roy's, Germans who might possibly be putting out significant peace feelers. The mission comes to nothing, but Eliot and Roy have one more intense period together.

The Light and the Dark lacks a political theme, has little to say about morality or society. Lewis discusses Nazism very abstractly, with no analysis of specific European developments or personalities, though he takes his usual interest in practical academic politics. It is a question of whether Roy, specialist in the recently recovered language Soghdian, should be elected a fellow, in preference to a productive young proletarian scientist named Walter Luke. But the novel is primarily a love story, as the concluding poignant memory of Roy directly tells us.

The New Men (1954) is a story of brothers, of Lewis and Martin Eliot. The sudden importance of Martin—nine years younger than Lewis—is a little startling. He has barely been mentioned in the series since their mother was indignantly pregnant with him a quarter of a century earlier in *Time of Hope*. Preoccupied with careers, Lewis

Eliot and Arthur Miles ignored their families. We have no
sense of how Martin grew up or what role, if any, he
played during the difficult years with Sheila.

Nor is it clear why at this point Snow introduces his
scientist brother as the "new man" when the series already contains first-rate scientists like Walter Luke and
Francis Getliffe, Herbert Getliffe's younger brother. Is it
an opportunity to split Snow's self-image in the novels into
two halves to dramatize the quarrel within the self?

But the split, so interpreted, becomes very confusing.
Lewis accuses Martin of cold, ruthless, calculating ambition, though Martin strikes the reader as impetuous and
variable, shifting from one extreme position to its opposite.
Martin accuses Lewis of being too self-indulgent in personal relations, of wasting himself in them, just at the time
when Lewis is moving most rapidly and forcefully into a
position of influence.

These are the war years. A cousin of Lord Bocastle,
put in charge of coordinating confidential scientific work,
chooses Lewis Eliot as his personal assistant. A series of
crises and decisions follows, presented without much thematic coherence. Should research into nuclear fission be
pushed, and specifically the research directed by Martin
Eliot and Walter Luke, even after the heartbreaking failure
of their first atomic pile? Later Luke and a young scientist
named Sawbridge nearly die of radiation sickness. When
America throws its tremendous resources into making the
bomb, should Britain close up Harwell (or Barford, as it is
called here) and use its scientists in other much needed
ways? Finally America explodes the bomb, and then drops
it on Hiroshima and Nagasaki. Almost to a man, according
to Lewis Eliot, British scientists find the bombings unnec-

essary and indefensible. They feel betrayed. Should they protest, and how?

On his own, Martin composes a strong letter to the *Times* which would certainly finish him for any public office. Lewis dissuades him from sending it. But when Sawbridge is suspected of leaking information to the Russians, Martin puts all his energies into breaking him down. Lewis angrily accuses Martin of playing this role to curry official favor and be made next head of Barford instead of Walter Luke, who scorns what he considers American-style fanaticism about security and Soviet spies.

When the post is offered him, Martin Eliot at the last moment turns it down. He wants to be free to think and speak as a man, not an official. The decision also shows that he is free of his youthful need to rival his older brother. And now his relationship with his wife is secure too. Against Lewis's advice, Martin had married Irene, an attractive, restless, vulnerable girl, much like Audrey or Sheila. Through most of the novel she is still involved with a lover out of her past, a slightly disreputable journalist who recalls Sheriff and some of the men to whom Sheila was attracted. Irene is able to give herself fully to Martin when she realizes that he loves her out of strength, not weakness. This provides the confidence that her deep self-distrust had never before let her feel, or even believe possible.

Though he sacrifices a top post in administration, to return to teaching science in competition with younger men more brilliant than he, Martin seems happy. But the novel fails in its attempt to present Martin's emotions, his science, and his dramatic shifts of position through his brother's eyes. Martin is too reticent with Lewis for that.

The science is inadequately explained, and the presumably dramatic inner life is seen only at one or two removes. Martin does not capture Lewis's imagination—or ours—as Roy Calvert does, or Sheila Knight.

The Conscience of the Rich (1958) also dramatizes renunciation and a quarrel between kin, in this case the painful widening breach between Charles March and his father. The Marches are an old, far-flung and respected Jewish banking family whose members in rotation entertain each other at huge dinners on Friday nights. Into this fascinating world Lewis Eliot is warmly received, and soon plays his usual confidant's role, especially with Charles's elderly widowed father, a talkative worrier with total recall. Mr. March is a mad, impetuous character who ranks as a creation with Sheila Knight's father.

Though he has a keener legal mind than Lewis Eliot's, Charles gives up law as soon as he has proved his ability at it. He cannot face the kind of success that his family connections will place in his lap. But a decision to become a doctor, after two years of restless, fashionable idleness, troubles his father even more. Mr. March decides to cut off Charles's inheritance. He rightly interprets his son's decision as a criticism of his own mode of life. "He could not begin to understand the sense of social guilt, the sick conscience, which were real in Charles." He suspects correctly that Charles has been influenced by Ann Simon, daughter of a wealthy Jewish physician. Ann is a Communist and supporter of a weekly, *Note*, edited by Humphrey Seymour, a witty upper-class ideologue. *Note* is modeled on *The Week*, edited by Claud Cockburn.

Mr. March has had a series of shocks when Charles

gave up law, when his daughter Katherine married a Gentile, Francis Getliffe, and when Charles married Ann Simon. Worse is in store. *Note* is using scandal, some of it rather dubious, to try to bring down the present government of appeasers. Part of this scandal concerns Herbert Getliffe and Mr. March's brother, Sir Philip, who holds a government post. Ann is in a position to stop what *Note* is doing, but Charles will not try to influence her. Both she and Seymour are, according to Lewis Eliot, "believers by nature. At times it gave them a purity and innocence that men like Charles never knew: at times it gave Seymour, and perhaps even Ann, a capacity to do things from which Charles, answering to his own conscience, would have been repelled."

When Ann falls dangerously ill, she rather implausibly provides Lewis Eliot with information for Charles to have after her death; it will enable him to stop *Note* if he wishes. After she begins to recover, she sends Charles, even more implausibly, to learn from Lewis what the information was. "She'd rather you told me than tell me herself."

At a big family conference Charles refuses to use the weapon in his hands. Though he is not a Communist and loves his father and sister, his respect for the integrity of Ann's beliefs is so great that he will not stop what *Note* is doing. The attitude is essentially unpolitical, as was Lewis Eliot's emotional acceptance of Roy Calvert at the time that Roy was a Nazi.

When he lets "personal things" be dominant for Charles, when he lets him be governed chiefly by respect for Ann's faith, Snow both avoids and confuses the issues. To stop *Note*, Charles would have had to turn over to the authorities certain documents in Ann's possession which *Note* had obtained improperly. This could have raised the whole troubling question—a central one for Koestler, Orwell, and Sartre—of liberal support of Communists, especially where the uglier aspects of Communist totalitarianism are concerned. Because Charles keeps silent for love of Ann, the issue is left in the same moral obscurity as the issue of Arthur Miles's integrity when he failed to reveal Sheriff's fraud.

The Conscience of the Rich is not a political novel; it is a study of Charles March's character. As in *The New Men*, the narrative method is an obstacle to understanding. Lewis tells us that Charles, like himself, had trouble accepting and reciprocating love, but the only woman we see him with is Ann, and they are in apparently complete rapport. We are told that Charles "had always been fascinated by the idea of goodness. Was it because he was living constantly with a part of himself which he hated?" But what he hated is not dramatized. Lewis is typically present with Mr. March and Sir Philip when a dispatch box arrives from the Prime Minister containing Sir Philip's dismissal from office. But he is not present in the depths of Charles's soul, where a successful struggle goes on for goodness, and against cruelty, isolation, and pride. All that is veiled from us.

In these four novels—*Strangers and Brothers, The Light and the Dark, The New Men,* and *The Conscience of the Rich*—four men turn aside, because of deeply personal needs or problems, from the kind of success that their situations and superior talents seem to offer. Until he enters government service during the war and begins a second career, this is Lewis Eliot's history also.

The Masters (1951), the most popular of Snow's novels, is a highly concentrated, step-by-step account of a college election, but it really fits the same pattern. Lewis Eliot throws himself completely into the attempt to get Paul Jago elected because he has so much more "humanity" than the aloof, correct, unimaginative scientist who is his rival. Jago is painfully eager for the job; when his chances are threatened, his friends redouble their efforts because they think defeat will destroy Jago as a man. Later, in *Corridors of Power*, Lewis acknowledges that support for Jago was wrong. "Sometimes my affections ran away with me. . . . They had made me forget function, or justice, or even the end to be served."

The novel begins with word that the master of the college is gravely ill of inoperable cancer; it ends when a new master is sworn in. All scenes take place in the college, all bear upon the contest. The highly limited, localized contest becomes a paradigm for nonviolent power struggles within all social institutions everywhere.

Immediately on news of the master's illness, parties form. Lewis Eliot, Roy Calvert, Arthur Brown, and Brown's friend Chrystal all support Jago. Arthur Brown, the tutor, loves to maneuver in the background, effect compromises, keep the college running well. Chrystal is a strong, statesmanlike character whose name, we learn at the final vote, is Charles Percy Chrystal. (C. P. Snow is Charles Percy Snow. The first sentence of the novel begins, "The snow had only just stopped . . ." Snow is made of crystals. It is in crystallography that Arthur Miles, Snow's first alter ego, begins his research.)

With Lewis Eliot presenting the situation, our interest focuses almost entirely on the lively play of personalities,

not on substantive issues. Curriculum, educational
theories, university government, student problems are
hardly mentioned. Francis Getliffe does rebuke Lewis for
supporting, in 1937, a stubborn conservative instead of the
liberal Crawford, but the issue is then dropped until near
the end. The student protest movements and the heated
intricate political arguments that would have been going
on in that year are totally ignored.

Tension is increased because the master lives longer
than was expected and because he must be shielded from
knowledge of the electioneering. All antagonisms, hopes,
and self-questionings are exacerbated. Should promotions
to other posts be used for bargaining? How much pressure
should be put on young Luke, who does not have tenure?
Should Jago be told to persuade his wife to stop acting as
if she were already mistress of the master's lodge?

Every casual meeting is a contest. Private conversations, especially between those in opposite factions,
arouse curiosity and suspicion. By the time the election
takes place a great many ample dinners have been eaten in
which the fellows have succeeded or failed in maintaining
gentlemanly relations between the factions; much fine
wine has been contributed ceremoniously by individual
fellows to honor this occasion or that. At times the obsession with the coming election seems slightly mad; the fellows appear to do nothing but caucus and eat.

An unsuccessful scientist named Nightingale, still expecting his totally unlikely election to the Royal Society,
shifts his support from Jago to Crawford and begins circu-
lating malicious statements about Jago's wife. Nightingale's early defection is followed much later by the return
from Europe of Pilbrow, an elderly lighthearted *bon vi-*

vant, who has been abroad during most of the maneuvering. Alarmed by the success of Nazism, he is absolutely opposed to putting in office someone with Jago's political views. At the last moment, for quite different reasons, Chrystal decides that he must support Crawford, though this means a painful rupture with his old friend Brown.

Jago takes defeat very hard, but when he forces himself to drink the health of the new master there is a sense of restored unity, of corporate survival. Other novels of the series have concentrated on individuals governed by impulses they could neither control nor fully understand. Now a group of such individuals, still so governed, decide on the future of the college. In such a committee process do the irrational personal motives cancel each other out? Do sensible men, acting democratically, usually reach sensible decisions?

This question is debated again, somewhat repetitiously, in *The Affair* (1960), set in the same college sixteen years later, with an overlapping cast of characters. Again an election for master is in prospect, with Arthur Brown and Francis Getliffe as the likely choices. But the fellows are more immediately split over a case that is as unrepresentative and as curious in its details as the charges against George Passant for swindling.

A rude, resentful, provisional fellow, Howard, of leftist leanings, has been quietly dropped for falsifying the scientific data in his thesis. He and his wife, a handsome Communist who sees human beings totally in strategic and ideological terms, campaign for a reconsideration of the case. Naturally they try to involve Lewis Eliot, an important man of affairs, but still close to the college, where Martin is now a fellow.

The issue is complicated not only by the prospective election of master but by the fact that nearly everyone dislikes Howard. Some of the conservatives feel justified in considering his political views, since they believe a Communist to be incapable of honesty. They charge, unfairly, that the liberals and leftists support Howard for political reasons. Since the war the proportion of conservatives has greatly increased.

The facts are hard to get at. Howard had done his research under an old scientist, now dead, uncle-in-law of one of the fellows. A photograph on which Howard's conclusions were based is discovered to have been "blown up" so that the dimensions are erroneous. An American notices that the tack hole, caused when the original negative was hung up to dry, is too large! This is about all the "science" we are vouchsafed. As usual, the character of the experiment on which so much depends is not explained.

By a circuitous route the old scientist's papers reach the college authorities. At some point a photograph has been removed from one of the notebooks. The inscription under it suggests that it might be the crucial photograph which Howard says he reproduced exactly as his professor gave it to him. Howard proves to be an exasperating witness in the hearings at which Lewis Eliot serves as his legal adviser. He is vague, truculent, can never give a straight answer. And he must be a poor scientist to hang everything on unchecked data supplied by somebody else. Finally Francis Getliffe, with his great authority, decides that it was not Howard who faked the photograph, and the case ends in a rather unsatisfactory compromise.

The facts are messy, unpleasing to all, including the

reader. By calling the novel, a little pretentiously, *The Affair*, Snow recalls the Dreyfus case, but in that case the ideological and social alignments—clerical and anticlerical, liberal and reactionary, socialist and traditionalist—were very clear. The baffling facts and Howard's unsatisfactory explanations suggest rather Trollope's *The Last Chronicle of Barset,* where Mr. Crawley has to surrender his incumbency when he gives so unsatisfactory an explanation of how he came by a lost or stolen twenty-pound check which he deposited to his account. He, also, is later exonerated.

The lack of clarity in the Howard case permits us once again to concentrate on the personal issues and the process itself.

As before, Nightingale is the villain. Handling such a colleague so as to achieve justice and yet not create an open scandal is a delicate business for Lewis and the Court of Seniors. Readers of *The Masters* are naturally interested to see how old acquaintances have fared. Under Crawford's mastership Arthur Brown has retained his quiet power. Chrystal is dead. Jago makes a brief, effective foray from the bitterness of his retirement. Gay, the aged, ebullient, Norse saga man of *The Masters* is incredibly still alive, still demanding to be heard.

The Affair too greatly resembles *The Masters,* and suffers the disadvantages of a sequel or reprise. Howard is poor stuff compared even to the overeager, insecure Jago.

In *Corridors of Power* (1964), on the other hand, Snow treats a public issue more directly and clearly than in *The New Men,* describing the exercise of great power on nearly the highest governmental level. Once again the "personal thing" gets in the way.

This time the central figure is not an old friend or brother, though plenty of old friends are involved, most of them now as titled and prominent as their creator, Lord Snow. Walter Luke and Francis Getliffe are knights; Lewis Eliot's former employer, Lufkin, who has steadily increased his industrial empire since the war, is a Lord, and Horace Timberlake, whose possible benefaction to the college was a complicating factor in *The Masters*, is Viscount Bridgewater. Now, in 1955, Lewis Eliot has been working for sixteen years as a fictionally convenient kind of free-lance assistant to Sir Hector Rose, Permanent Secretary of one of the war ministries. Rose, like most of the younger civil servants, is solidly conservative. A Tory government holds office.

The central character is Roger Quaife whom we first see pressing Lewis's good American friend, the physicist David Rubin, on the matter of nuclear policy. The name Rubin suggests that of Snow's friend I. I. Rabi. Quaife is particularly concerned with the arms race between the United States and Russia, and what kind of significant role, if any, Britain can play in preventing disasters.

A faithful reader of the whole Lewis Eliot series is not surprised that one of the first things Roger Quaife does, as soon as he is given a junior ministerial post, is to telephone Lewis Eliot and ask whether they might, in the next few days, "spend a bachelor evening at his club." Roger talks frankly to Lewis about power and the uses of power. Before he can act significantly in the atomic arms race, he must maneuver his way into a major governmental post.

"Remember," said Roger, "there are going to be real decisions. There won't be many of them, they're only too real. People like you, sitting outside, can influence them a bit, but you can't

make them. Civil servants can't make them. So far as that goes, as a junior Minister, I can't make them. To make the real decisions, one's got to have the real power."
"Are you going to get it?" I asked.
"If I don't," said Roger, "this discussion has been remarkably academic."

Lewis sets up for Roger an advisory committee of scientists, including the villain of the book, Brodzinski, a Polish refugee scientist of ability and fanatical determination. The inclusion of Brodzinski alarms Getliffe and Luke. In Luke's view Brodzinski is "a mad Pole, whose only uncertainty was whether he hated Russians as Russians more than Russians as Communists, and who would cheerfully die himself along with the entire population of the United States and Great Britain, so long as there wasn't a Russian left alive." Quaife persuades the others that to exclude Brodzinski would be to announce prematurely in what direction he hopes to direct policy.

Again after the Suez crisis he has to give Lewis and some of the others a little lecture on political realities. Thoroughly opposed though he was to the British military seizure, thinking it wrong and futile, Roger had kept silent at the time. He knew he could do no good, and he was determined not to endanger his position with the party and thus make impossible any effective action on the atomic bomb.

After a quiet interval, the uncontrollable Brodzinski suddenly begins making speeches in America attacking his British scientist colleagues. David Rubin tells Quaife that both the United States and Russia prefer to keep atomic bomb manufacture to themselves, but that the United

States would take it amiss if Britain seemed to be getting out of the atomic race for wrong or neutralist reasons, "to be sliding out of the Cold War."

In the prevailing climate of opinion it is easy for Brodzinski to arouse suspicion in America. Snow often refers in his later novels to the American anti-Communist obsession. Of a rich young American courting Francis Getliffe's daughter, Lewis Eliot says, "He could not get over his discovery that Sir Francis, so eminent, so strait-laced about domestic behavior was, when he talked about the world, by American standards wildly radical . . ." Lewis thinks that it will do an American no harm "to hear us talk about Communists as though they were human beings."

As a result of Brodzinski's charges, Quaife's advisers are double-checked by one of the security heads. Getliffe is furious, and at first refuses to go through it. Though Lewis manages to persuade him, it casts a shadow over their friendship. Lewis is angry with himself for seeming too conciliatory in his own interview. He had protested only at one circumstantial but false charge coming from an unidentified source which he assumed "was one of your ex-Communists."

In the interview Lewis refers to his engagement in political activities in the thirties, to speeches at I.L.P. meetings, for instance, which had not been dramatized in the novels. Again it is evident that Snow's purposes as a novelist do not include factional politics of the sort described by Orwell and Koestler. Eliot can always see both sides of any question, as in his attitude toward Russia and Stalinism. He had differed with Ann March and others over the "major horrors of power."

I always believed that the power was working two ways. They were doing good things with it, as well as bad. When once they got some insight into the horrors, then they might create a wonderful society. I now believe that, more confidently than I ever did. How it will compare with the American society, I don't know. But so long as they both survive, I should have thought that many of the best human hopes stand an excellent chance.

Despite Rubin's advice, Quaife, who has now become a privy councilor, decides to press ahead. Snow suggests that it is difficult for an ambitious man to analyze his own motives at such a time. Having a real cause makes him feel better about his ambition, gives him more confidence, provides him with arguments, and if he wins, puts him in the history books. Statesmanship and self-interest are not necessarily enemies.

Meanwhile, as in all Snow's novels, the "personal thing" has intervened. Roger's wife is vivid, wealthy, intelligent, the daughter of an earl, and effectively eager to help him win the highest position. But in mid-course he reveals confidentially to Lewis Eliot that he is in love with the former wife of a mentally ill colleague. He enlists Lewis's aid because the woman, Ellen, is being harassed by some unidentified person who knows their secret and might conceivably use it to do great harm politically. Lewis sees her a number of times both alone and with Quaife. Between Roger and Ellen "there was a link of the senses, so strong that sitting with them was like being in a field of force. Why it was so strong, I should probably never know." The "probably" is amusing on a number of counts.

In a review of one of Upton Sinclair's "weirdly readable" late novels, Snow, after remarking on Lanny Budd's "preposterous intimacy with the great," says, "I suspect that all addicts of this series (me among them) secretly wish to have been Lanny Budd." Being Lewis Eliot is next best. Everyone in the novels regards Lewis Eliot as both shrewd and wise, and seeks his advice. Since the reader is taken into confidence too, this is all highly informative. When, for instance, Francis Getliffe arranges a last luncheon at his club with his reckless, rebellious young daughter off on her own to America, Lewis, of course, must make a third.

Lord Lufkin, the airplane manufacturer, puts on a prestigious dinner party for political purposes. When the guests—"the Ministers, the tycoon, the Second Secretary, the P.R.S."—rise from table to go to the drawing room, Lufkin calls out sharply, "Wait a minute, Lewis, I want a word with you." Lewis leaves the party to seek Quaife, carrying a confidential message from Lufkin. Quaife, whose wife has now been informed of his affair, telephones Ellen. It is past one in the morning. He returns to say flatly to Lewis, "She wants me to go and see her. She asked me to bring you too!"

On the weekend at Bassett, a dispatch box arrives requiring immediate attention, and a secret meeting convenes in a bedroom. But the great are not comfortable without Lewis Eliot's presence. A handwritten note comes from the chief adviser to the Prime Minister: "I should be grateful if you could spare us a few minutes of your time. It would be a convenience if you could come without delay."

If these were daydreams, they anticipated what was to happen in real life. In an interview with the press in October, 1964, the new Lord Snow of Leicester—formerly C. P.

Snow, later Sir Charles Snow—told how his promotion occurred.

> "The Sunday after the election," Lord Snow said, "I received a phone call from 10 Downing Street, asking if I could see the Prime Minister in an hour's time. He offered me the post, and I asked for a night to think it over. Then I said yes."

The position he was offered, that of Parliamentary Secretary, was the same rank Roger Quaife held in the first part of *Corridors of Power*. Snow revealed that he did not plan to write any more novels for a while.

When *Corridors of Power* was published, Snow's political career on a ministerial level lay ahead of him. In the novel, Quaife's career comes to an end. After the long debate in Parliament, there are enough abstentions to indicate lack of confidence. Whether veiled allusions to Quaife's private life by one of the speakers had an effect is a question. Across the pool of light from a reading lamp in a darkened office, Roger reads to Lewis the draft of his letter of resignation. Clearly Roger believes deeply in what he tried to do. If he had not believed so deeply, he might have fared better. He also really loves Ellen, who is no Christine Keeler. When he divorces his wife his constituents no longer return him to Parliament. But the new marriage seems firm and good. Like Martin Eliot, he accepts with equanimity his greatly lessened position; like George Passant, he has not given up hope for himself or his ideas.

In *The Sleep of Reason* (1968), Lewis Eliot returns with his son to the town where he grew up, where his father and George Passant still live and where he himself serves as a visiting member of the governing board of his old college of art and technology, now expanded into a university. As usual, a difficult case comes before the board, with implications and involvements reaching back into earlier novels of the series.

Two student couples were found fornicating in the lounge of a university building. Should they be expelled? The daughter of the vice-chancellor (he is chairman of the board) is hopelessly in love with Martin Eliot's rather unreliable son Pat. She, in turn, is hopelessly loved by Francis Getliffe's son Leonard, also a member of the governing board. Though fond of the vice-chancellor, Leonard cannot in good conscience support him either as a scientist or in his handling of this case.

The board's deliberations are only peripherally related to two of the more dramatic sequences in the novel: Lewis Eliot's eye operation, and the murder trial of two young women. The eye operation, which leaves Eliot with impaired vision, has no immediate relevance except that, like other deaths and illnesses in *The Sleep of Reason* and *Last Things*, it reflects the fact that Snow, Eliot, and the "Strangers and Brothers" series itself are growing old.

In this city of his youth, a lesbian pair have been charged with the sadistic murder of a kidnapped child. One of the accused is a niece of George Passant; the other is sister to one of the students brought before the board. So everyone, of course, seeks Lewis Eliot's advice and help. Even the opposing lawyers speak freely to him. Rather pointlessly he twice visits Passant's niece in jail.

In using such material Snow was following unabashedly in his wife's footsteps, and underlining the fact that "Strangers and Brothers" was not governed by any preconceived plan. It had become a kind of public diary, reflecting Snow's current preoccupations, misfortunes, and triumphs. In 1966, Pamela Hansford Johnson, Lady Snow, had been asked by the *Sunday Telegraph* to attend the so-called Moors Trials. In that case the accused were heterosexual lovers. Readers of violent thrillers and pornography, including the works of Sade, the pair had tortured to death youths aged seventeen, twelve, and ten, recording on tapes the screams and pleading of their victims.

Deeply upset, Pamela Johnson published in 1967 a highly controversial book called *On Iniquity.* She challenged liberal assumptions about censorship and the nature of responsibility. The pervasive intellectual and institutional permissiveness had lost touch, she thought, with moral reality. "Affectless" violence, encouraged by the mass media, was one of the results.

In *The Sleep of Reason* Snow raises the same questions, but as usual in a somewhat more detached and ambivalent way. He entitles the final section of the novel "Responsibility." Martin Eliot, in the past more radical than Lewis, exclaims impatiently "I should have thought we'd had enough of the liberal illusions" about crime and its prevention. On the other hand, George Passant, far from being given increased doubts about his influence on the young, is roused by the trial and the guilty verdicts to something of his old liberationist spirit.

Like so many of the others, this novel ends with a moment of "sheer, simple joy" which has nothing to do with the social problems that we have just seen dramatized. This time it is Martin Eliot who experiences it. He is delighted that his son Pat is going to marry Muriel, Roy Calvert's daughter, stepdaughter of an influential Jewish entrepreneur, Azik Schiff, who soon becomes a lord. (In

the later Snow novels, the proportion of lords is very high.)
The marriage, Martin says, will be "the making" of Pat.

It does not make him. The results of the marriage, we
soon learn from *Last Things,* are a cause for sorrow. During Muriel's pregnancy, Pat has had affairs with other
women. She, being resolute, resourceful and without illusions, decides on a divorce. The two sets of parents are
disconcerted when Lewis's son Charles, still an under-
graduate, joins Muriel as resident lover in the smart es-
tablishment she has set up for herself in Chelsea. It is
even more disconcerting to find that Charles and Muriel
are part of a group of leftists who, in occupying university
offices during a protest, discover documents which suggest
that the government is subsidizing university research in
biological warfare. Members of the group and their associates are officially investigated as Lewis Eliot's associates
were a quarter of a century earlier when the atomic secrets
seemed in jeopardy.

Meanwhile (and this novel is even less coherent the-
matically than *The Sleep of Reason*) Lewis Eliot has refused a key government position and undergone another
eye operation. The operation, though more difficult and
dangerous than the first, is successful. Lewis wavers and
consults friends before declining the government post.
Some tell him his writing is more important than official
service. The post had been refused by Francis Getliffe and
is subsequently accepted by Sir Walter Luke.

Later Lewis and his son Charles sit in the gallery of
the House of Lords to hear Luke, now Lord Luke of Sal-
combe, fend off questions about the germ warfare reports.
After the session Luke has a lively talk with Charles about
the values of careers in and out of the sciences. Apparently

he did not know that Charles had been one of the leftist group. Although Luke had announced that none of the students involved in the purloining of papers would be prosecuted, Charles decides to leave both Muriel and his family for a prolonged stay in some of the trouble spots of the world. He is going to prepare to be a foreign correspondent.

The young depart; the old die. The next-to-last chapter of *Last Things* is called "Another Funeral." The narrative is followed by a curious appendix headed "Announcements—1964–68 (From the London *Times* unless otherwise stated)." It itemizes nine deaths, nine marriages, and five births. The deaths include those of Lewis's wife's father (he had previously attempted suicide); Lewis's own father; Francis Getliffe; and George Passant; all described in the novel. But added without warning is the shocking death by accident of Azik Schiff's twelve-year-old son, one of the most promising and most loved of the newest generation.

Lewis had been reflecting on obituary notices after seeing his son off on the plane. They were for other people. The dead man did not read them. There was no death for the "I," which "lived in a dimension of its own," and so long as there was consciousness, so also was there renewal, will, hope. The series ends with Lewis's thinking: "That night would be a happy one. This wasn't an end."

Snow's decision not to make *The Malcontents* (1972) and *In Their Wisdom* (1974) part of the "Strangers and Brothers" series is not easily explained. They achieve nothing which could not have been achieved as well or better within the series. Indeed, they strangely overlap with it. *In Their Wisdom* includes, though in very minor roles, characters both from "Strangers and Brothers" (the March family, Azik Schiff, Muriel Calvert) and from *The Malcontents* (Bishop Boltwood).

The Malcontents concerns a student leftist group very like that in *Last Things. In Their Wisdom* invites comparison with *Last Things* by exploiting even more fully Snow's intimate knowledge of the House of Lords, including its informal gathering place, the Bishop's Bar. Both narratives depend, as did *The Sleep of Reason,* on legal action to provide suspense and a public forum where opinions and commitments can be tested. Lewis Eliot has vanished, and we miss him. His general sense of things continues, but now there is no one to attach it to, except, of course, the author himself.

In *The Malcontents* Snow tries to recreate imaginatively the thoughts and emotions of the sexually and politically advanced youths of 1968 and after, but the effort is too much for him. The youth whose mind he principally enters turns out to be nearly as discreet and responsible and respectful of his elders as Snow himself. Snow cannot achieve for the 1970s an equivalent to the anguish, turbulence, and intermittent hopefulness of his own youth, recalled so very poignantly in the earlier novels.

In *The Malcontents,* a young leftist group, using questionably acquired evidence, tries to show that a high government official is a slum landlord, exploiting colored immigrants. Some members of the group are well-to-do or well connected, have fathers like Snow or Lewis Eliot, and upset their parents by their activities, even when the parents are liberals.

A few are of working-class background. One of these, son of Jewish refugees from Germany, falls from a high

window at a meeting of the group. Was it suicide or a
drug-induced accident? Since the group has already
learned indirectly that there is an informer among them, it
is conceivable that to test him, LSD was put secretly in a
drink. Murder within a revolutionary student cell inspired
Dostoevsky's *The Possessed*, exactly a century before.

Tensions, uncertainties, and splits in loyalty develop,
as the group gets ready to face a coroner's jury. Prosecu-
tions are likely to follow. Drug use and the mysterious
death have played nicely into the hands of those whom the
group were trying to expose. In Snow's novel itself they
divert attention from the social conditions which the group
was setting out to expose and correct.

After their defeat, though they have been treated fairly
gently by the authorities, members of the separate group
go their different political and emotional ways. To their
parents' relief, two from upper middle-class families decide to marry each other. One wonders why Snow felt impelled to write this book, since in *Last Things* he had already dealt with youth and leftist politics, using almost the
same inconclusive ending slightly less inconclusively.

In Their Wisdom (1974) dramatizes a prolonged legal
action which has no moral or social significance except to
remind us that respectable people, more prudish in talking
about money than about sex, "thought about money more
than they admitted, and badly wanted it." Like its predecessors, *In Their Wisdom* uses skillfully the swiftly moving "and then, and then, and then" pattern that E. M. Forster, in *The Art of the Novel*, made the essence of good
storytelling. In most respects C. P. Snow has become increasingly indifferent to the demands of his medium, especially to nuances—or even the bare elements—of language

and style. But he can still lure us on with a calculated succession of surprises and reversals, of questions so answered that even more questions are raised. And he fully exploits his knowledge of those British settings—courts, universities, Parliament, the homes of the rich—whose abiding appeal attracted huge audiences to the TV series, "Upstairs, Downstairs."

Like so many detective stories, *In Their Wisdom* begins with the reading of a will. Although the two did not get on particularly well, a rich stubborn old man had always in his previous wills handsomely recognized his only child, a daughter. But in his last he cuts her off without a shilling. Most of his money instead goes to the rather useless grown-up son of a strong-minded woman who has apparently taken over the old man's life in his final years. The disinherited daughter works for a charity sponsored by an upstart tycoon who decides, for the fun or mischief of it, to fight her case through the courts, even if necessary to the House of Lords. Sooner or later a number of lords become involved, including a penniless one whom the nonheiress marries. Since the chief interest is in personal histories rather than politics, more scenes occur in the Bishop's Bar than in the Chamber itself. And since the lords are mostly old, these histories are heavy with serious illnesses and deaths. Actually *In Their Wisdom* is dedicated to the American surgeon who presumably coached Snow in the details of the brain operation which here takes the place of the eye operations in the last two "Strangers and Brothers" volumes.

By the end of *In Their Wisdom*, the contest over the will (which the daughter finally lost) is pretty well forgotten. Although the novel seems at first to be about the social obsession with money, a Balzacian theme, and although a number of the life peers had bought their titles with political contributions, Snow has little of Balzac's energetic need to know and show directly how fortunes are acquired and then used in trafficking for place and power. Yet he was writing at a time when financial scandals involving government leaders in England were reaching almost American proportions. On the final page, one of the lords reflects on history, but comes only to the unstartling conclusion that "the present couldn't imagine the ideas of the future" and that future men could not relive "the existence of any present."

Such bland comprehensiveness occurs outside the novels as well. Snow's heart may be in the right place, but his mind recoils from the highly structured or the precisely differentiated. When Snow was interviewed on television by Malcolm Muggeridge in 1962, the following exchange occurred:

Muggeridge: How Left would you regard yourself politically, Charles, in terms of our set-up here?
Snow: Well, I think the word's almost ceased to have meaning in our set-up here, hasn't it? I mean it's perfectly reasonable to be a Conservative in the present flavour of the Conservative Party (of the front bench of the Conservative Party at least), or a member of the Labour front bench, and there's almost nothing between it. For certain things I believe, as a matter of fact, that the Conservative Party could have done and in some ways has done slightly better than the Labour Party would have done for ten years.
Muggeridge: But you haven't, in the context of this country, got any very strong political feeling?
Snow: No, not in the context of this country, no. In a sort of world context, certainly yes. That is, I am strongly for the poor.

Though it is his most directly political novel, Snow's *Corridors of Power* ends diminuendo, like most of its fellows, not with politics but with personal relationships and moods: "The memory of the struggle, even the reason for it, dimmed down. We talked of the children and were happy. . . . We talked as though the future were easy and secure, and as though their lives would bring us joy."

Despite the wistful irony, "happy" and "joy" are the proper terms. Ever since Sheila said that she believed in joy, we have known that the series was primarily concerned with individual happiness. Those characters are happy who are realistic about the chances of attaining what they seek, who can renounce ambition when it sets too high an inner price, who can suffer limitation and even defeat without bitterness. They choose marriage and parenthood because they value them for the right reasons and are clear about what may be expected in return. A surprising number of the principals in Snow's novels achieve happiness on these moderate and even stoic terms.

Joy is another matter. Joy is not the child of measure and compromise. It is Dionysian, ecstatic, and brooks no barriers. It occurs when the self is in free, outgoing, confident rapport with ideas, objects, persons, situations, and moments. In Snow's novels it springs chiefly from science, sex, or success.

Of what particularly produces these first two kinds of joy we have only glimpses or glimmerings. We meet joyful lovers as we meet joyful scientists, but the rites of the bed are as veiled from us as the rites of the laboratory. Snow is no Puritan; neither is he D. H. Lawrence or Henry Miller. Lewis Eliot alludes fairly frankly to his early and more troubled relations with women, though with no physical details. As the series continues, gentlemanly reticence becomes total. After he marries Margaret Davidson, we should as little expect to learn specifically about their sex life or even about any serious emotional difficulties between them as to learn similar facts from the *Times* about the royal couple.

Aside from general references to sex and sickness, the physical life shared by men, plants, and animals counts for little in Snow's imagination. The sufferings of the war years are not recreated, or the excitements of combat or hunting or swimming. No one kills a bull or climbs Kilimanjaro or plants crops or—even in laboratories—does much with his hands. To link Snow and Tolstoy, as one or two critics have done, seems particularly strange when we consider the openness, the geographic expanse of Tolstoy's world, and the wide range of emotional, sensory, intellectual, and religious experience.

A comparison with Proust, which Snow himself invites, also reveals more contrast than kinship. Proust's sensibility is richest in areas where Snow is unresponsive—in, for instance, painting, music, architecture, botany, women's dresses, philology, literary style, Bergsonian metaphysics. Proust's richly charged imaginative evocations, working through analogy and association, require a nuanced and involved prose totally unrelated to Snow's simple and sometimes careless plainspeaking. Snow has a handful of favorite figures—"lemur-eyed," for example—which he works rather hard. Even analogies drawn from science occur more in Proust than in Snow, and where Snow's version of the Dreyfus case is confined to a few college fellows, Proust shows the anti-Dreyfusard poison spreading all through the veins of French society.

A third joy is the joy of success—competitive success in examinations, in court, in bureaucratic, academic, and parliamentary politics. Here we can usually watch things happening with a specificity not accorded us in sex or science. Though early in their careers Snow's heroes dream of power in the abstract, their author is not really interested in power *qua* power. He does not, through symbols or a vast conspectus, give heroic character to natural, social, or industrial forces as Zola did in *Germinal* or Dos Passos in *U.S.A.* We do not see any charismatic leaders— Hitler, de Gaulle, Churchill, Roosevelt—directing or riding historic forces. We do not meet the masses to whom these men made their empowering appeal. We do not visit Lord Lufkin's factories or drop in at a rally of Roger Quaife's constituents. In *The Masters,* we get the impression that the thirteen fellows outnumber the students.

In one respect Snow is a naturalist. Each individual seems to him endowed with an unchangeable temperament which he must manage as best he can. There is no point in expecting him to be different from what he is. When Snow—or Lewis Eliot—accepts a person, he accepts him totally. It does not matter to his friendship that Roy Calvert is a Nazi sympathizer or Ann Simon a Communist. It would not have mattered if the trial had proved George Passant to be intentionally dishonest. This principle fails to work only with Sheila, about whom Lewis complains so bitterly, but that is because he is bound to her by a temperamental need of his own that he cannot control and that he finds an intolerable burden.

Snow's novels are popular partly because his psychology is a classically humoral one. The Norse scholar Gay is happy and productive all his long life because it is in his sanguine nature to be so. Despite a happy marriage and success in the war, Nightingale misbehaves with the same bilious malice in *The Affair* as in *The Masters*. Roy Calvert is doomed by ineradicable and unsatisfiable yearnings that are at the very root of his melancholic being.

When Lewis does judge those close to him, it is always a particular practical judgment about how they will function in a given situation to achieve a given end. When a group of individuals is concerned, seeing how they will behave, how they will act and react to each other, takes on the fascination of a game of chess. Each man is limited by his nature to certain kinds of moves; but with enough pieces in play, and with some natures still unrevealed, all sorts of unpredictable combinations can occur.

Which side or issue wins does not count so much as the game itself and what it tells about the pieces or players. Those portions of the prose that are not straight dialogue consist largely of aphoristic comments on the rules of the game or a careful assessment of the contending forces within each man's psyche. There are a few added observations, characteristically general, of social changes in England in the past quarter-century.

Omitted in the later novels is any indication of how Lewis Eliot himself is to be judged, or what price he has had to pay for his own success. He seems simply to have drifted upward into a position of influence and universal respect. And yet the psychic costs of success are amply evident elsewhere in the series. Perhaps Lewis Eliot's increasing blandness and self-satisfaction show what is happening, though here again we have the problem of separating Eliot from his creator. Snow has been made famous by his novels and his widely acclaimed public statements. He obviously delights in this public role, but it cannot have been entirely free from tensions, embarrassments, and moments of doubt. Neither for the joys or stresses and self-searchings has Snow found adequate equivalents in the later career of Lewis Eliot.

The new age of bureaucracy, where most things are done by committees, is ideal for the confrontations and character testings that Snow dramatizes so well. On the other hand, his interest in the individuals who confront each other is thoroughly traditional. Since he is not trying to say anything new psychologically, intellectually, or imaginatively, Snow is not driven to the technical extremism, the distortions in perspective, the "antihumanity" he condemns so roundly in most major twentieth-century writers. His fiction provides a comfortable compromise between new conditions and old forms. With it readers repelled by Beckett and Henry Miller, Genet and Burroughs, can feel thoroughly at home. What a relief to have a narrator who is happily married, socially responsible, and reasonably confident about the future!

Abstractly and indirectly, Snow's world is a world of darkness and strangeness. Men are imprisoned in their own temperaments, are essentially alone when they suffer anguish of mind or body, and face a death of utter extinction. Concretely and immediately it is often a world of brotherhood and light. Men can learn to control or live with their temperaments. They are sustained by friendship, by love, by respect for institutions, by work, by shared ideas of justice and the common good. The sensible, unideological compromises of Snow's committee meetings are his model for that hoped-for understanding between the United States and Soviet Russia toward which so much of his public activity is directed. His private goal is different, though perhaps not incompatible. The nostalgic personal symbol in his novels is one of homecoming, of return with a wholly accepting and accepted companion to a small, warm—but very well-lighted—room.

DANIEL B. DODSON

Malcolm Lowry

> Yet is the service which arises
> from fear not to be depreciated,
> for fear leads to love.
> Moses de León, *Zohar*, II, 216

Poet, short-story writer, novelist, movie scriptwriter, legendary alcoholic, jazz musician, sailor, golfer, student of the Cabbala, mythopoeist, and indefatigable jester, Malcolm Lowry died at the age of forty-seven in 1957 in Ripe, near Lewes, Sussex, according to Douglas Day's account, following an argument with his wife, Margerie, and drinking most of a bottle of gin braced with twenty sodium amytal tablets. He was buried in the churchyard of St. John the Baptist in Ripe following an inquest by the coroner who pronounced the cause of death, "Misfortune." The epitaph tells something of his life as well, for misfortune, no doubt invited, seemed to pursue him. His manuscripts were lost or burned in conflagrations; he was accident-prone, and though physically very strong, suffered from a series of shattering illnesses; he spent turbulent, dark nights and darker days in an alcoholic penumbra filled with demonic "familiars." He led a life, for the most part, of poverty and frustration and died known as the author of a single book,

Under the Volcano. There is a certain justice in this fact since he himself thought of his lifework as a single cycle, first as a modern *Commedia* of which *Under the Volcano* was to be the *Inferno*, then as a five-part series, and later as a cycle of seven novels. And though infrequently he published poems and short stories, his lifework was the product of a singular devotion to one idea and one work of art—Malcolm Lowry. He was his own greatest mystery and his own mysterious god whom he spent a relatively short lifetime trying to understand and explain.

Born to convention and affluence in 1909, Lowry attended the Leys School near Cambridge. In 1927 he went to sea as a cabin boy on the Oriental run, an experience which was to have a profound effect on both the man and the artist. After a brief period of study in Bonn, he went up to St. Catharine's, Cambridge, having during the preceding summer visited Conrad Aiken, with whom he had begun a correspondence, in Cambridge, Massachusetts. He shipped out again as a fireman on a Norwegian freighter in the summer of 1930, and in 1932 received his B.A. degree with third-class honors in the English tripos.

In Spain in 1933 with Aiken he met and married Jan Gabrial and in 1935 left for the United States, alone. After a period in New York City and Los Angeles, late in 1936 he was in Cuernavaca, Mexico, with his wife, and by 1937 had completed not only a first draft of the lost novel, *In Ballast to the White Sea,* but also an entire version of *Under the Volcano,* which had begun as a short-story idea. With his marriage breaking up, after the departure of his wife he returned to Los Angeles and was there rescued from a colossal drinking bout by the American writer Margerie Bonner. In 1939 Lowry and Miss Bonner moved to Vancouver, B.C., and in 1940, after his divorce from Jan Gabrial, they were married and moved into a fisherman's shack in Dollarton, B.C., where they were to live and work with absences in Mexico, Haiti, and Europe, until the final departure in 1954. Here Lowry wrote and rewrote *Under the Volcano* until he withdrew it from his agent, Harold Matson, in 1941 after it had been rejected by twelve publishers, to begin yet another version. In 1944 the Lowrys' house burned down, destroying the manuscript of *In Ballast to the White Sea,* but in 1945 with their own hands they rebuilt the only real home they were to know. The period between 1940 and 1945 was one of extraordinary suffering and courage, gaiety and deprivation, sickness and accident. Living on a very small allowance from his father, but forced to borrow from friends, Lowry spent the war years as an English subject resident in Canada, suffering the severity of wartime restrictions. Throughout, however, he was working with the high dedication of the artist in exile, convinced of the merit of his vision. In the fall of 1945, after finishing the final version of *Volcano,* Lowry took his wife to Mexico to the scene of the book, Cuernavaca, and here on New Year's Eve in 1945 he received a letter from Jonathan Cape, to whom he had submitted the manuscript, not precisely rejecting the book, but requesting extensive changes. In despair Lowry made a suicidal gesture, but after recovering, spent two weeks writing one of the most exacting letters in the history of modern literature, defending and explaining his book in detail. Joyce had Stuart Gilbert to accomplish the initial task of exegesis on *Ulysses.* Lowry was both creator and exegete.

In that singularly dramatic fashion in which he believed destiny organized his life, he received letters accepting *Volcano* for publication unaltered from both Reynal and Hitchcock in New York and Jonathan Cape in England on the same day in the spring of 1946. Nine years had passed since the completion of the first version. On publication in February of 1947 the book was almost unanimously acclaimed as a masterpiece in the United States but received very little notice in England. Translations into German, French, Italian, Norwegian, Swedish, Danish, and other European languages followed.

Early in 1946 the Lowrys were back in Dollarton and later that year they sailed from New Orleans for Haiti. In New York for the publication of *Volcano* early in 1947, they returned to Dollarton and later the same year sailed for Europe in a French freighter which took them through the Panama Canal and across the stormy, wintry Atlantic. From this experience Lowry derived the material for one of his most vivid stories. In 1949 they were in Dollarton where Lowry began work on the stories later to be collected in *Hear Us O Lord from Heaven Thy Dwelling Place*, and on a film-script of *Tender Is the Night* which has so far not been produced. Between 1950 and 1954 he worked tenaciously on the stories and on a novel, *October Ferry to Gabriola*, which was still unfinished at the time of his death.

In August, 1954, they left Dollarton for the last time to sail from New York for Genoa, spending the winter in Italy and Sicily. In June of 1955 they moved to England where in Ripe, in a final rage, Lowry apparently committed suicide on June 27, 1957.

Vastly condensed, these are the facts of a tortured and yet hilarious life, drawn from Margerie Lowry's outline and the biography by Douglas Day. The turbulence, the lifelong addiction to alcohol, and the gravely unpredictable behavior should not blind us to the evidence offered by friends and associates of Lowry's immense charm, vitality, slyness, and capacity for discerning the ridiculous, particularly when that vision, as it so often was, was the reflection in a mirror.

Ultramarine (1933) is the novel that every sensitive young man who goes to sea dreams of writing. Aside from the actual adventure of shipping out, in large measure substance for the book came (as did so many of Lowry's early, formulative ideas) from Conrad Aiken, specifically from Aiken's novel *Blue Voyage* (1927), from which he borrowed prose rhythms, narrative and stylistic devices, as well as many fictional ideas. Other obvious guiding spirits are Joseph Conrad and Eugene O'Neill, with Shakespeare and Eliot mixed in liberally and often infelicitously.

Dana Hilliot, the first version of the recurring Lowry *persona*, ships out as an act of self-discovery in the search for manhood. Resented as a toff, bullied and ridiculed by his shipmates for his class and his ineptness as a sailor, he ultimately achieves, if not acceptance, a precarious accommodation. In an elemental sense this quality of strangeness, of isolation, of failure to adapt to the social, psychological, and metaphysical environment is the initial ingredient of Lowry's world, as it is of Kafka's. The resultant, hovering suggestion of evil, unspecified but ubiquitous, remains one of the characteristics of the Lowry vision.

Young and uninitiated though he is, Dana Hilliot is excessively ridden with fancies and fears which prevent him from entering the primitive fraternity of the sea except through the doors of alcohol. Mechanically the young Lowry arranged the traditional equipment of the *Wanderjahre* novel: the girl at home to whom, though both are sexually intact, his erotic and romantic fancies stray, providing him an excuse to remain aloof from the prostitutes, though not the drinks, of the East; the exaggerated contrast between his own cultural attainment and that of his primitive shipmates; the threat of a homosexual advance; the well-observed exotica of Eastern ports; and the intermittent stream of self-conscious irony punctuated by shards of Eliot and Shakespeare, allowing a display of purple prose (Conrad Aiken, professor of the pun to an apt student, suggested *Purple Passage* as title).

Lying below these traditional elements, however, is an inchoate sketch of the world of *Under the Volcano* to come. Dana Hilliot, like his creator, is an anguished syphilophobe who drowns the painful urging of his sexuality in the profound stupor of alcoholic escape, but responding to the suspicious taunts of his shipmates, he erects an adolescent's mariolatry, a mixture of sexual and religious inspiration. He insists that he will remain true to Janet at home, though their relationship has consisted of nothing more bestial than clutched hands and the brush of chaste lips. Fearing sex and contamination, Dana Hilliot turns to alcohol and onanism, but on this perverse sanctity creates a vaguely realized religion of threatening retribution.

Hear me, Janet. . . . Did you know I was liable to stigmata? Yes, the blood flows from my feet, from the upper surface as well as the soles, and from the palms and back of my hands.

Technically the book is less experimental and less interesting than Aiken's *Blue Voyage*. Except for chapter 3, which is told in the first person (and which Lowry apparently intended to revise), the narrative is third person with the fashionable, in 1933, stream of consciousness carrying the interior monologue of Dana Hilliot across the cruder surfaces of life in the forecastle. Contrapuntal rhythms in the dialogue of the seamen are more borrowed from O'Neill, particularly from "The Hairy Ape" (which Lowry admired), than recorded from life, but Lowry's fascination with conversational counterpart to suggest the fragmentation of auditory experience was to remain with him until he mastered it in *Under the Volcano*.

More impressive first novels have been written by twenty-one-year-olds, but *Ultramarine* is a recognizable first chart of the Lowry element with both its hilarity and its demonology.

An early draft of *Lunar Caustic* was accepted by Whit Burnett for *Story* magazine under the title of "The Last Address" in the mid 1930s, but Lowry recalled it for amplification, apparently undecided whether to leave it as a long short story or to refashion it as a part of a full-length novel. In his correspondence he refers to it as a "short novel, written in 1936," but in the last years of his life he was engaged in reworking it from two versions, one of which had appeared in French translation in *L'esprit* in 1956. After his death, still another version was published by the *Paris Review* in 1963, and a final version, edited by Earle Birney and Mrs. Lowry, appeared from Jonathan Cape in 1968.

Lunar Caustic is an account of a brief period of self-commitment (according to Lowry's explanation) in Bellevue Hospital in New York City, following a prolonged al-

coholic nightmare. But this brief (76 pages in the Cape
edition) fragment is an arresting study in comparative
nightmares. The first chapter follows with cinematic eye
the dazed wandering of an anonymous drunken sailor
through the lower East Side of New York, staggering from
bar to alley, clutching his bottle, on an erratic pilgrimage
around a magnetic center, the hospital. Beginning with
chapter 2 the vantage point is from within the new nightmare, the hospital, looking out on the old, the city from
which Bill Plantagenet, English sailor off the S.S. *Lawhill*,
has escaped. From the delirium of *tremens* we are introduced to the delirium of the institution for the mentally
infirm, the derelict spawn of the great city.

Again contrapuntal dialogue is used, but with much
more skill and compassion, as a demented old man, a
mythomaniacal boy, and a song-crazed Negro intrude for
recognition. And again emphasis is placed upon the cultural and educational incongruity of Bill Plantagenet self-
incarcerated in a psychiatric ward while a sympathetic
doctor initially discusses his symptoms and then reluctantly ejects him as a noncitizen. The short book ends with
Plantagenet again on the outside, again drinking, huddled
in autistic withdrawal in the corner of a bar.

The quality of the marine imagery suggests that Melville was very much on Lowry's mind while writing *Lunar
Caustic,* and brief as the book is, it shows a marked development over *Ultramarine*. Earlier gaucheries have almost
disappeared, and a somber landscape of the damned
begins to emerge, illuminated briefly by pentacostal lightning. The silhouette of the skyscraper was to be replaced
by the spectral eminences of Popocatepetl and Ix-

taccihuatl, however, before the nightmare was to achieve its full, authentic power.

Lowry's major achievement, *Under the Volcano* (1947), is also one of the major achievements of English literature in the second quarter of the twentieth century, but like *Ulysses*, to which it has repeatedly been compared, it is an excessively complex book which requires intense study and exegesis. Scattered articles and academic studies of the novel have been appearing since the early fifties, but only when this brief commentary was well under way did a book-length analysis of one aspect—a very important aspect—of the novel, its dependence upon the Cabbala, reach publication: Perle Epstein's *The Private Labyrinth of Malcolm Lowry*.

With impressive documentation from studies in the Cabbala, Mrs. Epstein has argued ably, if at times over-ingeniously, that far from being mere window dressing for the book, the cabbalistic mysteries are the articulating mythic substance of the account of Geoffrey Firmin's apocalyptic journey to death on the Day of the Dead (November 2) in Quauhnahuac (Cuernavaca), Mexico, in 1938. Suggestive evidence of Lowry's use of cabbalistic studies of course may be detected even by the uninitiated in the novel itself, and are more clearly hinted at in his explanatory letter to Jonathan Cape of January 2, 1946, but Mrs. Epstein's work suggests that Lowry consciously used the hieratic numerology, rituals, ritual objects, and symbols of the Cabbala ("tradition") as a structural center of the book, much as Joyce used Homeric substance in *Ulysses*. In effect, and vastly simplified, Geoffrey Firmin's aspiration toward divine knowledge and atonement lies not in the way of the White but rather of the Black Magician, self-destructive, spiritually doomed, in search for *Kether,* or light. Lowry himself clarified this central movement of the book by describing Firmin, the Consul, as one who has misused the divine gift of wine, symbolically and blasphemously, thereby betraying the uttermost Mysteries of cabbalistic knowledge. However, the allegorical intention is plainly conceived since in his fall Geoffrey Firmin, yearning for a return to purity and innocence, carries the burden of atonement for all men.

The question of deliberate structural and methodological affinity with *Ulysses* is difficult to decide upon since it is complicated by Lowry's own, not always reliable, testimony. In the letter to Jonathan Cape in which he is protesting the singular obtuseness of Cape's reader, he cautions that the book was written on "numerous planes," and insists that his approach was opposite to that of Joyce, "i.e. simplifying, as far as possible, of what originally suggested itself in far more baffling, complex and esoteric terms." This would seem to suggest that the infinite complexities of cabbalistic ritual are enacted symbolically and consciously in the Consul's daylong progress toward death, whereas Stephen Daedalus and Mr. Bloom quite unconsciously perform mythic mimicry.

Five years after the publication of *Under the Volcano,* however, Lowry wrote to Albert Erskine: "I read *Ulysses* through—essentially—for the first time . . . it was my first intelligent and complete reading." It is conceivable that Lowry's memory was accurate in this instance since his book was written and rewritten during the period of intensive Joycean studies, and Lowry may well have got his

Joyce secondhand from Conrad Aiken. At any rate the reader of *Ulysses* will find himself in a technically familiar landscape in *Under the Volcano* with its complex hierarchy of symbols, correspondences, and anticipations.

The action of *Volcano* is embedded in time past, time already thoroughly played out, as chapter 1 opens on November 2, the Day of the Dead, in 1939, with a prologue provided by the Frenchman Jacques Laruelle, a former movie director and childhood friend of the Consul, now preparing for a final departure from Mexico the following morning to return to France on the eve of World War II. Laruelle's function is not only choric, but actor in, and *metteur en scène* of, the epic of Geoffrey Firmin's day of death.

Leaving his tennis partner, Dr. Vigil, Laruelle walks slowly into town pursuing a significantly circular path, encountering various symbolic objects, men, animals, elements, to the local cinema which has been plunged into darkness as the result of an impending storm. Invited by Sr. Bustamente, the manager of the cinema, he has a drink in the adjoining bar, and Sr. Bustamente returns to him the Consul's collection of Elizabethan plays, including Marlowe's *Dr. Faustus*. Laruelle misreads the lines of Faustus' final soliloquy, "Then will I headlong *fly* into the earth," and turns accidentally to the famous concluding chorus, both of which passages apply, he realizes, to the Consul. A long spiritual memorandum in the form of an unsent letter written some years earlier by the Consul to his then estranged wife, Yvonne, falls from the book; Laruelle also reads the letter—and burns it. The chapter—the first of twelve—ends with Dantesque cadences, "*Dolente . . . dolore,*" and a glimpse of the luminous Ferris wheel, erected for the fiesta, turning backwards, carries us to the same day of the previous year.

Chapter 2 begins the narrative proper in the bright morning light at 7 o'clock precisely a year earlier, on the Day of the Dead, 1938, as the Consul's now divorced wife returns to Quauhnahuac to discover Geoffrey in the drunken sobriety of the confirmed alcoholic, drinking at the Bella Vista bar after an entire night of indulgence. The novel consists, then, of a cluster of intricately related ironies: a homecoming and a final leave-taking; restoration and deprivation; love offered and love betrayed; life affirmed while it is being brutally denied; and a quest which has already ended.

The reunion itself so desired by both the Consul and his wife is a failure from the beginning. Geoffrey and Yvonne leave the bar to walk home, passing through the spectral sunlit streets of the village, itself suffering from massive hangover, observing various emblems of their separation, a sun-split stone, an advertisement for the movie *Las Manos de Orloc,* and observed by a mysteriously persistent man in dark glasses. The Consul tells Yvonne that his half-brother, Hugh, recently arrived from the States, is staying with him, and that he, the Consul, has continued a precarious friendship with Jacques Laruelle. A pariah dog follows the Consul.

The garden of the Firmins' house, once so carefully tended by Yvonne, is now a jungle of desuetude. Suffering from the mutilated pleasure of their reunion, Geoffrey considers resuming the life together which both had found essential but insupportable. In order to appease his badly lacerated nerves he has yet another drink, but Yvonne's re-

fusal to join him revives old tensions contributing further
to the psychic dissonance. Soon, with scarcely controlled
restraint, they are arguing about trivialities, and when the
telephone rings the Consul's brief and mysterious conversation so unsettles him that he rushes out to find a cantina.
In the Calle Nicaragua he passes out and is discovered
lying face down in the street by an astonished British mo-
torist, who, after satisfying himself that the Consul is not
injured, gives him a drink of Irish whiskey. Returned
home Geoffrey discovers Yvonne having breakfast in bed
and, stimulated more by the expectations of custom than
physical desire, he tries to make love to her but discovers
he is impotent. He retires to the porch where he suffers a
hallucination and falls asleep "with a crash."

Wearing the Consul's jacket with a copy of a cable-
gram he himself has dispatched to the *Daily Globe* on anti-
Semitism in Mexico, Hugh Firmin, the Consul's half-
brother and alter-ego, encounters Yvonne attempting to restore order to the wilderness of the garden. Hugh has long
loved Yvonne but out of loyalty to his brother he has never
spoken his love; yet while affirming his devotion to both,
in the long day's pilgrimage he involuntarily betrays both.
After some cryptic discussion of his experiences in China
and Spain and his plans to ship out, Hugh suggests they
take a walk which leads them by a stable where they hire
horses for a ride into the countryside. Under the level of
deceptively frivolous banter Hugh thinks about Yvonne
and the Consul and about the disaster of the Civil War in
Spain. While descending to cross the river they pass a
sleeping Indian whose horse, branded with the number 7,
is cropping grass nearby. The ride becomes an idyllic can-

ter into freedom away from the Consul, briefly relieving
Hugh of his sense of betrayal and Yvonne of her oppres-
sive awareness of failure.

The Consul, still asleep on the porch, dreams of a Hi-
malayan landscape of overwhelming beauty which alters
into a scene of water, stimulated by his compelling but insatiable thirst, and dissolves into visions of empyreal
brightness. He awakens with a cosmic hangover, remembers he has hidden a bottle of tequila in the wasted
garden which he finds and drinks from, seeing both a
snake and the familiar pariah dog. Observing for the first
time an admonitory sign, he reads:

> ¿LE GUSTA ESTE JARDÍN?
> ¿QUE ES SUYO?
> ¡EVITE QUE SUS HIJOS LO DESTRUYAN!

Without confidence he attempts a translation. Mr. Quincey, his American neighbor, watering his orderly adjacent
garden, has been observing him with amused contempt
and now speaks to the Consul, who is suffering from both
hiccups and an open fly. After the Consul has discoursed
learnedly on the Garden and the Expulsion, Dr. Vigil,
with whom he had spent the previous drunken evening,
comes down through the garden and together they start for
the porch where Hugh and Yvonne, returned from their
ride, are seated. But before Geoffrey manages to reach
them he blacks out and at 12:15 finds himself sitting in the
bathroom with a glass of flat beer in his hand, listening to
the conversation of Yvonne, Hugh, and Dr. Vigil. He is
threatened by hallucinatory *tremens* and voices arguing
over his destiny.

After a swim and luncheon Hugh, lying on the porch daybed, recognizes that he is in the middle of life's journey—he is twenty-nine—and recalls his abortive career as musician, composer, seaman, student, journalist, lover of other men's wives, and incompetent activist in the struggle against Fascism. But he has made up his mind to atone for his political impotence by sailing later in the month from Vera Cruz with a shipload of dynamite for the Loyalists in Spain. His guilt-ridden meditations are interrupted by the Consul who, suffering from the shakes, has been trying to shave in the bathroom. Hugh lathers and begins to shave his half-brother, sneaks him a therapeutic drink, and in passing through the Consul's bedroom observes his library of occult literature. The Consul warns Hugh of the *Union Militar,* a Fascist organization allied with the Military Police who are infiltrating positions of authority in the state during the strike of the regular police. Leaving the bathroom they pass through the Consul's bedroom where Geoffrey points to a picture of a Q-Boat, the *Samaritan,* he allegedly commanded in World War I. With rising spirits the three Firmins set out to attend a bull-throwing in Tomalín.

The entire remainder of the novel consists of a quest for atonement, proffered in the love Yvonne brings to the Consul, which he rejects in a series of symbolic gestures even while professing his hope for reconciliation.

Before they are able to escape from Quauhnahuac yet a fourth actor in their destinies intervenes briefly, Jacques Laruelle, who, in the Firmins' earlier life in Quauhnahuac, had betrayed Geoffrey with Yvonne. Two incidents occur here which illustrate the symbolic function of Lowry's narrative technique: the postman delivers to Geoffrey a post card from Yvonne, expressing her desolation at their separation, mailed at least a year earlier, but gone vastly astray; and in Laruelle's towered house where they retire for drinks, Geoffrey, without consciously understanding his own motives, hides the card under Laruelle's pillow.

The journey by bus to Tomalín is preceded by Geoffrey's encounter with a dominant symbol in the novel, the Ferris wheel, both anticipating and repeating the device with which the transition from chapter 1 was made. In the carnival center of Quauhnahuac, Geoffrey, still avoiding the narcotic mescal, has a drink with Laruelle and, though pursuing his appointment with Hugh and Yvonne, avoids them to step onto the gigantic *Máquina Infernal*. Wound up as Cocteau's *Machine Infernale* is wound to unroll a human destiny, the wheel violently rotates the drunken and helpless Consul while his pockets disgorge possessions and symbols of identity. The circular ride suggests movement without progression, eternal recurrence, as well as man's drunken plunge to disaster. When the Consul is returned to stable earth again, gaping children surprisingly return all his belongings except his passport, which he cannot now be certain he has brought with him. Again avoiding the dreaded mescal, he has another drink of tequila at the cantina El Bosque (Dante's dark wood), and addresses a pursuing pariah dog with an unfinished prophecy. Leaving the cantina he narrowly misses Sr. Bustamente, Dr. Vigil, and M. Laruelle, who, he imagines, are seeking him. It is proclaimed that the Pope's death is inevitable.

Finally the bus to Tomalín begins its journey bearing the three Firmins and various other passengers, mainly Indian women. Of major importance are two figures encoun-

tered on this hot, dusty ride which permits occasional
glimpses of the towering eminences of Popocatepetl and
Ixaccihuatl above while they move slowly through the
town, passing another sign, "¿Le guste este jardín. . . ?"
At the first stop they pick up an apparently eccentric drunk
wearing two hats (suggesting layers of disguise) and eating
a melon (the fruits of Mexico) whom the Consul designates
to Hugh as a Spanish Fascist involved in the *Union Militar*, a *pelado* ("peeled one" or "one who is broke") who
becomes symbolically involved in the next encounter.
After passing through savage desert landscapes they are
stopped suddenly by a detour. Hugh, however, has caught
a glimpse of a man lying under the hedge and notifies the
driver. The three Firmins, accompanied by two male passengers and the *pelado,* dismount to examine the evidently badly injured Indian whose sombrero has been
placed over his face. Prompted by naïve compassion, the
desire of the politically motivated liberal to aid, Hugh
starts to remove the sombrero, but is warned that such a
gesture is illegal. Impetuously the *pelado* does uncover
the wounded man's face, disclosing an ugly abrasion on
his temple and several coins in his collar. A confused discussion about medical aid and the police takes place, and
Hugh and the Consul examine the man's horse, whose
saddlebags are missing, and discover it is branded with
the number 7. Three vigilantes arrive, Hugh argues with
them, but they force him back onto the bus, which then
leaves. But before they arrive at Tomalín the Consul draws
Hugh's attention to the bloodstained coins the *pelado* is
clutching in his hand—stolen from the wounded Indian.
The insidious power of a flourishing and corrupt political
force, in other words, permits aggression against the

wounded and the deprived, the helpless indigens of the
country, whereas the sentimental politics of the Anglo-
Saxon world is reduced to impotence. In Tomalín they
leave the bus before the tavern Todos Contentos y Yo
También, and as Geoffrey becomes progressively drunker
the great circular movement continues toward the bull-
throwing.

At the Arena Tomalín a festival spirit returns, and
Yvonne regains her composure after having wept at the
sight of the wounded Indian. The first bull appears
bravely, but soon loses its spirit. Yvonne remembers her
father, who, like Geoffrey, had been a consul, the American representative in Chile, also an alcoholic and a hopeless venturer into various catastrophic business enterprises
in Hawaii and the States. At the age of thirteen she had
become a movie actress in Westerns and serials, leading
lady to a cowboy star. After an unsuccessful first marriage
and the death of her child, significantly named Geoffrey,
she had returned to Hollywood, promoted by tawdry public relations to initiate a new movie career. In this venture,
however, she had been spectacularly unsuccessful. Meeting Jacques Laruelle in Quauhnahuac the first time had
permitted her to share with him a professional enthusiasm
she had never been able to enjoy with the egocentric Consul. In fact, she had seen one of Laruelle's films in New
York and had closely identified with the heroine, again
significantly, named Yvonne. While the now spiritless
bull-throwing continues the Firmins nip at a bottle of ha-
banero, and Yvonne dreams of removing Geoffrey to Vancouver, B.C., as Hugh has described it, where they would
live simply and Geoffrey could continue his book on At-
lantis. Her reverie is interrupted by the glimpse of a man

in dark glasses whom she believes she has seen that morning in Quauhnahuac. The totally degenerated spectacle in the arena is suddenly given life by Hugh's vaulting the railing and successfully riding and throwing the bull. Briefly alone together, Yvonne and the Consul share a passionate revival of their love for one another. Rejoined by Hugh they leave the arena and return to the tavern Todos Contentos y Yo También, from which emerges an elderly Indian bearing (as Aeneas bore Anchises) a still more elderly and lame Indian on his back.

At the Salón Ofélia (suggesting another spurned woman) while Yvonne and Hugh swim in a natural pool, the Consul, caught up in the sweep of self-destructive action, finally capitulates and begins ordering mescal. The owner of the Salón, Sr. Cervantes, hovers spectrally about the drinking Consul and leads him to an inner shrine of the Virgin and one way of redemption, reminding Geoffrey of another Maria Dr. Vigil had escorted him to, "The Virgin for those who have nobody with." While Geoffrey prays for a return of his purity, for a renewed chance of happiness with Yvonne, his devotions are punctuated contrapuntally by the voices of Hugh and Yvonne gaily planning an ascent of Popocatepetl (anticipating the hallucination Geoffrey is to experience at the moment of his death).

Rejoined, the Firmins order dinner after reading the curious bill of fare and listening to Sr. Cervantes' ribald version of the food available. The Consul, "flying" once more on mescal, thinks of the mountainous accumulation of bottles he has left behind him in the course of his life and suddenly finds himself seated once more in a toilet, hearing Yvonne and Hugh discuss the Indian and the horse branded with the number 7 they had seen on their morning ride and later on the roadside. Sitting on the toilet and half-listening to their conversation the Consul reads from a mutilated-English travel folder of the history and geography of the district, Tlaxcala. Fragments of voices and impressions of the day's experience now filter through his mind, supplemented by the conversation in the dining room.

After several mescals consumed from a lemonade bottle in the toilet he emerges in a drunken trance and directs an outrageous attack on Hugh's moderate Marxist political philosophy which then changes into a violent accusation against Hugh and Yvonne in Othellian imagery in which he levels the charge that they are planning to cuckold him. Paying for the dinner, he announces that he "loves hell" and is running toward it, and in fact does begin to run toward the Farolito (the little lighthouse described earlier by Dr. Vigil as an *"infierno"*) in Parián which has been drawing him during the entire day's pilgrimage.

Under the ominous sky of an approaching storm Hugh and Yvonne pursue the Consul, stopping at various cantinas on the way to Parián to see if he has passed by. After searching at the Todos Contentos, Yvonne ominously chooses the longer way since on that route are situated two more cantinas. By the thunder of a great waterfall Hugh asks for information of the Consul in yet another cantina while Yvonne, waiting outside, discovers a caged eagle which she releases. The freed bird rises into the dark blue evening sky. Hugh reports that the Consul has not been seen and they continue their search while Yvonne with her interest in astronomy begins to recognize the constellations of the southern sky. The approaching storm is heralded by thunder and high-piled clouds. At another bar they continue the search for the Consul, and Yvonne, conceding a power to Geoffrey, decides to try mescal. After a brief disappearance Hugh returns with an electric torch, a guitar, and an old menu, on the back of which in the Consul's handwriting is a signed chit for drinks and a scarcely legible poem whose concluding line, "Who once fled north," is a haunting memory of the legend which described the death of Geoffrey's father. Once more, at twelve minutes to seven, they set out for the Farolito in Parián. Following the path upwards through the jungle they are met by the advancing storm while Hugh sings Loyalist songs as he follows Yvonne. They hear three pistol shots in the distance—it is now seven o'clock—and as Yvonne climbs a ladder over a fallen tree and reaches the top, the sound of a fleeing animal comes to her. In the darkness she slips and is trampled to death by the hysterical horse branded with the number 7. In the moments before her death she feels herself lifted skywards toward the Pleiades.

In the twelfth and final chapter of the book Geoffrey has returned to the Farolito, for on a previous, drunken occasion there he had abandoned important symbols: one a favorite pipe, phallic in its significance; and closely related, a bundle of Yvonne's letters. He is too drunk to read the letters, but he succumbs to the invitation of a young whore, another Maria, whose shrine he does successfully enter (and immediately thereafter is approached by the pimp who reports that the time is "half sick by the cock"), whereas his sexual attempt with Yvonne earlier in the day had resulted in impotence. Suffering remorse for this ultimate betrayal of Yvonne, as well as for its unprophylactic nature, he wanders drunkenly outside and discovers the

horse branded with the number 7 once more, and is accused by a police sergeant of intended theft. Forced inside
again, he is confronted with a chorus of drunken accusers:
Diosdado ("God-given"), owner of the Farolito who reports that Geoffrey has suspiciously drawn a map of Spain,
and sinister members of the constabulary identified as the
Chief of Municipalities, Chief of Rostrums, and Chief of
Gardens. Mescal and tequila are served and consumed in
abundance by all while a macabre, hallucinatory scene
takes place. Warned in broken English by the pimp on one
side, and by the old woman he had seen that morning in
the Bella Vista bar on the other, wheedled by a drunken
sailor who claims that Mozart wrote the Bible, and observed at a distance by a drunken American, Weber, an ex-
legionnaire who had also been in the Bella Vista bar that
morning, accused by the Chiefs of being a Jew, a Bolshevik, and a member of the International Brigade, the Consul is deprived of his money, Yvonne's letters, and the
telegram on anti-Semitic organizations in Mexico written
by Hugh and left in the Consul's jacket. Without his passport and in spite of the telegram signed "Firmin" (not he,
but Hugh), he insists that he is William Blackstone (not
the jurist, but an English exile among American Indians,
also a "searcher"). Finally in a drunken rage the Chief of
Rostrums now alleges that he is a spy, but Geoffrey, demanding the return of Yvonne's letters, strikes the ominous Chief of Gardens and accuses them of having murdered the Indian and stolen his horse. He is pushed
brutally outside, staggers toward the horse, which bolts for
the rendezvous with Yvonne in the dark woods below the
Farolito, and is shot three times by the Chief of Rostrums.
In the moments before his death he has a fantasy that he is

climbing Popocatepetl with Hugh and Yvonne, but dying, realizes he is "flying," plunging into the barranca. A dead pariah dog is flung in after him.

The three epigraphs which Lowry chose for his novel define the scope as well as the antinomies of the highly compacted experience of the Consul's last day. The first, from the *Antigone* of Sophocles, is the eulogy on man who has successfully contended with all the forces of his environment save only his mortality; the second, from Bunyan's *Grace Abounding*, is the cry uttered by the soul recognizing its refusal of deliverance; and the third is Goethe's well-known "Wer immer strebend sich bemüht, den können wir erlösen." The mystery of Geoffrey Firmin lies somewhere within the triangle formed by these opposed visions, and his failure derives from his incapacity to resolve the psychological dilemma which these forces impose upon him. Consequently his way of becoming, *immer strebend,* leads to an avid but terrified acceptance of damnation. But the mystery is both a Mystery revealed and a cathexis on self.

Reconstructing the Consul's life from the fragments offered by himself and the three attendant human beings who observe his plunge into hell is necessary for a confident exploration of the novel's vision. Born in Kashmir, Geoffrey had been deprived of the maternal image by the early death of his mother; and while he was still very young his father, after remarriage, had simply disappeared, "fled North" into the Himalayas. Geoffrey's stepmother, Hugh's mother, had also died shortly thereafter, and the two brothers had been shipped off to England where Geoffrey had been domiciled with the English poet Abraham Taskerson, father of numerous, athletic, heavy-drinking sons. In the company of the Taskersons he had met Jacques Laruelle on a vacation in France, and Jacques, of an equal age with Geoffrey, had accompanied the Taskersons back to England. Here the two boys had become close friends and together in intact adolescence had made tentative explorations in sex, picking up girls to take for walks on the golf course adjoining the Taskersons' property. On one of these nocturnal excursions Jacques and his girl discover Geoffrey and another girl in the notorious "Hell Bunker" on the eighth fairway. After embarrassed readjustments of clothing the four had proceeded to an inn, "The Case Is Altered," for a drink, refused by the proprietor on the grounds of their minority. After that incident of love in an abyss and discovery, the relations between Geoffrey and Jacques had deteriorated, and they had gone their separate ways, Geoffrey to school and legendary exploits in "some obscure capacity" as commander of a Q-boat in World War I, both decorated and court-martialed, and Jacques to film-making. They had not met again until many years later in Quauhnahuac, Geoffrey at the end of long consular service in various parts of the world, and Jacques retired from film-making.

The incident which precipitated the court-martial is important to any psychological analysis of Geoffrey Firmin's inadequacies. Allegedly (he himself in drunken moments later in life both denies and accepts culpability) while in command of the disguised gunboat, he had captured a German submarine and condemned the officers thereof to incineration in the ship's furnaces. No more precise information may be discovered in the novel, and the specific date of the incident is not disclosed.

With all his attention to detail and the meticulous functioning of symbol and correspondence, Lowry was very careless with fact. Numerous errors occur in *Volcano* (unfortunately perpetuated in later editions) and in his other work, some of them trivial, possibly typos in manuscript, but others more serious. In two of the stories of *Hear Us O Lord from Heaven Thy Dwelling Place*, for example, the narrator, or monologist, standing at sea level in the Vancouver, B.C., area, insists upon identifying a peak as Mount Hood, an 11,245-foot mountain in northern Oregon 275 miles away, thus invisible, and screened by Mount Rainier in Washington, 14,108 feet high. Trivial possibly, but indicative.

The Consul has committed, or believes he has committed, a crime against humanity by consigning German officers to a fiery death, and the destructive sense of guilt which pursues him, in part at least, allegedly stems from this horrifying incident of his past. However, at the time of the action of *Volcano*, 1938, the Consul recalls that he is twelve years older than Hugh, who is twenty-nine, and is therefore forty-one, establishing his birth date as 1897 (though in chapter 1 Laruelle remembers him as being fifteen in 1911, which would put his year of birth at 1896). At the beginning of World War I, therefore, he would have been seventeen or eighteen, and at the end in 1918, twenty-one or twenty-two, an impossibly tender age to have been commander of a gunboat. Is this another example of Lowry's carelessness? Or, as seems more likely, has the Consul's spiritual requirement for guilt fabricated his involvement in the episode? Is he a supralapsarian mythopoeist who insists that guilt is available and must be allocated? The analogy to *Lord Jim* is obvious, but Jim spends the rest of his brief life attempting to atone for a moment of instinctive cowardice, while the Consul's career is marked by progressive degeneration. In his search for identity he admits that "there is no explanation for my life," and speculates that "in one of those lost or broken bottles, in one of these glasses, lay, moreover, the solitary clue to his identity."

The profound sense of guilt, then, that hovers over Geoffrey Firmin driving him on to self-destruction and the destruction of those whom he loves, or believes he should love, functions on at least three well-defined, but carefully fused, levels: that of psychic arrestment resulting in narcissistic containment; closely related, political capitulation to the apparently victorious dark powers of Fascism about to devour the world, and literally destroying the Consul himself; and in the broadest sense possible, theological, the Calvinistic sense of primal transgression and implication in cosmic guilt. These levels, however, are intricately woven together in the day's pilgrimage by the use of symbol and sign, animate, inanimate, political, religious, geographical, and institutional, only a few of which may be commented on here.

The barranca, or ravine, which runs across the countryside through Quauhnahuac and which according to ancient Indian myth split open on the day of the Crucifixion relates back to the "Hell Bunker" of Geoffrey's youth and the sexual definition of that experience, but it is also the hell which both attracts and repels him, is finally his grave, and is symbolic of his separation from Yvonne. It has its correspondence in the sun-split stone the Consul and Yvonne see in a store window in chapter 2.

Essential to the articulation of the novel is the use of both familiar and occult numerology, the twelve chapters corresponding to the months of the year, the twelve hours of the book, and the twelve labors of Hercules; 7, of cabbalistic significance, is first introduced branded on the rump of the horse which Jacques Laruelle sees in chapter 1 bearing a drunken rider, a symbol of the now deceased Consul, and which reappears through the day and ultimately figures spectrally in the death of both the Consul and Yvonne; that number is also the hour on which the day of the book begins and ends; 3, with its usual trinitarian weight, has multiple applications to the three attendants to Geoffrey's passion, the three men surrounding Yvonne, and the three-legged retreat from Geoffrey of the obsequious little pariah dog in the cantina El Bosque. Other more arcane numbers such as 666 and 34 lead off into the complexities of cabbalistic lore.

Animals, reptiles, and birds play a major role in the field of symbolic references in the book. The apocalyptic horse of death seen in many moods and many settings during the twelve hours of the book's action is perhaps the most prominent. Geoffrey is described several times as being "strong as a horse," and in effect he releases the horse which kills Yvonne. Hugh and Yvonne escape briefly from the Consul on horses, and Yvonne, who had been a movie cowgirl, had once been threatened in a canyon by 200 stampeding horses, and has a premonitory vision of a horse about to trample her to death. The pariah dog, or dogs, which insistently attach themselves to the Consul would seem to have a dual reference: one, a relation to the satanic black poodle which follows Goethe's

Faust, and two, the symbol of the totally abject humility which, though he aspires fervently toward it, is forever inaccessible to the Consul.

"For God sees how timid and beautiful you really are, and the thoughts of hope that go with you like little white birds—"
The Consul stood up and suddenly declaimed to the dog:
"Yet this day, pichicho, shalt thou be with me in—" But the dog hopped away in terror on three legs and slunk under the door.

At the day's end, of course, the Consul and the dog are joined not in heaven but in hell.

Appropriate to an allegory of Eden and the Expulsion, a snake, real it would seem, appears in the Firmins' sinister garden. Scorpions are passed which the Consul repeatedly declares "will only sting themselves to death," as he continues to absorb the death-sting of alcohol. A goat bearing the symbolic order of tragedy, *cabron* (cuckold), and scapegoat attacks Hugh and Yvonne. And among the most effective of many bird symbols, including hovering vultures, is the caged eagle which Yvonne releases in chapter 11. Since one of the suggested meanings of Quauhnahuac is "where the eagle stops," in freeing the eagle Yvonne is finally relinquishing her hold on the Consul, to watch the winged symbol mount into the dark blue sky where she herself is about to be lifted in death.

In the thoroughly animistic world which surrounds the Consul forces contend obscurely for his attention. A sunflower, one of God's spies, stares at him fiercely all day, registering its disapproval. The deserted garden tries to "maintain some final attitude of potency . . . the plan-

tains . . . once emblematic of life, now of evil phallic
death"; the elements themselves, as in Conrad, are responsive to the human drama, and the final scenes are
played before jagged lightning and the roll of thunder.

Technically a symbolist novel, *Volcano* returns to the
primal myth of Western man, the allegorized enactment of
the Fall and Expulsion. The Consul's garden, now an evil
jungle, was once well tended by the departed Yvonne.
Upon her return, divorced from the Consul now, she
makes a few tentative gestures, interrupted by Hugh, to restore this lost paradise, but the separation is complete before the day's journey begins. Both mythic structure and
sexual trauma are intended here. And the Consul alone in
his garden speculates to Mr. Quincey, his disapproving
God next door, on the possibility of Adam's having been
left sole, impotent tenant presiding over the primal waste-
land.

"What if his punishment really consisted," the Consul continued
with warmth, "in his having to *go on living there,* alone, of
course—suffering, unseen, cut off from God?"

Man expelled from Eden assumes the myths of two literary explorers of hell in Lowry's allegory: Dante in the
dark wood preparing for descent, and Faustus having bar-
tered his soul, accompanied by his warring familiars, preparing for the full, even gleeful exploitation of his bargain.
"I love hell. I can't wait to get back there," the Consul
calls out to Yvonne and Hugh as he runs toward the final
circle of his descent.

Warnings are posted in this earth-Garden against
those who despoil it and waste its fruits.

¿LE GUSTA ESTE JARDÍN?
¿QUE ES SUYO?
¡EVITE QUE SUS HIJOS LO DESTRUYAN!

The complete sign (or fragments of it) appears on various occasions in the course of the book and stands alone as epilogue facing the last page. But again, since memory and alcohol constantly distort perspectives, no dependable separation of myth and actuality is possible. At his first glimpse of the sign the Consul translates tentatively, "You like this garden? Why is it yours? We evict those who destroy!" Palpably unsound, though he later concedes that it seemed to have too many question marks. On the second occasion the superfluous question mark after "jardín" and the inverted mark before "que" are omitted, and the Consul translates, "Do you like this garden that is yours? See to it that your children do not destroy it!" The final appearance in block capitals repeats this version.

In the letter to Jonathan Cape, referred to above, Lowry admits that the Consul slightly mistranslates on his first attempt, and adds that the "real translation can be in a certain sense even more horrifying." Precisely what he is referring to is not clear, unless it is the ambiguity of the possessive pronouns "suyo" and "sus," which in block capitals could be either "yours" and "your," or "His," that is, God's. A discussion of the meaning occurs in *Dark as the Grave* in which Wilderness-Lowry confesses that he had in fact not only miscopied the sign but mistranslated as well, but insists again that the "real translation is even worse." In the second alternative, horror certainly is suggested—"Does this Garden which is His please you? Prevent His sons from destroying it!"—in the fact that the Consul, man playing out an allegory of the Fall, betraying the Mysteries entrusted to him and rejecting salvation, has been irredeemably expelled from the Garden to wander eternally without hope of atonement. Appropriately it is finally the Chief of Gardens who presides over Geoffrey's execution.

One more emblem thrust up in the convulsive world of Geoffrey Firmin's final day offers commentary on the Consul's self-destructive instinct. Its message is introduced as a leitmotif in the second chapter as Yvonne approaches the Bella Vista bar, hearing the Consul's voice announce that "a corpse will be transported by express." Death is ironically pronounced at the moment of Yvonne's arrival, a dissonant introduction to what immediately follows, but also supplying the theme of sterility (the corpse is that of a child), not Yvonne's sterility, for she has had a child by her previous marriage, but the total sterility of the Consul's love. Immediately juxtaposed amid the auditory fragments, also suggesting death in the voice of the Fascist Weber who twelve hours later will attend the Consul's death, is the bartender's "Absolutemente necesario." Only after she is in the bar does Yvonne realize that it is not death, not the transportation of the child corpse, which is referred to, but love: the bartender's statement refers to the picture of a woman in an advertisement for *caféasperina*.

Amid all the symbols of separation, sterility, and death, this theme is repeated futilely to the Consul's deliberately dulled sensibilities. As Geoffrey and Jacques follow Hugh and Yvonne through the fiesta, "absolutemente necesario" is yoked together with the clearest possible statement of the theme, written on a housefront: "no se puede vivir sin amar."

Geoffrey has abandoned Yvonne, that is, love, and despite his anguished prayers for her return, every act he performs during the long day's decline when she does appear is symbolically part of a ritual murder, finally successful when he releases the horse of death to trample her in the dark woods below the Farolito. Whereas the movement of the book is circular, ritualistic, propelled by the insistent momentum of fragmented days and nights of the protracted descent, the Consul's professed intention is to reacquire the love, respect, and dignity of a now futile vision: thus the action is disjunctive, for lying between action and professed intention is the shadow of a metaphysical perversity which alters each gesture into uxoricidal, suicidal effect.

Lowry has been described as a monologist, a novelist of a single point of view, and there is some justice in the repeated accusation that he was not a successful creator of "character." In his letters he tried to answer this criticism by agreeing in principle, but at the same time pointing out that the four main characters of the novel are all aspects of one person: he did not add Malcolm Lowry, but that is the sense of the claim.

But it is only a partially defensible claim. Yvonne is the inadequate shadow of a human being, which all his women are, whether their name is Primrose, Tansy, Yvonne, or whatever. As a symbol in the tragedy of Geoffrey Firmin she is functional, but when "her" chapter comes up at the bull-throwing in Tomalín our expectations are cruelly disappointed. Quite simply she works as a symbol but not a psyche. It is possible that Lowry intended to convey a reciprocal psychological disorder by suggesting that Geoffrey is a double of her father, who had been a consul and was also an alcoholic, factors which determine her destiny as an Electra whose "one true love" remains her father beyond whom she cannot proceed.

Jacques Laruelle is much more worthy of consideration as the failed artist whose past films have been forgotten and who dreams of making a modern version of Marlowe's *Dr. Faustus* while in fact the contemporary Faustus plays out his destiny before Laruelle's eyes. In a sense it would seem that Lowry intended to grant Laruelle certain powers of definition: it is he who, when they are children, comes upon Geoffrey's amatory explorations of the Hell Bunker, and again he who has cuckolded the Consul with Yvonne (an autobiographical incident here involving Lowry's first wife apparently supplied the fictional idea). The downfall of Geoffrey Firmin, it might be argued, is the script of a film to be made by Jacques Laruelle.

Hugh, on the other hand, is an essential ingredient in the total, subdivided personality which Lowry carried over into the fashioning of the novel. The marine and musical exploits of Dana Hilliot in *Ultramarine* are Hugh's in *Volcano*. Far more important, however, is his role as the political conscience of the book. As Geoffrey suffers a psychological and metaphysical guilt, Hugh speaks and suffers for the political guilt of the decade of nonengagement when the battle of the Ebro was being lost, China was suffering rape by the Japanese, Mexico was being despoiled by the Sinarchists, and sleeping England was rousing from the long dormancy which led up to World War II.

A feckless sort of energy has driven Hugh from his marine days through an abortive career as a songwriter, student, an early anti-Semite and later overcompensating Semitophile, seducer of other men's wives, journalist, and

finally defector from the political scene. Driven by guilt
for this defection, he has determined to sail on a freighter
laden with dynamite for the Loyalist cause in Spain, a per-
ilous, but not necessarily suicidal (as claimed by Mrs. Epstein), mission. No evidence exists in the book to suggest
that he has actually slept with Yvonne (as generally is
claimed), though obviously he desires her and therefore
considers himself Geoffrey's Judas, and in the drunken
scene of chapter 10 played out by the three of them, he is
accused by the Consul of infidelity, an accusation the Consul requires to proceed with the act of self-destruction.
Deeply and rather mysteriously embedded within the
mythic structure of the book, however, Hugh's role as
Judas is substantiated, for ironically he has flown down to
Quauhnahuac with Weber, the American Fascist, whose
activities in the *Union Militar* seem obscurely to contribute to the death of the Consul. In fact there is substantial
though unillumined evidence that the Consul dies in
Hugh's place.

   Lowry's narrative technique inevitably reminds us of
Ulysses, as do several specific scenes. Throughout he
maintains the third-person perspective, permitting his
characters the flow of memory and interior monologue. In
spite of heavy demands on the reader, primarily because
of the deliberate suppression of narrative detail into the
mysterious and threatening background, and the profusion
of literary allusion, *Volcano* is a singularly emotional, subjective cry—with moments of lacerated humor—of agony,
which Joyce's novel certainly is not. Witty, deeply read,
urbane, and doomed, Geoffrey Firmin cannot speak his
love, refrains from acting, and dies. The service which

arises from fear leads him toward love, but love remains beyond his grasp.

A thin volume of Lowry's poems, most of which had previously appeared in various journals, was published by City Lights Books in 1962, representing, his editor and friend Earle Birney tells us, approximately a fourth of the verse in manuscript. Inevitably the imagery and subject matter of the sea dominate the earlier work, nature's storms appealing to the storm of the heart. But as the landscape changes, following Lowry's life-itinerary, intensive introspection begins to darken the mood and tonality of the poet's vision. Mexican bars, cantinas, and jails in livid morning light provide an oblique poetic glimpse of the familiar demonology.

Be patient for the wolf is always with you.

As might be expected, when Lowry turned to verse the cry of the wounded soul becomes more audible, if less articulate. In spite of invocations to Yeats, Rilke, and Eliot, the spirit of Hart Crane, one of Lowry's favorite poets, moves through these utterances effecting cryptic compression; indeed, some of them give the impression of a single phrase subjected to repeated, tortuous variations: "Pure scavenger of the Empyrean," or "The midtown pyromaniac, sunset." In others, attempting an austerity of form as in the villanelle "Death of a [sic] Oxaquenian," Lowry has succeeded in achieving a nondiscursive litany very moving in its incantatory effects.

It should be added that occasionally the alcoholic

gloom and cycles of repentance were broken through for
comedy's sake, as in the "Epitaph":

> Malcolm Lowry
> Late of the Bowery
> His prose was flowery
> And often glowery
> He lived, nightly, and drank, daily,
> And died playing the ukulele.

The seven stories edited by Mrs. Lowry and Harvey
Breit which were published as *Hear Us O Lord from
Heaven Thy Dwelling Plaçe* (1961) are uneven in quality
and effectiveness, but one technical characteristic which
they all share removes them from traditional categories of
short fiction: they are essentially monologues on travel,
memory, art and life, marital love, and atonement. They
lack the drama and economy of the short story as generally
practiced, but with perhaps two exceptions they are eman-
cipated from the restrictions of mythic archetypes and consequently range with freedom and self-conscious humor
over the mind's reflexive terrain. The monologist, whether
he is named Sigbjørn Wilderness, Sigurd Storlesen, Kennish Drumgold Cosnahan, or Roger Fairhaven, is always a
thinly disguised *persona* for Lowry. And the woman
whose physical presence or distant effect is both admonitory and supportive is the familiar figure of Yvonne in *Volcano* relieved of the role of a participant in a *Totentanz*,
but otherwise virtually unaltered. Yet the invitation to
share the subtleties of a tortured, gifted mind recognizing
the humor and absurdity of its anxieties is a courageous
gesture and one well worth accepting. The cosmic threat
remains, but the tone is quite different.

Of the two major achievements in the collection, "Through the Panama" and "The Forest Path to the Spring," the latter is a brilliant sketch of an intended *Paradiso* in the cycle of novels which Lowry planned to call *The Voyage That Never Ends*, the *Inferno* section of which was to be *Under the Volcano*. Both of these stories, or novellas, deserve more detailed examination than may be given them here, but the artistic intentions are clearly admirable. "Through the Panama" is an imaginatively construed, factual account of the voyage the Lowrys made from Vancouver, B.C., through the Canal to France on a French freighter in November, 1947. After a peaceful passage down the western coast of the United States and Mexico, the *Diderot* traverses the canal and, leaving Curaçao, is tossed into the fury of a violent storm in the winter Atlantic, the rage of which seriously threatens to sink the ship. Both "Typhoon" and *The Nigger of the Narcissus* come to mind in the fine descriptive passages, but the sombre music of Conrad is altered to comedy. Comedic, or low mimetic, too, are the desperate stratagems employed by Sigbjørn Wilderness to protect and replenish his failing supply of liquor by buying *pinard* from the steward and inducing the captain to extend invitations for apéritifs. But the comedy is a glittering facet on a contour which again encloses a mythic substructure, that of the mariner, Coleridge's Ancient Mariner, carrying his burden of culpability. Using selections from Coleridge's own gloss to his poems, Lowry constructs of the *persona* Sigbjørn Wilderness, in a third fictional remove, a surrogate in one Martin Trumbaugh, a character in a novel planned by Wilderness. Through such an elaboration, reminding us of both Gide and the involuted narrative perspective of

Conrad's *Chance*, Lowry equates the effect of the sin of the Mariner to the sense of literary isolation, alienation from his own artistic contemporaries, which through the Lowry alchemy becomes a Calvinistic conviction of guilt. This sense of being alone in artistic endeavor, of nostalgia for Melville, O'Neill, Kafka, even Poe, of trying unsuccessfully to understand "The Love Song of J. Alfred Prufrock" and "The Waste Land" (even after he himself had written a prose Waste Land), of recognizing "more sense of life actually felt in Wolfe than all Joyce," imposes on Lowry-Wilderness-Trumbaugh the role of the Ancient Mariner of modern art.

But such aesthetic skirmishes do not obscure the vitality and lively cadences of the novella, which is one of the most volatile of Lowry's works. The recurring rhythm of "Frère Jacques, frère Jacques" to describe the beat of the ship's engines (a musical association which absolutely haunted Lowry), the incisive and yet compassionate insights into suffering fellow passengers and crew, the magnificent descriptive passages as well as the fascination with posted directions, fragments of exhortation (here without the sinister significance of those in *Volcano*), and the humor coalesce to produce a wonderfully suggestive, marine prose poem.

Testifying to its popularity, "The Bravest Boat" has been reprinted more frequently than any other of Lowry's short stories. The reasons are not difficult to understand, for with the exception of the much more complicated "The Forest Path to the Spring" it is the closest thing to a love-idyll that Lowry wrote, but even here he has used an appropriately moderated allegory. The toy boat which Sigurd Storlesen releases as a child with a note enclosed braves twelve years of sun, tempests, and strandings to be found by Astrid, who later becomes his wife. As man and wife now, twenty-nine years after that launching, they commemorate this magic berth by walking through the wild beauty of a Canadian lagoon, occasionally encountering the contamination produced by the small village nearby, marveling at the perseverance of a destiny which has brought them together. In no other work has Lowry so simply illustrated his faith in a transcendent order which arranges man's life for fortune or disaster as in this little parable of a ship come home to port.

"Strange Comfort Afforded by the Profession" is an artist's confession of the reward which may be found in the precedents of misery, struggle, and poverty. Sigbjørn Wilderness, in this metamorphosis an American writer on a Guggenheim fellowship in Rome, makes the traditional inspection of Keats's last home on the Piazza di Spagna, compulsively taking notes on the various mementos and Severn's letters describing Keats's final days. Retiring to a bar for a grappa, he begins to read the accumulation of notes he has made in Rome on the Mamertine Prison where prisoners in the lower area suffered various violent deaths, and, juxtaposed to those notes, records of generations of artists—Gogol, Ibsen, Mann, and Eliot—who had lived in or visited Rome. Several grappas later he retraces his note-taking expeditions back to the United States, to Richmond and the Valentine Museum with relics of another addict of art, Edgar Allan Poe, and reads his transcript of an anguished letter from Poe begging for aid. Searching further in the record of his past he comes across the rough draft of a letter of his own, recording the spiritual and economic anguish he suffered as a virtual prisoner of his father-appointed guardians in Seattle, Washington. "Comfort" offers the knowledge that the artist shares a community with his predecessors severe and humiliating though it may be, even if one is (or believes oneself to be) quite alone in the contemporary landscape.

"Elephant and Colosseum" is unique among Lowry's stories, the sole example of pure ironic comedy, a sustained joke on himself. As such it gives evidence of a growing objectivity, the developing capacity for the distance which irony exacts. Kennish Drumgold Cosnahan is a displaced Manxman—and the name itself suggests the Gaelic tonality of comic fantasy—a "successful" writer of an amusing book describing his experiences as a deck hand on a freighter returning from Singapore with a collection of animals destined for European zoos, and in particular an elephant named Rosemary which he had tended. Now many years later in Rome without his wife, whom he misses, he is suffering from post-success impotence, performing the tourist's rites at the Colosseum, on the Via Veneto, experiencing the singular loneliness of the tourist alone, grieving his failure to reach his mother, a nonprofessional sorceress, on the Isle of Man before her death, and trying to generate the energy to locate the offices of his Italian publisher. Again the mode in the beginning is low mimetic, almost that of the clown, as Cosnahan, terrified of traffic (one of Lowry's pervading fears), with his inadequate Italian, little knowledge of Rome, and without the publisher's address, which he had failed to bring with him, attempts to locate the publisher and, when he does, discovers that the main office to which he should have directed himself is in Torino. Fortuitously his steps take him to the zoo where an instinct—he had inherited but lost some of the maternal sorcery—leads him toward the elephant cage. Here he recognizes Rosemary, who has survived Fascism, war, and defeat, being fed and following her antic custom of depositing wisps of hay on her head as protection against the sun. A sudden glory descends upon Cosnahan, a Manx ecstasy, releasing him from the heavy weight of his mother's unmourned death, restoring his fertility, and he is "as happy as some old magician who had just recovered his powers." The clown, the pure fool, has his innocence restored.

Though not without the charm of a sly pun, "The Present Estate of Pompei" is less successful, depending as it does on a tourist's cliché, the tour of the preserved ruin by Roger and Tansy Fairhaven in the charge of a stereotypic Italian guide, significantly named Signor Salacci, with his routine speech on archaeology delivered in unpredictable English. But very predictably he leads them to the brothels in the Vico dei Lupanare, lingers raffishly over the priapic emblems, and with genuine nostalgia laments the vanished luxury of the Empire. Responding to this vanished *beauté, luxe, calme, et volupté,* Roger Fairhaven views the ruins as suggesting that perhaps a "precious part" of man had disappeared from the earth.

The Wildernesses are on what appears to be a mysteriously repugnant mission in "Gin and Goldenrod." Trying to locate a house in a jerry-built community in the familiar Dollarton terrain for reasons which remain questionable and slightly threatening until the end, Sigbjørn and Primrose wander through the narrowing margin between civilization and nature, debris and flowers, responding with increasing irascibility to the disagreeable search for an address. Perhaps more clearly here than in any other part of the work the inadequacy of the male-female relationship in Lowry's world is explored—unconsciously, one is tempted to add. It is apparent from the beginning that the mission has been prescribed by Primrose, agreed to reluctantly by Sigbjørn, who erects small barriers to their progress, but who, like the guilty son under the admonishing eye of his mother, is urged on and rewarded with encouragement and praise after each minor victory. The mystery revealed consists of a debt to be paid for several bottles of gin bought from a bootlegger the previous Sunday, a large proportion of which had been drunk on the premises with Sigbjørn standing drinks to several Indians and consuming immense quantities himself. He had subsequently disappeared with a bottle, apparently slept in the forest, returning home the next morning. With the debt paid, the Wildernesses begin the walk home through the goldenrod and the carbon monoxide fumes of civilization, immense relief flooding Sigbjørn's chastised soul. Primrose's ultimate reward to her son-husband is the information that the bottle of gin had not been lost but retrieved and hidden by her. With this promise of a cocktail awaiting them at home, they step into their own woods where "a kind of hope began to bloom again."

"The Forest Path to the Spring" gives every evidence of having been planned as a major, complementary work, as suggested above, the *Paradiso* to the *Inferno* of *Volcano*. In its present form it consists of a rapturous conclusion only, a prose poem on man in nature, a Wordsworthian benediction on nature's benevolent power to transform the heart capable of seeing and receiving.

In the final month of his life, June 1957, Lowry and Mrs. Lowry spent a fortnight at Grasmere while he

engaged in revising the stories in this volume, and Wordsworth was on his mind and in his letters. The theme of
the "other Being" is subtly reflected in "The Forest Path,"
as are those haunting presences of *The Prelude:*

> I heard among the solitary hills
> Low breathings coming after me, and sounds
> Of indistinguishable motions, steps
> Almost as silent as the turf they trod.

And yet with his naturalist's and poet's eye sharply
focused on the immensity as well the minutiae of nature's
rhythms, Lowry saw more deeply than the bland, pan-
theistic affirmation of the Wordsworthian vision. A man
who has walked through hell does not forget the landscape
or the citizenry.

"The Forest Path," as is fitting, is a *Paradiso* on the
other side of hell, but hell is still visible in the distance:
across the bay the Shell Oil Company erects a sign above
the wharves, but for weeks it is complete except for the
"s." And the scars of that earlier journey heal slowly, as his
"thoughts [chase] each other down a gulf." With an instinct that is clearly extraordinary Lowry has managed to
establish a symmetrical relationship between the literal
and archetypal narrative, the Dantesque structure of the
experience, with illuminating psychological insight.

The scene is again the Dollarton area, and in the quest
for drinking water a spring is finally discovered to which
the nameless narrator carries a canister each day. On one
such trip he becomes aware of a cougar—a mountain lion,
rare that close to civilization—perched above him in a
maple tree. After a tense moment's hesitation the animal
returns to the forest. Of the three heraldic beasts encoun-

tered by Dante in Canto I of the *Inferno,* the lion is rage, the psychological incontinence which leads to self-betrayal. The encounter described by Lowry leads to self-transcendence and realization of the symbolic path,

paths that lead to a golden kingdom, paths that lead to death, or life, paths where one meets wolves, and who knows? even mountain lions, paths where one loses one's way.

But this becomes the path of wisdom when rage disappears, permitting "something perfectly simple, like a desire to be a better man, to be capable of more gentleness, understanding, love." What the Consul could not encompass becomes salvation in Paradise, a new baptism from the waters of the little spring: "Feeling its way underground it must have had its dark moments."

According to those who have examined the Lowry collection in the University of British Columbia Library, there remains a massive accumulation of incomplete manuscripts, notes, and drafts, and it is possible that from this residue there may still emerge material enough for another volume: the fragments of *Eridanus* and *La Mordida.* However, if the last two of Lowry's complete but posthumous novels, *Dark as the Grave Wherein My Friend Is Laid* (1968), and *October Ferry to Gabriola* (1970) are representative, future publication will be of interest only to those who believe that anything written by the author of *Volcano* is worth the labor of editing what is apparently monstrous confusion.

Such a conclusion is not unfair to Lowry, since as Douglas Day explains in the introduction to *Dark as the*

Grave (edited by him and Mrs. Lowry) Lowry's work habits were expansive but at the same time meticulous. He preferred to work on many projects simultaneously since he conceived of them as part of a large unity, and he was never entirely satisfied that a book was quite finished. Since *Dark as the Grave* was not more than a rough draft of a novel when its editors decided to prepare it for publication, any judgment on its final potential must remain provisional.

As it stands it is a severe disappointment. It is also probably unique since it is not only a painstaking gloss on *Volcano* but an intimate exposure of the author's methods of composition and a distressing vision of the naked heart. It is also a *recherche* into an earlier man who lived through the experience which produced *Volcano* and a commentary on the artist who (as it turned out) had accomplished his work but had not yet received the reward. For someone who does not know *Volcano* it approaches meaninglessness. For someone who does, it is a fascinating, incestuous account of the artist returned to his vomit to speculate on the value of the ingestion. It professes to be the search for a friend—Juan Fernando Martinez, the Dr. Vigil of *Volcano*—but it is much more obviously the continuing quest for the spore of self. Above all it is a very human search, for Sigbjørn Wilderness (again) leaves Dollarton with Primrose to visit the scene of *The Valley of the Shadow of Death* (Lowry's original title for *Volcano*) before the book has been accepted, nine years after it had been begun, in order to show her the world he has written about, which she has seen only through the book. It is almost as though, convinced that the world had refused his vision, in order to retain his artistic sanity he must at least convince Primrose, his wife, of the accuracy of that dark descent.

The Lowrys-Wildernesses left Vancouver in December, 1945, to fly to Mexico City and thence by bus to visit Cuernavaca for what turned out to be a disastrous journey, though the real humiliation of the disaster (recounted in the letters) is wisely eliminated from the novel. Allegedly the purpose of the visit was to search out Juan Fernando Martinez, of whom Lowry had created a legendary hero, but the fact that, after writing many unanswered letters, Lowry had not bothered to ascertain Fernando's precise location, or even if he were still living, suggests the other compulsive reasons for the journey. Fernando was in fact dead, he had been dead for several years. The novelistic version of this journey ends here upon the discovery of the death on a note of shock and sorrow, as the Wildernesses retreat into a church, kneel to pray for the dead man's soul, and begin the journey back to Cuernavaca, passing through the rich fields of flourishing cereals, the granary of Mexico, in part the results of Fernando's selfless labors as bank courier.

It is not at all certain that the novel, even if Lowry had lived to finish it, would have been a successful work of art. There is even less "action" in the traditional sense than in *Volcano*, which, as suggested above, has more movement on the literal level than is generally accorded, though much of it remains mysterious. There is a linear, chronological development here, fashioned quite simply from observations made on the flight, then the trips by bus, the hotels stayed in, and the residence—for Sigbjørn highly portentous—in the house in which he had chosen to quarter Jacques Laruelle in *The Valley of the Shadow*.

This aspect of the book resembles a narrative assembled from travel notes, and that is precisely what it derives from, notes made by both Lowry and Mrs. Lowry.

Of infinitely greater interest to the student of Lowry, with the exception of the name Wilderness, is the total abandonment of the *persona:* Lowry speaks here as clearly and as personally as he does in his letters. His neurotic fears and weaknesses, his morbid superstition, his obsession with certain themes and phrases, and with coincidence, his love of latinisms ("sublacustrine"), his occasional deficiencies in taste, and finally his conviction that life is indeed a forest of symbols are all exposed here without artifice. The time for artistic sublimation was not permitted him, and the unadulterated substance of his world is conveyed to us directly, half-humorously and half in terrible earnestness. Those moments in *Volcano* when the Consul engages with almost talmudic subtlety to rationalize the need for still another drink are here plainly presented as the alcoholic's dreadful but irresistible requirement for sustenance. The trivial quarrels which take on the nature of a cosmic disorder in *Volcano* are here stripped of mystery and related directly to psychological incontinence, the petty furies of the mind inclined to paranoia. Paranoiac, too, is the furious lamentation over the publication of Charles Jackson's *The Lost Weekend* (also reflected bitterly in the letters), a competent, analytical dramatization of the alcoholic, the appearance of which was inflated by Lowry into one of those coincidences arranged by malign powers to reduce the accomplishment of *Volcano.* There was indeed objective evidence which contributed to Lowry's gross devaluation of *Volcano:* Cape's unfortunate reader and others inevitably drew the parallel, but that Lowry should have confused the merits of the books again suggests the erratic pattern of his aesthetic and psychic response.

October Ferry to Gabriola had its origins in another trip, this one which the Lowrys made in 1946 from Vancouver to Victoria Island, by bus to Nanaimo, and thence by ferry to Gabriola Island, British Columbia. As Margerie Lowry explains in her editorial note, the first version was a short story, a collaboration, which Lowry refashioned into a novella in 1951. Letters written to Harold Matson and Albert Erskine in 1953 describe his characteristically desperate struggle with intractable material which is essentially not the substance from which a great novel could be fashioned. In 1957, less than three months before his death, he reported from Sussex, England, to Ralph Gustafson that he was "writing a huge and sad novel about Burrard Inlet called *October Ferry to Gabriola.*" Mrs. Lowry picked up the fragments later, editing and selecting, and quite correctly refusing to make additions which would have developed lines merely introduced into the book, but finally releasing the manuscript for 1970 publication.

Huge the novel is not (332 pages), and sad, only because of the aesthetic failure and the clear indication that Lowry was suffering from artistic paralysis owing, in part at least, to the increasingly disastrous state of his health. Set within the structure of the familiar quest-myth, the book has some formal resemblance to Virginia Woolf's *To the Lighthouse.* At the beginning, the Llewelyns, Ethan and Jacqueline, threatened with eviction from their cabin, are on a bus on the second leg of their journey to Gabriola Island in search of a new home; the final pages describe their arrival by ferry, though from a newspaper they learn

they have been reprieved from eviction. But all in between is the turbulent disorder of familiar obsessions, conflagrations and, by now, outworn themes and rhythms.
Brilliant fragments emerge occasionally, particularly in the
description of nature and in subtle introspective analysis,
but Ethan and Jacqueline are automata wrenched about
gratuitously by their creator's despairing attempts to cast
them into significant roles, the immensity of which they
are unable to achieve.

Ethan Llewelyn, like Jean-Baptiste Clamence in
Camus' *La Chute*, has retired from the law in consequence
of having innocently defended a client guilty of atrocious
homicide. He has also assumed spiritual complicity for
perhaps contributing to the suicide of a schoolmate twenty
years earlier. Neither of these transgressions provides the
weight which Lowry apparently intended, and in fact,
with the exception of a fire (once more) which has destroyed Ethan's ancestral home in Niagra-on-the-Lake, and
the threat of eviction from their cabin on the inlet in Eridanus (Dollarton), Ethan and Jacqueline seem to lead relatively happy, most modestly drunken, if indigent lives
together.

Quite apparently Lowry was retreating further into the
perils of solipsism in the final years of his life, resisting (or
insulated from) the assimilation of new experience, and re-
using the material of earlier impressions without the sustaining chord of tragic magnitude which makes *Under The
Volcano* a major work.

Criticism has been directed at *Under the Volcano* on
various grounds and from various reservations, but it is
hoped that the wiser of those negative earlier reviewers
who saw the book as an anthology of literary styles and ref-

erences have had the time to reconsider Lowry's major work. The accusation that the theme of drunkenness led to highly exclusive parochialism of interest, attractive only to depraved minds or to those suffering from similar weakness, suggests a total misunderstanding of the book. Obviously Lowry, sharing his Consul's illness, invited such a confusion since the book is in all senses a highly subjective statement. But he was writing neither a sociological document on alcoholism nor a confession of his own personal inadequacies. Drunkenness is indeed the theme, but the drunkenness of Geoffrey Firmin is the correlative of the drunkenness of the world as seen by both Dostoevsky and Hesse, a world reeling down the corridors of disaster filled with the sins of both commission and, particularly, omission, a world which had apparently condemned itself to impotence in the dark night presided over by palpable evil.

SAMUEL HYNES

William Golding

I am very serious. I believe that man suffers from an appalling ignorance of his own nature. I produce my own view, in the belief that it may be something like the truth. I am fully engaged to the human dilemma but see it as far more fundamental than a complex of taxes and astronomy.

William Golding wrote these words in reply to a literary magazine's questionnaire, "The Writer in His Age." The questionnaire raised the question of "engagement": should the writer concern himself with the political and social questions of his time? Golding's answer is unequivocal: the job of the writer is to show man his image *sub specie aeternitatis*. It is in this sense of engagement, not to the concerns of the moment but to what is basic in the human condition, and in the forms that this engagement has led Golding to create, that his uniqueness lies; he is *the* novelist of our time for whom the novel matters because of what it can mean, and what it can do.

In the note from which I quoted above, Golding described himself as "a citizen, a novelist and a schoolmaster." The latter term is no longer literally applicable, but

there is still a good deal of both the citizen and the schoolmaster in the novelist. The citizen is concerned with "the
defects of society"; the schoolmaster is concerned to correct them by proper instruction; the novelist finds the appropriate forms in which man's own nature may be embodied, that he may learn to know it. One consequence of
this will-to-instruct is that Golding is an unusually disciplined, schematic writer; he thinks his novels out very
slowly, and in careful detail (he wrote *Lord of the Flies*, he
said, "as if tracing over words already on the page"), and
he is willing, even eager, to discuss what they mean. Another consequence is his desire to have his works read
with the same kind of conscious intelligence, and his distrust of irrational and intuitive views of literary creation.
He clearly thinks of his novels as the expressions of conscious intentions that existed before the writing began.
Indeed he has twice spelled out what those intentions
were. This does not, of course, imply that they took the
form of abstract moral propositions which were then
clothed in plot; but it does suggest that for Golding the entire plan of the work, *and* the meaning of that plan, were
worked out first—that he started with meaning rather than
with character or situation. Golding's own glosses of the
meanings of *Lord of the Flies* and *Pincher Martin* have not
seemed satisfactory to most readers—the teller in fact supports Lawrence's view of the creative process, and not
Golding's; nevertheless, the fact that Golding thinks of his
books as he does tells us something useful about the forms
that they have taken.

    There is no adequate critical term for that form. Gol-
ding himself has called his books both *myths* and *fables*,
and both terms do point to a quality in the novels that it is

necessary to recognize—that they are unusually tight, conceptualized, analogical expressions of moral ideas. Still, neither term is quite satisfactory, because both imply a degree of abstraction and an element of the legendary that Golding's novels simply do not have, and it seems better to be content with calling them simply *novels*, while recognizing that they have certain formal properties that distinguish them from most current fiction.

The most striking of these properties is that Golding so patterns his narrative actions as to make them the images of ideas, the imaginative forms of generalizations; the form itself, that is to say, carries meaning apart from the meanings implied by character or those stated more or less didactically by the author. "In all my books," Golding has said, "I have suggested a shape in the universe that may, as it were, account for things." To direct the attentions of his readers to that shape, Golding has chosen situations that isolate what is basic, and avoid both the merely topical and the subjective existence of the author. All but one of his novels employ a situation that is remote in time or space, characters who are radically unlike the author, and a narrative tone that is removed, analytical, and judicial. Consequently we must look for human relevance to the patterned action itself; if we "identify," it must be with the moral—with the conception of man and the shape of the universe—and not with this character or that one.

The forms that Golding uses carry implications both for the kind of action selected and for the kind of characters involved in it. Since Golding proposes to embody general truths in his novels, he is committed, one would think, to select those human experiences that can be viewed as *exemplary*, not merely as *typical*; it is not enough to pro-

pose that a fictional event might happen. To be justifiable
in a Golding novel an event must also bear its share of the
patterned meaning. Consequently the novels tend on the
whole to be short and densely textured, and the characters,
while they are usually convincingly three-dimensional
human beings, may also function as exemplars of facets of
man's nature—of common sense, or greed, or will (one of
Golding's most impressive gifts is his ability to make characters exemplify abstractions without *becoming* abstractions).

What we acknowledge if we choose to call Golding a
fabulist is not that the total story is reducible to a moral
proposition—this is obviously not true—but rather that he
writes from clear and strong moral assumptions, and that
those assumptions give form and direction to his fictions.
But if Aesop and La Fontaine wrote fables, we need another term for Golding. We might borrow one from scho-
lastic aesthetics, and call them *tropological,* meaning by
this that the novels individually "suggest a shape in the
universe," and are constructed as models of such moral
shapes. Or if tropological seems too rarefied, *moral models*
will do. The point, in any case, is to suggest the patterned
quality of Golding's work, and to recognize the assumptions which that quality implies. Golding accepts certain
traditional ideas about man and his place in the world: that
mind, by meditation and speculation, may arrive at truth;
that it may find in the past, meanings which are relevant to
the present, and available through memory; that it may appropriately concern itself with metaphysics and with
morals. Not all of these ideas are current now, certainly
not in the avant-garde, and consequently Golding's work
may seem, in the context of his time, more didactic and

moralizing than in fact it is. For though Golding is a moralist, he is not a moral-maker, and his novels belong, not
with Aesop's fables, but with the important symbolic
novels of our century—with Camus's and Kafka's.

Golding has founded *Lord of the Flies* on a number of
more or less current conventions. First of all, he has used
the science-fiction convention of setting his action in the
future, thus substituting the eventually probable for the
immediately actual, and protecting his fable from literalis-
tic judgments of details or of credibility. A planeload of
boys has been evacuated from an England engaged in
some future war fought against "the reds"; after their departure an atomic bomb has fallen on England, and civilization is in ruins. The plane flies south and east, stopping
at Gibraltar and Addis Ababa; still farther east—over the
Indian Ocean, or perhaps the Pacific, the plane is attacked
by an enemy aircraft, the "passenger tube" containing the
boys is jettisoned, and the rest of the plane crashes in
flames. The boys land unharmed on a desert island.

At this point, a second literary convention enters. The
desert island tale shares certain literary qualities with
science fiction. Both offer a "what-would-happen-if" situation, in which real experience is simplified in order that
certain values and problems may be regarded in isolation.
Both tend to simplify human moral issues by externalizing
good and evil; both offer occasions for Utopian fantasies.
Golding's most immediate source is R. M. Ballantyne's
Coral Island, a Victorian boys' book of South Sea adventure, but Ballantyne didn't invent the island dream; that
dream began when man first felt the pressures of his civili-

zation enough to think that a life without civilization might be a life without problems.

The relation of Golding's novel to Ballantyne's is nevertheless important enough to pause over. In *Coral Island,* three English boys called Ralph, Jack, and Peterkin are shipwrecked on a tropical island, meet pirates and cannibals, and conquer all adversities with English fortitude and Christian virtue. We may say that *Coral Island* is a clumsy moral tale, in which good is defined as being English and Christian and jolly, and especially an English Christian *boy,* and in which evil is un-Christian, savage, and adult. The three boys are rational, self-reliant, inventive, and virtuous—in short, they are like no boys that anyone has ever known.

Golding regards *Coral Island* morality as unrealistic, and therefore not truly moral, and he has used it ironically in his own novel, as a foil for his own version of man's moral nature. In an interview Golding described his use of Ballantyne's book in this way:

What I'm saying to myself is "don't be such a fool, you remember when you were a boy, a small boy, how you lived on that island with Ralph and Jack and Peterkin." . . . I said to myself finally, "Now you are grown up, you are adult; it's taken you a long time to become adult, but now you've got there you can see that people are not like that; they would not behave like that if they were God-fearing English gentlemen, and they went to an island like that." There savagery would not be found in natives on an island. As like as not they would find savages who were kindly and uncomplicated and that the devil would rise out of the intellectual complications of the three white men on the island itself.

One might say that *Lord of the Flies* is a refutation of *Coral Island,* and that Golding sets about to show us that

the devil rises, not out of pirates and cannibals and such
alien creatures, but out of the darkness of man's heart. The
Coral Island attitude exists in the novel—Jack sounds very
like Ballantyne's Jack when he says: "After all, we're not
savages. We're English; and the English are best at everything." And the naval commander who rescues the boys at
the end of the book speaks in the same vein: "I should
have thought that a pack of British boys—you're all British
aren't you?—would have been able to put up a better show
than that—I mean—" But Jack and the commander are
wrong; the pack of British boys are in fact cruel and murderous savages who reduce the island to a burning wreck-
age and destroy the dream of innocence.

The fable of the novel is a fairly simple one. The boys
first set out to create a rational society modeled on what
"grownups" would do. They establish a government and
laws, they provide for food and shelter, and they light a
signal fire. But this rational society begins to break down
almost at once, under two instinctual pressures—fear and
blood lust. The dark unknown that surrounds the children
gradually assumes a monstrous identity, and becomes "the
beast," to be feared and propitiated; and hunting for food
becomes killing. The hunters break away from the society,
and create their own primitive, savage, orgiastic tribal society. They kill two of the three rational boys, and are
hunting down the third when the adult world intervenes.

This fable, as sketched, is susceptible of several interpretations, and Golding's critics have found it coherent
on a number of levels, according to their own preoccupations. Freudians have found in the novel a conscious dramatization of psychological theory: "denied the sustaining
and repressing authority of parents, church and state, [the

children] form a new culture the development of which reflects that of genuine primitive society, evolving its gods and demons (its myths), its rituals and taboos (its social norms)." The political-minded have been able to read it as "the modern political nightmare," in which rational democracy is destroyed by irrational authoritarianism ("I hope," said V. S. Pritchett, "this book is being read in Germany"). The social-minded have found in it a social allegory, in which life, without civilized restraints, becomes nasty, brutish, and short. And the religious have simply said, in a complacent tone, "Original Sin, of course."

It is, of course, entirely possible that Golding has managed to construct a fable that does express all these ideas of evil, and that what we are dealing with is not alternative interpretations, but simply levels of meaning. The idea of original sin, for example, does have political, social, and psychological implications; if it is true that man is inherently prone to evil, then certain conclusions about the structure of his relations to other men would seem to follow. The idea of original sin seems, indeed, to be one of the "great commonplaces," one of those ideas which are so central to man's conception of himself that they turn up, in one form or another, in almost any systematic account of human nature. It describes one of perhaps two possible accounts of the nature of human behavior (*Coral Island* assumes the other one).

Since the novel is symbolic, the best approach would seem to be to examine first the "meaning" of each of the major characters, and then to proceed to consider the significance of their interactions. Ralph—in *Coral Island* the first-person narrator—here provides the most consistent point of view, because he most nearly speaks for us, rational, fallible humankind; Ralph is the man who accepts responsibility that he is not particularly fitted for because he sees that the alternative to responsibility is savagery and moral chaos. He tries to establish and preserve an orderly, rational society; he takes as his totem the conch, making it the symbol of rational, orderly discussion.

Ralph's antagonist is Jack, who represents "the brilliant world of hunting, tactics, fierce exhilaration, skill," as Ralph represents "the world of longing and baffled common-sense." Between them there is an "indefinable connection"; like Cain and Abel, they are antithetical, but intimately linked together—man-the-destroyer confronting man-the-preserver. Jack is the hunter, the boy who becomes a beast of prey (and who uses *kill* as an intransitive verb, an act which is for him an end in itself). He is also the dictator, the authoritarian man-of-power who enters the scene like a drill sergeant, who despises assemblies and the conch, and who becomes in the end an absolute ruler of his tribe. He devises the painted mask of the hunter, behind which a boy may hide, "liberated from shame and self-consciousness," and by painting the boys he turns them into an anonymous mob of murderous savages, "a demented but partly secure society." Jack is the first of the bigger boys to accept "the beast" as possible, and the one who offers the propitiatory sacrifice to it; he is the High Priest of Beelzebub, the Lord of the Flies.

Associated with each of these antagonists is a follower who represents in a more nearly allegorical form the principal value of his leader. Piggy, Ralph's "true, wise friend," is a scientific-minded rationalist, who models his behavior on what he thinks grownups would do, and scorns the other children for "acting like a crowd of kids."

He can think better than Ralph, and in a society in which thought was enough he would be supremely valuable; but on the island he is ineffectual; he is incapable of action, and is a physical coward. His totem is his spectacles, and with them he is the fire-bringer; but when Jack first breaks one lens and then steals the other, Piggy becomes blind and helpless, a bag of fat. His trust in the power and wisdom of grownups is itself a sign of his inadequacy; for if the novel makes one point clearly, it is that adults have no special wisdom, and are engaged in a larger scale, but equally destructive, version of the savage game that the hunters play. (When Ralph wishes that the outer world might "send us something grown-up . . . a sign or something," the adult world obliges with the dead parachutist, an image of terror that destroys Ralph's rational society.)

Beside or slightly behind Jack stands Roger, around whom clings "the hangman's horror." Roger's lust is the lust for power over living things, the power to destroy life. In the beginning he is restrained by "the taboo of the old life . . . the protection of parents and school and policemen and the law." Jack and the paint of savagery liberate Roger from these taboos, and "with a sense of delirious abandonment" he rolls the rock down the cliff, killing Piggy, his opposite.

One character, the most difficult to treat, remains. Simon, the shy visionary, perceptive but inarticulate, occupies a central position in the symbolic scheme of the book. It is Simon who first stammers that perhaps the beast is "only us," who sees the beast in terms of "mankind's essential illness," and who goes alone to confront *both* beasts, the grinning pig's head and the rotting airman, because, as he says, "What else is there to do?" Golding has described Simon as a saint, "someone who voluntarily embraces this beast, goes . . . and tries to get rid of him and goes to give the good news to the ordinary bestial man on the beach, and gets killed for it." He would appear to be, then, at least in Golding's intentions, the embodiment of moral understanding. If this is so, those symbolic scenes in which he appears will be crucial to an understanding of the novel.

I have said that one distinction between Golding's novels and allegory is that the novels are meaning-in-action, general truth given narrative or dramatic form by the creative imagination. In considering the meaning of *Lord of the Flies*, one cannot therefore stop at an examination of character—meaning must emerge from character-in-action. In the narrative action certain scenes stand out as crucial, and most of these announce their importance by being overtly symbolic. There is, for example, a series of scenes in which Jack's hunters evolve a ritual dance. On the first occasion, in chapter 4, a child *pretends* to be the pig, and the hunters *pretend* to beat him. A chapter later the dance has become crueler, "and littluns that had had enough were staggering away, howling." After the next hunt Robert, acting the pig in the dance, squeals with real pain, and the hunters cry "Kill him! Kill him!" After the dance the boys discuss ways of improving the ritual: " 'You want a real pig,' said Robert, still caressing his rump, 'because you've got to kill him.'

" 'Use a littlun,' said Jack, and everybody laughed." In the final ritual dance, the sacrificial function is acknowledged; the boys' chant is no longer "Kill the pig," but "Kill the *beast!*" and when Simon crawls from the forest, the boys fulfill their ritual sacrifice, and by killing a human being, make themselves beasts ("there were no words, and no movements but the tearing of teeth and claws"). Ironically, they have killed the one person who could have saved them from bestiality, for Simon has seen the figure on the mountaintop, and knows that the beast is "harmless and horrible."

Simon's lonely, voluntary quest for the beast is certainly the symbolic core of the book. The meaning of the book depends on the meaning of the beast, and it is that meaning that Simon sets out to determine. His first act is to withdraw to a place of contemplation, a sunlit space in the midst of the forest. It is to the same place that Jack and his hunters bring the pig's head, and leave it impaled on a stick as a sacrifice to the beast they fear. When they have gone, Simon holds hallucinatory conversation with the Lord of the Flies, Beelzebub, the Lord of Filth and Dung. The head, "with the infinite cynicism of adult life," assures Simon that "everything was a bad business," and advises him to run away, back to the other children, and to abandon his quest. "I'm part of you," it tells him (in words that echo Simon's own "maybe it's only us"), "I'm the reason why it's no go." Simon, apparently epileptic, falls in a fit. But when he wakes, he turns upward, toward the top of the mountain, where the truth lies. He finds the airman, rotting and fly-blown, and tenderly frees the figure from the wind's indignity. Then he sets off, weak and staggering, to tell the other boys that the beast is human, and is murdered by them.

How are we to interpret this sequence? We may say, first of all, that the beast symbolizes the source of evil in human life. Either it is something terrifying and external, which cannot be understood but must simply be lived with (this is Jack's version), or it is a part of man's nature, "only us," in which case it may be understood, and perhaps controlled by reason and rule. Simon understands that man must seek out the meaning of evil ("what else is there to do?"). By seeking, he comes to know it, "harmless and horrible." Thus far the moral point seems orthodox enough. But when he tries to tell his understanding to others, they take *him* for the beast, and destroy him in terror. Another common idea, though a more somber one— men fear the bearers of truth, and will destroy them. This has both political and psychological implications. A "demented but partly secure society" (read: Nazi Germany, or any authoritarian nation) will resist and attempt to destroy anyone who offers to substitute reason and responsible individual action for the irresponsible, unreasoning, *secure* action of the mass. And in psychological terms, the members of a "demented society" may create an irrational, external evil, and in its name commit deeds that as rational men they could not tolerate (the history of modern persecutions offers examples enough); such a society *has* to destroy the man who says, "The evil is in yourselves."

At this point, I should like to return to the argument that this novel is a symbolic form but not an allegory. One aspect of this distinction is that Golding has written a book that has a dense and often poetic verbal texture, in which metaphor and image work as they do in poetry, and enrich and modify the bare significances of the moral form. Golding's treatment of Simon's death is a particularly good case in point. At this instant, a storm breaks, the wind fills the parachute on the mountain, and the figure, freed by Simon, floats and falls toward the beach, scattering the boys in terror before passing out to sea. The storm ends,

stars appear, the tide rises. Stars above and phospho-
rescent sea below fill the scene with brightness and quiet.

Along the shoreward edge of the shallows the advancing
clearness was full of strange, moonbeam-bodied creatures with
fiery eyes. Here and there a larger pebble clung to its own air
and was covered with a coat of pearls. The tide swelled in over
the rain-pitted sand and smoothed everything with a layer of silver. Now it touched the first of the stains that seeped from the
broken body and the creatures made a moving patch of light as
they gathered at the edge. The water rose farther and dressed
Simon's coarse hair with brightness. The line of his cheek sil-
vered and the turn of his shoulder became sculptured marble.
The strange attendant creatures, with their fiery eyes and trailing
vapors, busied themselves round his head. The body lifted a frac-
tion of an inch from the sand and a bubble of air escaped from
the mouth with a wet plop. Then it turned gently in the water.
Somewhere over the darkened curve of the world the sun
and moon were pulling, and the film of water on the earth planet
was held, bulging slightly on one side while the solid core
turned. The great wave of the tide moved farther along the island
and the water lifted. Softly, surrounded by a fringe of inquisitive
bright creatures, itself a silver shape beneath the steadfast constellations, Simon's dead body moved out toward the open sea.

This is Golding's rhetoric at its richest, but it works. The
imagery of light and value—*moonbeam, pearls, silver,
brightness, marble*—effect a transfiguration, by which the
dead child is made worthy, his death an elevation. In
terms of allegory, this sort of metaphorical weighting
would perhaps be imprecise and deceptive; in terms of a
symbolic novel, it seems to me a legitimate application of
a skillful writer's art.

In discussing the actions of *Lord of the Flies* I have
again and again slipped from talking about boys to describ-

ing the characters as men, or simply as human beings. It is true that as the action rises to its crises—to the *agon* of chapter 5, Simon's confrontation with the beast, the murders, the final hunt—we cease to respond to the story as a story about children, and see them simply as *people*, engaged in desperate, destructive actions. Consequently, Golding can achieve a highly dramatic effect at the end of the book by bringing our eyes down, with Ralph's, to a beach-level view of an adult, and then swinging round, to show us Ralph from the adult's point of view. The result is an irony that makes two points. First, we see with sudden clarity that these murderous savages were civilized children; the point is not, I take it, that children are more horrid than we thought (though they are), but rather that the human propensity for evil knows no limits, not even limits of age, and that there is no Age of Innocence (Ralph weeps for the end of innocence, but when did it exist, except as an illusion made of his own ignorance?). Second, there is the adult, large, efficient, confident—the "grown-up" that the children have wished for all along. But his words show at once that he is a large, stupid *Coral Island* mentality in a peaked cap, entirely blind to the moral realities of the situation. He may save Ralph's life, but he will not understand. And once he has gathered up the castaways, he will return to his ship, and the grown-up business of hunting men (just as the boys have been hunting Ralph). "And who," asks Golding, "will rescue the adult and his cruiser?"

To return briefly to the question of levels of interpretation: it seems clear that *Lord of the Flies* should be read as a moral novel embodying a conception of human depravity which is compatible with, but not limited to, the

Christian doctrine of Original Sin. To call the novel religious is to suggest that its values are more developed, and more affirmative, than in fact they are; Golding makes no reference to Grace, or to Divinity, but only to the darkness of men's hearts, and to the God of Dung and Filth who rules there. Simon is perhaps a saint, and sainthood is a valuable human condition, but there is no sign in the novel that Simon's sainthood has touched any soul but his own. The novel tells us a good deal about evil; but about salvation it is silent.

The Inheritors is Golding's most brilliant tour de force—a novel written from the point of view of Neanderthal man. Golding has set himself the task of rendering experience as it would be apprehended by this subhuman, subrational intelligence, and his success, within the severe limits implied, is extraordinary. But, being Golding, he has not assumed such difficulties simply to demonstrate his skills; *The Inheritors*, like *Lord of the Flies*, is a moral fable, and the quality of the observing consciousness employed is a part of the morality.

The Inheritors also resembles *Lord of the Flies* in the way it relates to a book out of Golding's childhood. *Lord of the Flies* used Ballantyne's *Coral Island*, not as a source of plot or character, but as the embodiment of an attitude—a symbol out of childhood of a whole set of wrong beliefs about good and evil. *The Inheritors* uses H. G. Wells's *Outline of History* in a similar way. Wells, in the eighth and ninth chapters of his book, described Neanderthal man, and his extermination by *Homo sapiens*. The key passage, from which Golding drew the epigraph to his novel, is this:

We know nothing of the appearance of the Neanderthal man, but this absence of inter-mixture [with *Homo sapiens*] seems to suggest an extreme hairiness, an ugliness, or a repulsive strangeness in his appearance over and above his low forehead, his beetle brows, his ape neck, and his inferior stature. Or he—and she—may have been too fierce to tame. Says Sir Harry Johnston, in a survey of the rise of modern man in his *Views and Reviews:* "The dim racial remembrance of such gorilla-like monsters, with cunning brains, shambling gait, hairy bodies, strong teeth, and possibly cannibalistic tendencies, may be the germ of the ogre in folklore. . . ."

One can see how Wells, with his rationalist's faith in evolution and the virtues of "an intelligence very like our own" would be unpalatable to a man like Golding. In an interview Golding described the *Outline* as "the rationalist gospel in excelsis," and went on to recount his reaction when he returned, as an adult, to Wells's book:

When I re-read it as an adult I came across his picture of Neanderthal man, our immediate predecessors, as being these gross brutal creatures who were possibly the basis of the mythological bad man, whatever he may be, the ogre. I thought to myself that this is just absurd. What we're doing is externalising our own inside. We're saying, "Well, he must have been like that, because I don't want to be like it, although I know I am like it."

We might say, then, that Golding and Wells are most basically opposed in their views of the nature of "the ogre"; Wells, the rationalist, wishes to separate this figure of terror from Homo sapiens, and to place him in a repulsive, hairy body, now extinct except in folklore; Golding says the ogre is in our own insides. The two positions are essentially antithetical ideas of the nature of evil: the rationalistic, and the religious. Golding has used a view which he deplores as a foil for his own.

Neanderthal and "true men" are the antagonists of Golding's novel; the plot is summarized in one sentence of Wells:

Finally, between 40,000 and 25,000 years ago, as the Fourth Glacial Age softened towards more temperate conditions . . . a different human type came upon the scene, and, it would seem, exterminated *Homo Neanderthalensis*.

The Inheritors is an account of that extermination, seen from the point of view of the exterminated. In creating his two primitive species, Golding has on the whole been anthropologically accurate, but he has taken certain significant liberties. He says of his Neanderthals that they have opposed toes, and have not learned to shape the stones that they use for tools; he says of Homo sapiens that he can make clay vessels, bone instruments, and canoes. He has made Neanderthal man *more* primitive, and Homo sapiens more advanced, thus emphasizing the intellectual and cultural gap between the species. And he has widened that gap in order to construct, out of Wells's one-sentence plot, an anthropological version of the Fall of Man.

Virtually the entire novel is narrated from the point of view of Neanderthal men, "the people." We see them first, we observe their tribal behavior, and then only gradually are we made aware of another species. Golding sets out to make two basic points about the people: the quality of their intelligence and (a related point) the quality of their innocence. They are introduced in migration from winter to summer quarters, and immediately a problem arises—a log across a marsh, which they have always used as a bridge, is gone; how are they to cross the water, which they fear? They are baffled, they cannot think consecutively, their minds wander, they have little command of either memory or causality. Finally, Mal, their old leader, remembers a wise man who *made* a bridge with a fallen log, and the people are able to resume their journey, though Mal falls into the water, and later dies of the exposure. The episode of the log is important to the novel as a model of the Neanderthal mind; the most significant feature of that mind is this, that it cannot conceive of relationships, and we might take this as a tentative definition of the State of Innocence: man cannot sin until he can both remember and anticipate.

The innocence of the people is dramatized in a number of ways. We see Lok and his mate, Fa, hunting for food; they find a doe killed by a cat, and take the carcass for food, but only after Fa has said, "A cat has sucked all her blood. There is no blame." Far from being the cannibals that Wells describes, these creatures have a reverence for life that forbids killing or eating blood, and they dislike the taste of meat. Their deity, Oa, is an earth goddess who gives and preserves life, and who is worshiped in natural forms—a root shaped like a woman, and female-looking ice formations. And—one further aspect of their innocence—they share a collective identity that is not yet fully differentiated into separate personalities; thus they share thoughts and emotions, and lack the antagonisms that personalities imply.

Into this prelapsarian collective consciousness there gradually intrudes a sense of "other"—another mysterious species somewhere near. The way in which Golding slowly builds this awareness in the minds of the people gives to his novel some of the excitement of other fictional forms involving unknown antagonists—mystery novels, for instance, and ghost stories use similar devices of dramatic anticipation. Beginning with the missing log (what hands moved it, and why?), Golding offers a series of hints and mysteries, as baffling to us as to the clumsy minds through which we experience them. Lok, for example, smells what he takes to be the fire that the old woman carries on their migration. He turns toward it, and almost falls over a cliff. There is another fire, then, but Lok cannot imagine this, and we are left with his bafflement and fright. Gradually "other" becomes defined—first a scent, then a creature, a lump, a nobody, and finally "the new people."

The new people are simply *us*—postlapsarian man, with all his capacities for creation and for evil, his fears and desires and guilts. For most of the novel we see these creatures from the outside, with the eyes of innocence. But not really—rather, we receive the data of those innocent eyes, and interpret it as our own familiar behavior. The crucial scene in this respect is the long sequence, taking up almost a quarter of the book, in which Lok and Fa, hidden in a tree, watch an encampment of the new people, and uncomprehendingly witness lust, drunkenness, cruelty, cannibalism—a Goldingesque demonstration of the benefits of "an intelligence very like our own." We also observe the new people's religion, and the contrast to the worship of Oa is significant. The new people's religion is totemic—a man dressed as a stag, a stag drawn on the earth—and sacrificial—the stag requires an amputated finger from a victim chosen by lot. The point seems to be that while innocence can worship natural forms, and the principle of life itself, fallen man constructs mimetic religions, which at least in part worship his *own* capacity to mime, and that his deity is male (in this book the females preserve, the males act and destroy).

The ultimate effect of the meeting of these species is, as Wells said so casually, the extermination of *Homo Neanderthalensis;* but the intermediate effects of their awareness of each other are also significant. The feelings of the people toward the new men are powerful and ambivalent: Lok thinks that "the other people with their many pictures were like water that at once horrifies and at the same time dares and invites a man to go near it. He was obscurely aware of this attraction without definition and it made him foolish." *Pictures* is the Neanderthal's word for thought, and the attraction that the others have is clearly the attraction that knowledge (including the knowledge of good and evil) holds out to innocence. Being innocent, the people do not understand any fear that is not a physical response to a physical threat; they surrender to "the indefinable attraction of the new people," but they do so "with a terrified love."

The effect of contact with knowledge is necessarily the loss of innocence; after Lok and Fa have watched the new people's orgy, they creep into the abandoned camp, where they get drunk on mead and discover lust. But experience also teaches Lok to think; out of loss and suffering and responsibility he discovers the basic element of thought—likeness. But the only use to which he can put this new tool is to understand the irresistible power of the new people; "they are like the river and the fall," he thinks, "they are a people of the fall; nothing stands against them." And indeed they are the people of the Fall—that is what the novel is about.

For most of the novel we see the new men's reaction to the people only from a distance; we know that they are frightened, and that they try to destroy what they fear, but only at the end of the novel, when the last of the people lies dead, and the new men are in flight, do we know the nature and extent of their fear. They have discovered objective images of their terrors, and have called them devils, and in their terror they have committed evil deeds that have changed them—a child has gone mad, and a woman is literally possessed of a devil. They are fleeing from the darkness that will henceforth be man's symbol for what he fears, though what he fears is not really back there in the forest—it is, as *Lord of the Flies* tells us, "the darkness of men's hearts." Tuami, the new man, is looking into the still unwritten history of his species when, in the last paragraph of the book, he looks at the line of darkness along the horizon.

It was far away and there was plenty of water in between. He peered forward past the sail to see what lay at the other end of the lake, but it was so long, and there was such a flashing from the water that he could not see if the line of darkness had an ending.

The moral of the novel is not a very complicated one, and certainly it is not what one critic has called it, "blazingly heretical." It offers an anthropological analogue of the Fall, which distinguishes between prelapsarian and postlapsarian man in terms of knowledge of evil and capacity for thought. The book is original in that no one had previously thought of Neanderthal man as a possible analogue for Adam, but the originality is in the fictional conception of the moral, not in the theology (which in a novel is surely as it ought to be). This originality is also the novel's limitation: in so far as *The Inheritors* is an imaginative creation of primitive consciousness it is an unusual achievement, but it is an achievement that succeeds *by* limitation. Golding has written a novel in which his principal perceivers cannot understand or reason about what they perceive, and has thus denied himself the use of important areas of discourse traditionally open to the novelist—introspection and abstract thought cannot be directly expressed as parts of the characters' conscious activities. And since introspection and abstraction are parts of our usual mental equipment, the discourse of *The Inheritors* is strange to us, and sometimes extremely obscure. It is also occasionally rather grotesque in the locutions that it contrives in order to avoid anything that might be construed as reasoning, as when Lok "watched the water run out of her eyes." Is weeping so difficult an abstraction?

But if the style imposes limitations, it also has its expressive strengths. The innocent eye sees actions that we might regard as common for the first time, and the newness becomes a part of our own awareness—as when, for example, Lok and Fa look down from their tree upon human evil. And because Golding is a poetic writer, his treatment of the unfiltered sense data of these innocents is often poetically moving, as when Lok hunts for his lost mate, or when the people bury their old leader, Mal. But beyond these advantages, the point of view of the novel provides another that is perhaps even more essential—the limited perceptions of the observing characters make possible an informing mode of dramatic irony that is steadily and powerfully effective. Dramatic irony depends upon our recognition of limits in characters' perceptions—limits to which we are superior; in *The Inheritors* we observe as Neanderthal man observes, but we interpret as rational, fallen man interprets. Thus we see, from the first action of the novel, that innocence is doomed to yearn toward and be destroyed by thinking, guilty experience. Then in the last chapter Golding cunningly reverses the point of view, and establishes a new irony as Homo sapiens, fleeing his own inner darkness, looks back in terror at the forest of innocence, the remembrance of which "may be the germ of the ogre in folklore . . ." The final irony is in the way the Wellsian epigraph has been realized.

The Inheritors is, as I have said, an extraordinary tour de force, and one which could scarcely be repeated. But one of Golding's virtues as a novelist has ·been his eagerness to regard each novel as a new approach to new problems, and his unwillingness to imitate himself. "It seems to me," he has said, "that there's really very little point in writing a novel unless you do something that either you suspected you couldn't do, or which you are pretty certain that nobody else has tried before." Both of these conditions are met by *The Inheritors;* both apply equally to Golding's third novel, *Pincher Martin,* a novel with a single character, who dies on page two.

Both formally and intellectually, *Pincher Martin* is the most impressive of Golding's novels. It is also the most difficult, because its form is an involved representation of time and consciousness, and because what it has to say about death is heterodox and complex. It bears certain family resemblances to the two preceding novels: it uses the literature of survival in much the same way that *Lord of the Flies* uses island literature, and it treats an unusual condition of consciousness, as *The Inheritors* does. Like the earlier two, it is a novel with a moral "program," which deals schematically with the problem of evil and its consequences.

But it is also different from the others in important ways. The primary difference is that the form of *Pincher Martin* does not compel a moral interpretation from the beginning; rather it offers first a vivid survival-adventure, and then reverses itself, and says: What you have been taking as objectively true is in fact false—or true in another, paradoxical sense. This is an uncommon fictional technique, but by no means a unique one; satires like *Gulliver's Travels* play tricks with our expectations, and so do the symbolical tales of Poe and Kafka. The difference in Golding's technique is that he goes to considerable trouble to make the apparent seem particularly real *before* he allows the symbolic quality of the action to appear overtly. As a result the grounds of reality shift within the novel, and the reader's relation to the action is unstable and ambiguous; this in turn compels a more attentive reading (or rereading) of the book—the symbolic meaning is more difficult to grasp, because it appears in the final chapters as a *new* interpretation of data which we have already interpreted in a conventional, realistic way.

The action of the novel thus divides into two parts, with a coda. The first part takes Christopher Martin from the moment when a torpedo blows him off the bridge of his destroyer through the events of his efforts to survive on a barren rock. In these ten chapters Golding creates, in sharp, circumstantial detail, the conditions in which Martin's extraordinary will-to-survive operates. The sea, the rock, the creatures that live on it, the weather—all are meticulously set down. So, too, is Pincher Martin, fiercely acting out his ego; and the vividness with which Golding has drawn this figure is in itself a remarkable achievement, since we do not see Pincher's personality reflected from any other human being, but only in relation to hostile nature, and to itself.

This lonely survivor we must regard as admirable, simply because he clings to life so tenaciously, and against such odds (how can we *not* side with Man, against Nature?). His endurance, his will, his ingenuity are all heroic—he is man opposing adversity, refusing to be annihilated. And when he cries "I am Prometheus," we see what he means—he is a man trapped on a barren rock, defying the fate that put him there.

But woven into this heroic narrative are flashbacks of Martin's past that establish a character who is the opposite of heroic—an unscrupulous egoist who has stopped at no depravity, no betrayal of love and friendship, to nourish his own ego. By seeing *this* character developed parallel to the Promethean survivor, we are forced to acknowledge that the same qualities that have kept him alive against such odds are the qualities that make him morally repulsive. And so in the middle of the eleventh chapter we face a moral dilemma: on what grounds can we condemn those qualities by which man survives?

The answer comes in the following three chapters, beginning with the moment when Martin looks down into the sea from his rock, and sees a *red* lobster, and realizes that perhaps his whole effort to survive—rock and all—has been a subjective creation, an act of the will asserting itself against necessity. He has invented it all, ingeniously, but not perfectly; he has forgotten that only boiled lobsters are red, and that guano is insoluble, and he has arranged the rocks on which he survives like the teeth in his own mouth. From this point on, the apparent reality of Pincher's survival begins to dissolve, and with it his own surviving personality, until at the end he is reduced to two hands, red and grasping like lobster claws, and symbolic, as his nickname is symbolic, of his essential nature. And then even these claws are worn away, and Pincher Martin as a personality is annihilated.

But what does it all mean? The coda is there to give us some clues. In the last chapter, as in the final chapter of *The Inheritors*, Golding provides a new perspective, a shift in point of view out and away from the agent of the action, by which we can regard the action more deliberately and objectively. We are on an island in the Hebrides when a naval party lands to pick up the body of a drowned sailor (Pincher Martin). An islander, called Campbell, is moved and disturbed by the experience, and asks the officer in charge of the party, "Would you say there was any—surviving? Or is that all?" The officer, like the one at the end of *Lord of the Flies*, misunderstands the question, and replies: "If you're worried about Martin—whether he suffered or not. . . . Then don't worry about him. You saw the body. He didn't even have time to kick off his seaboots."

If Pincher didn't have time to kick off his seaboots, then the moment in the first chapter when he apparently *did* kick them off was illusory, and if that was illusory, then so was everything that came after, and we must go back and reinterpret what we have read. Survival in *Pincher Martin* is not survival in the ordinary sea-story sense after all; Golding has used the "man-against-the-sea" conventions here just as he used the desert island conventions in *Lord of the Flies*, to provide a system of expectations against which to construct a personal and different version of the shape of things.

Some readers have felt cheated by this last-sentence reversal of their assumptions about the nature of reality in the novel. But in fact Golding has placed a number of clues to Pincher's state earlier in the novel, and the seaboots should come as the clincher; the clues are scattered and concealed, like the clues in a mystery novel, in order that the reader should discover the truth late in the book, and with surprise, but they are there. This device of discovery is dramatic, but it is more than that; it is a way of making an important point about the meaning of death. Though Martin dies on page two, this physical death is passed over: there are kinds of dying that are more important than that instant of merely physiological change. (Golding's American publisher made this point clearer by calling the novel *The Two Deaths of Christopher Martin*.) An audience for which Campbell's question about eternity was a vital one would surely have no trouble in understanding the paradoxes of living-into-death and dying-into-life that inform the novel; it is only to rational materialists (for whom Pincher is a type) that a novel about varieties of dying will seem an outrageous violation of reality.

Pincher Martin is so tightly and intricately interwoven as to read like a difficult poem; one must attend to its symbols and images in order to understand its narrative action, and indeed there is little that one could call *plot* in the book. The sequence of events is determined, not by the interaction of character and environment as in conventional novels, but by the necessities of the symbolic form in which Golding has expressed his theme. So many readers found this form difficult that when the novel was dramatized on the B.B.C. Third Programme, Golding provided his own account of the theme:

Christopher Hadley Martin had no belief in anything but the importance of his own life; no love, no God. Because he was created in the image of God he had a freedom of choice which he used to centre the world on himself. He did not believe in purgatory and therefore when he died it was not presented to him in overtly theological terms. The greed for life which had been the mainspring of his nature, forced him to refuse the selfless act of dying. He continued to exist separately in a world composed of his own murderous nature. His drowned body lies rolling in the Atlantic but the ravenous ego invents a rock for him to endure on. It is the memory of an aching tooth. Ostensibly and rationally he is a survivor from a torpedoed destroyer: but deep down he knows the truth. He is not fighting for bodily survival but for his continuing identity in face of what will smash it and sweep it away—the black lightning, the compassion of God. For Christopher, the Christ-bearer, has become Pincher Martin who is little but greed. Just to be Pincher is purgatory; to be Pincher for eternity is hell.

We must, of course, be cautious about accepting an artist's own version of his work; in Golding's case, the novels tend to expand and live beyond his programs. Nevertheless, this account gives a lead into the novel. We may start with the question of what it is to be Pincher.

It is, first of all, simply to be a man called Martin in the Royal Navy; "Pincher" is a nickname habitually attached to sea-going Martins, just as in the American services all Mullinses are called "Moon." But Pincher *is* a pincher—his Deadly Sin is Greed, and he eats everything he touches. Pincher is a devourer of life, "born with his mouth and his flies open and both hands out to grab." The grabbing hands, which are imaged in the novel as lobsters, are the last part of Pincher to disappear at the end.

This supreme greed is expressed in the novel in a parable, the Parable of the Chinese Box. One of Pincher's victims describes how the Chinese, when they wish to prepare a rare dish, bury a fish in a tin box. Maggots eat the fish, and then one another, until finally "where there was a fish there is now one huge, successful maggot. Rare dish." Pincher is the huge successful maggot, devouring the other maggots and crying, "I'll live if I have to eat everything else on this bloody box!"

Pincher's greed, however, is not a motive in itself; it is the means by which he preserves the only value in his world—his own personality. Those human attributes that assert identity—speech, thought, the consciousness of consciousness—are his goods; and loss of identity—as in sleep and ultimately death—is his evil. In his past life he has used other people to reassure himself of his own existence, as he has used photographs and mirrors. But on the rock there are no mirrors, and his identity-card photograph is blurred, and there is no one to touch; his existence there is therefore one fierce effort to preserve his personality, to assert that "I am what I always was," and later simply "I am! I am!" Pincher, in his efforts to assert that because he thinks, he is, is simply the modern heir of Descartes, man proving his own existence from the inside out. Starting with mind, he creates his own world in which all meaning and value is in *self;* and all outside self is meaningless mechanism, the material upon which mind plays, and on which self feeds.

This egocentric version of reality not only relates Pincher to the Cartesian tradition; it also connects with his "I am Prometheus." Prometheus is *the* mythic hero of humanistic, liberal man: he is the man-befriender, the God-defier, the indestructible life-worshiping identity whose own existence gives meaning to his suffering, and whose suffering affirms his existence. One might expect that Golding, the disillusioned ex-liberal, would consider Prometheus a symbol of that conception of man which he finds most immoral; and *Pincher Martin* might well be subtitled "The Case Against Prometheus." Golding establishes this point by making Pincher's Promethean heroism simply one more case of his self-creating egoism; Pincher *plays* Prometheus (he is, after all, a professional actor), to appropriate imaginary background music by Tchaikovsky, Wagner, and Holst: "it was not really necessary to crawl," Golding observes, "but the background music underlined the heroism of a slow, undefeated advance against odds." This is not heroism, but a parody of it; and indeed *parody* describes pretty well the overall relationship between what Pincher imagines himself doing and the reality—he is a parody Robinson Crusoe, a parody Hamlet, a parody Lear, a parody Lucifer. But he is one reality—Pincher, the clutching claws.

Strictly speaking, there is no character in the novel except Pincher; his isolation is complete from beginning to end. The naval officer and Campbell in the last chapter have no particular definition, and even the persons who people Pincher's memories and visions are not really characters, because Pincher has regarded them not as separate human beings but as things to be devoured. One figure, however, stands in an important symbolic relation to Pincher; the existence of his friend Nathaniel is interwoven with Pincher's in the way that good is interwoven with evil, dark with light. Nathaniel is a religious man and something of a mystic; he lectures on "the technique of dying into heaven," and he warns Pincher to prepare for death. Like his biblical namesake he is a man "in whom is no guile"; no doubt we are also meant to recall Christ's words to Nathaniel: "Hereafter ye shall see heaven open, and the angels of God ascending and descending upon the Son of man." Nathaniel is the opposite of Pincher; he can love selflessly and without thought, and he therefore wins the love of Mary, the girl for whom Pincher feels an obsessive lust.

The most important single scene in the novel is probably the one in which Nathaniel explains his eschatology to an amused Pincher. Man must learn, says Nathaniel, the technique of dying into heaven, in order to make himself ready for heaven when death comes. "Take us as we are now and heaven would be sheer negation," he says. "Without form and void. You see? A sort of black lightning, destroying everything that we call life . . ." If we do not prepare ourselves for heaven (*heaven* here meaning simply eternity described spatially), then we will die into the sort of afterlife that our natures invent. This, it is clear, is what has happened to Pincher; the rock is the heaven he has invented for himself, a barren rock like a tooth, without life except of the lowest sort, a place in which the only possible value is bare survival. Pincher's heaven is the appropriate fate of a man who has lived as he has lived; but because it is his own invention, it is not eternal. It exists by an act of will, and when his will fails, and he admits that he cannot believe in the objective existence of his invention, then the black lightning comes and annihilates him.

The final incident of Pincher's existence is a visionary interview with a mysterious figure in seaman's clothes, who is God. "What do you believe in?" God asks. "The thread of my life," Pincher replies. "I have created you and I can create my own heaven." "You *have* created it," says God. And in God's presence the world of rock and sea stops moving, becomes painted paper, cracks, and drops into "absolute nothingness."

Pincher Martin is an eschatological novel, a myth of dying; nevertheless, it is more concerned with life than with death (perhaps this is true of all such works), and Golding uses the ambiguities of time and reality in Pincher's survival narrative to make moral points about man's attitudes toward death as they affect his attitudes toward life. From the right view of the selfless act of dying, the right moral principles will follow; Nathaniel is a somewhat obscure embodiment of those principles, Pincher of their negation. The central point of the novel seems to be simply this: death is the end of identity. If we accept this, we will prepare for the end of identity, and will value what is personal and individual in our existences less (as saints have always done), and we will fear death less because the loss of identity will be familiar and acceptable to us. Whether indeed we will live in a "heaven" of our own invention if we die unprepared is of no importance, except as a symbolic way of representing the terrors of death to an identity-preserver, a Pincher.

When Golding was asked about the "mythical aspect" of Pincher, he replied that Pincher was "a fallen man . . . Very much fallen—he's fallen more than most. In fact, I went out of my way to damn Pincher as much as I could by making him the most unpleasant, the nastiest type I could think of, and I was very interested to see how critics all over the place said, 'Well, yes, we are like that.' I was really rather pleased." He should not have been surprised that responsive readers found in this "nastiest type" an image of their own natures. Like all of Golding's major characters Pincher is an embodiment of a proposition about human nature, rather than an individual; in so far as we recognize greed as a sin to which we are prone, we *must* say, "Yes, we are like that."

But this generalized quality in the central figure is also the principal limitation of the novel. Pincher is not a credible, individualized character as we understand character in most fiction; he exists in conditions that strip him of personality—indeed that is the symbolic point of the action—and leave him simply *a* human creature. The rock is the most real thing in the book, and Pincher is most real in his survivor-relation to it; when we see him in flashbacks with other persons he becomes a stock melodramatic villain, the Handsome Seducer. The symbolic action engages us—and engages us with more force than either *Lord of the Flies* or *The Inheritors* does—because it is barer, more entirely symbolic. But it does so at the expense of other expectations that are part of our general feeling for fiction—that there shall be persons with whom we can ally ourselves, existing in a believable world, that we shall experience life being lived. *Pincher Martin* is an extraordinary achievement, a moral document that is also a work of art, in which moral meaning is entirely embodied in artistic form. But its excellence is also its limitation, and it is not an excellence that could be repeated. Clearly Golding had to seek another fictional form for his moral preoccupations; and that is what he did in *Free Fall.*

Free Fall, Golding's fourth novel, might be regarded as his answer to Kingsley Amis. Amis had said of *Pincher Martin:*

it is the narrowness and remoteness of that world . . . which rob the novel of the universality it appears to claim. Although Martin is in some sense doing duty for man, the context of this performance is too remote from the world of man to excite that continuous recognition and self-recognition upon which depends the novelist's power to persuade.

Perhaps Golding felt this same limitation in his previous work; at any rate, in *Free Fall* he addressed himself, for the first time, to the world of men, and wrote a novel that is immediately striking, to a reader who comes to it from the earlier work, for the density and detail of its social texture. The world of *Free Fall* is ordinary and actual and grimy—and the man through whose eyes we are enabled to see this world is an ordinary, unheroic man who insists on his representativeness. The other novels depended for their expressive power upon a spine of significant action that Golding calls *fable* or *myth;* in *Free Fall* he abandoned that useful device, and wrote a novel in which meaning is embodied in events treated literally, and interpreted in recollection by a first-person narrator. The result is a novel that is slow-paced and reflective, and comparatively speaking, *realistic*—a novel that resembles the novels of Joyce Cary more than it does Golding's earlier work.

The change to a new formal problem is of course characteristic of Golding; certainly no two Golding novels are alike in their specifics, and *Free Fall* is particularly striking in its formal departures. But on the other hand, all five novels are clearly the products of the same "incompetently religious man" (Golding's phrase for himself), and show the same moral preoccupations and themes. *Free Fall* has a notably different surface, but it is concerned, like the other novels, with freedom and necessity, guilt and responsibility, reason and irrationality, and the nature of evil. The principal character, Sammy Mountjoy, is a more attractive man than Christopher Martin, but he has also been a pincher, and his narrative is, like Martin's, a mixture of recollected events and current reflections; only the proportions have been reversed. Pincher Martin's *present* condition is what holds us in that novel, while Sammy Mountjoy's attention is altogether on the past, and his present is sketchy and ambiguous. This reversal is an appropriate one, since Sammy is consciously searching in his past for its meaning; but the point to be made now is that the meanings he finds are consistent and continuous with the previous novels—there is no innovation in ideas.

Free Fall is a long reflection by the narrator upon the events of his past. The events are offered, not as they occurred, but in the order of their importance to Sammy Mountjoy. This ordering is difficult, and sometimes obscure, but if we piece together the details we will arrive at a history for Sammy that will run something like this: born in 1917, in a slum somewhere in Kent, the bastard son of a promiscuous charwoman, father unknown. Adopted, after his mother's death, by the local vicar, and educated in the local grammar school. Went to London to study art, became a painter, and briefly, a member of the Communist Party. During World War II served as a combat artist, was captured by the Nazis and imprisoned. Married, one child. To this should be added two less creditable incidents: as a child, Sammy attempted to desecrate the altar of the parish church; and as a young man he seduced his childhood sweetheart and later abandoned her, perhaps contributing to her eventual madness.

This narrative has chronological sequence, but it has no other pattern, and therefore no meaning. In reexamining his past, Sammy is searching for a pattern which will give experience moral coherence; "I am looking," he says, "for the beginning of responsibility, the beginning of darkness, the point where I began." Man is, in Golding's view, a pattern-making animal; Christianity is a pattern, Marxism is a pattern, scientific rationalism is a pattern. But experience itself is patternless, and it is this fact that provides the central issue of the novel—pattern-making man confronting patternlessness. "The difference between being alive and being an inorganic substance," Golding remarked in an interview in 1958, "is just this proliferation of experience, this absence of pattern." And he went on to say of *Free Fall*, then about to be published, "This time I want to show the patternlessness of life before we impose our patterns on it."

Sammy's particular search is for the answer to one question: "Where did I lose my freedom?" Examining his present moment, he concludes that he is not free—he is the victim of the mechanics of cause and effect. Turning back to his earliest memory, he recalls a moment when he sat in a park at the center of a fan of radiating paths, and knew that he could take any one. At that moment freedom was as real as the taste of potatoes; somewhere between that time and Sammy's present he must have lost his freedom, must have made a choice that ended the possibility of choice. The novel records his search through memory for that decisive moment.

It did not happen in childhood. Sammy examines his early past, and concludes that there is a radical discontinuity between himself and the "infant Samuel" who stole fag-cards from smaller boys and tried to desecrate the altar. It had already begun when he betrayed the love of the innocent Beatrice. As Sammy recalls each episode, he asks himself, "Here?" And replies, "Not here."

There is only one point at which that question does not invoke an immediate and negative answer. At the end of the twelfth chapter Sammy, leaving school for the last time, walks in the woods and catechizes himself.

> What is important to you? (he asks himself).
> "Beatrice Ifor."
> She thinks you depraved already. She dislikes you.
> "If I want something enough I can always get it provided I am willing to make the appropriate sacrifice."
> What will you sacrifice?
> "Everything."
>
> Here?

The appropriate sacrifice, it would seem, is freedom; by choosing to involve himself completely in another person ("I want to be you," Sammy tells Beatrice), he has entered the adult world of guilt, and Golding seems to propose that the beginning of guilt is the end of freedom. But such a proposition is scarcely an answer, since it contains a fundamental paradox—without freedom, how can a man be guilty?

The terms of the paradox are apparent in the title of

the novel—*Free Fall* is both a theological and a scientific reference: it alludes to Adam's (and man's) freedom of choice, and therefore implies a moral thesis; and it also refers to that state of neutralized gravitational pull that is a condition—and a hazard—of space travel, and hence a part of our contemporary scientific mythology. Golding's imagination seems to have been engaged by this idea of man falling freely and endlessly through space, as a metaphor for the scientific conception of man's place in the universe. These two versions of man—the religious and the scientific—oppose each other in the novel, and in Sammy Mountjoy's mind. In his childhood they are represented by two teachers, Nick Shales, the science teacher who is innocent and good and full of love, and Miss Rowena Pringle, the teacher of Religious Knowledge, a sadistic, life-denying spinster. These two, Sammy says, are his "parents not in the flesh," and in so far as Sammy is all of us, the point is obvious enough—we are all the children of science and religion, parents who don't get on together. Sammy sees the two as offering alternative "patterns," either of which would provide a kind of answer to his question, but both of which cannot be true. The objective world that we see and the subjective world that we feel contradict each other—that, I take it, is the point and the problem: "we live in freedom by necessity." The answer that Sammy seeks is really an answer to this paradox.

I have said that the action of *Free Fall* is not fabulous. There is, however, one long central episode that does resemble in form and in forcefulness the actions of the earlier novels. Sammy, a prisoner of war in a German prison camp, is interviewed by Dr. Halde, a Nazi psychologist. Halde is the Devil to Sammy's Christ ("I have taken you

up to a pinnacle of the temple," he says, "and shown you
the whole earth"); he explains Sammy to himself, and
offers him a Nazi answer to his question—a world made
tolerable by simplification, a world from which freedom,
and therefore guilt, have been eliminated. When Sammy
refuses to betray his comrades, Halde has him put in a
dark, solitary cell.

The chapter that describes Sammy's terrors in the
prison cell is the most powerful in the novel; in its realization of subjective torment it resembles the previous solitary action, that of *Pincher Martin*. Like Martin, Sammy
tries to preserve himself by reasoning about his circumstances; and like Martin, he fails. But here the resemblance ends. Pincher ends insanely defying God; Sammy,
in his extremity, cries, "Help me! Help me!"

The paragraphs that follow are the most difficult in the
novel; they are also the most important. "My life has re-
mained centered," Sammy says, "round the fact of the next
few minutes I spent alone and panic-stricken in the dark."

My cry for help was the cry of the rat when the terrier shakes it, a
hopeless sound, the raw signature of one savage act. My cry
meant no more, was instinctive, said here is flesh of which the
nature is to suffer and do thus. I cried out not with hope of an ear
but as accepting a shut door, darkness and a shut sky.

But the very act of crying out changed the thing that cried.

Because man cries out instinctively, he can seek for a
source of help. In Sammy's circumstances, the physical
world offers "neither help nor hope of weakness that
might be attacked and overcome"; he cannot escape from
the dark cell. He turns to time past, and finds there "only

balm for a quieter moment"; the search for the answer
through memory has therefore failed, because the past
cannot sustain man in the urgency of present need. What
is left? Only the future. Sammy "turned therefore and
lunged, uncoiled, struck at the future" (in a passage that
sounds very like the existential leap into the abyss). When
he does so, the cell door bursts open, and he emerges "a
man resurrected," who sees the world of matter as infused
with miracle—"a universe like a burst casket of jewels."
The two worlds of science and belief are still both separate and real, and there is no bridge between them; they
are two fields of equal gravitational pull, between which
man hangs, in a condition of free fall. "Cause and effect,"
Sammy thinks.

The law of succession. Statistical probability. The moral order.
Sin and remorse. They are all true. Both worlds exist side by
side. They meet in me. We have to satisfy the examiners in both
worlds at once.

This can scarcely be regarded as a resolution; it is nevertheless an answer, and the only answer that the novel offers. Men live at an intersection of incompatible worlds,
both of which they must inhabit; they are both compelled
and guilty; they torture each other, but they may also
forgive each other. We are all free and falling.

Free Fall is a dark, obscure novel, but its difficulty
does not lie in the ideas that it offers. Golding's views on
man's moral nature, and the moral structure of the universe, have not changed much; the schoolboys of Free Fall
are not morally distinguishable from those of Lord of the
Flies, and Sammy Mountjoy is Pincher Martin with a bet-

ter developed moral sensibility. The difficulties are formal, and it is in these difficulties that the weaknesses of the novel seem to me to lie.

Yeats once wrote that "we assent to the conclusions of reflection but believe what myth presents." This remark provides an apt distinction between *Free Fall* and the preceding novels; the first three are mythlike, and we believe what they present because meaning is embodied in significant action, but *Free Fall* takes as its form "the conclusions of reflection," and we give to those conclusions, at most, our assent. Because Golding has not composed a myth, the action does not carry the meaning, except in the single prison scene, which is different enough in method to seem a violation of the formal unity of the book. Consequently Golding has had to insert passages of generalization and interpretation into Sammy's first-person stream of consciousness. These passages have two unfortunate effects: they expose Golding's ideas to the kind of cold, philosophical scrutiny that one gives to didactic moral writing; and they impede the movement of the novel. *Free Fall* is vastly more expository than any previous Golding novel, and while this is perhaps inevitable in a first-person novel on a moral theme, it is nevertheless a formal weakness.

Another apparent flaw in the novel is the order of the incidents. Scene follows scene in a sequence devised for didactic reasons (Sammy tells us that he is recalling past events in order of their importance to his question); but because the scenes do not compose a myth or fable, they must be read, and must find their connections, on the literal level of action. Consequently there are frequently inexplicable gaps in the narrative, and obliquities of narration that seem merely willful. Characters enter obscurely, to be explained only later, actions are darkly alluded to before they occur, and often in a style that seems gratuitously lush and ambiguous.

One must judge cautiously and generously when dealing with a book like *Free Fall*, though; it is recent, it is difficult, and it is the work of a serious writer of demonstrated imaginative gifts. With such a work, critical understanding sometimes grows slowly, and must pass through many minds before it comes to anything like a just judgment. But until that process has taken place, one must record the difficulties, and say tentatively that in this novel Golding's worthy desire not to repeat himself led him astray, and into a form inappropriate to his preoccupations. The novel has the virtues of intelligence, moral passion, and intermittent dramatic force. But Golding has created his own high standards, and compared with his earlier novels, this one is not successful.

The Spire is in many ways a return to the method of the earlier novels, and an abandoning of the developed, contemporary social context that distinguished *Free Fall*. Golding has once more selected a situation that distances and isolates the action; *The Spire* is set in fourteenth-century England, but more than that it is set almost entirely within a cathedral close, which circumscribes the action and restricts the *dramatis personae* as severely as desert island or primitive forest did. It is an action set in the historical past, but the novel is not an historical novel in the ordinary sense of that term: Golding has not attempted to re-create the age of Edward III, or to fill his pages with the kind of contemporary detail that most historical novelists depend on for verisimilitude. He has rather written another symbolic novel, and has used time and cathedral close to preserve a narrative bareness, and to focus attention on the central symbolic action. (He calls attention to the *un*historical character of his novel by calling his cathedral town Barchester, though it is clearly Salisbury.)

The spire of the title is the spire of Salisbury Cathedral, and the principal action of the novel is the building of that spire. Salisbury, as all the guidebooks tell us, is built on marshland without sufficient foundation to support a structure of such weight; the spire nevertheless stands, as it has stood for 600 years, and so it is said to be "built on faith." Such a spire is a symbol of compelling potentialities: it reaches toward heaven, but rises from untrustworthy foundations on earth; it is made by man, in praise of God; it is beautiful and dangerous, and more dangerous as it rises higher; it is a landmark and a lightning rod, it threatens and summons. Golding, starting with the symbol of the spire, has constructed a novel that takes its form from the gradual evolution of the symbol's meanings.

The story line of the novel is simple enough: Jocelin, Dean of Barchester Cathedral, believes himself chosen of God to build a spire on the cathedral, and by force of will compels the spire to be built, against the judgment of both clergy and builders. The novel begins with the first stages of construction, and ends with the spire built, and Jocelin dead. But the focus of this story is not either on character or on action, but on symbolic significances; once more, as in the earlier novels, Golding has conceived his own kind of myth—fiction understood as the symbolic form given to moral meanings. Jocelin dominates the novel, not as a character but as a growing moral awareness; and the spire dominates Jocelin. As he reaches toward the meaning of the spire, so the reader approaches understanding of the meaning of the novel.

Some of the symbolic meanings of the spire are immediately and conventionally apparent. One thinks of Gothic architecture as expressing spiritual aspiration, and this is Jocelin's first understanding of his vision: "The building is a diagram of prayer; and our spire will be a diagram of the highest prayer of all." But the cathedral is also a diagram of man. In its first appearance—a description of a model of the building that occurs in the first chapter—it diagrams physical man, sexual and suffering:

The model was like a man lying on his back. The nave was his legs placed together, the transepts on either side were his arms outspread. The choir was his body; and the Lady Chapel, where now the services would be held, was his head. And now also, springing, projecting, bursting, erupting from the heart of the building, there was its crown and majesty, the new spire.

These meanings—man-as-phallic and man-as-crucified— are not at first clear to Jocelin, but before the spire is built he knows a good deal more about both, and acknowledges that both have played a part in motivating his vision.

But if the cathedral symbolizes man's physical nature, it also symbolizes his spiritual dimension; it is "an image of living, praying man." Jocelin, in moments of self-condemnation, thinks of himself as "a building with a vast cellarage where the rats live" (one recalls the dark symbolic cellar in *Pincher Martin*) but he is also a building with a spire. If he is a suffering animal, he is an animal who can pray.

A final meaning derives from the fact that the spire

goes up contrary to all reasonable principles of construction; it is called Jocelin's Folly, but Jocelin tells the master mason:

The folly isn't mine. It's God's Folly. Even in the old days he never asked men to do what was reasonable. Men can do that for themselves. They can buy and sell, heal and govern. But then out of some deep place comes the command to do what makes no sense at all—to build a ship on dry land; to sit among the dunghills; to marry a whore; to set their son on the altar of sacrifice. Then, if men have faith, a new thing comes.

God commands man to folly, for His sake, and Jocelin understands his compulsion to build the spire as such a command; but God also asks man to sacrifice what he loves most, as He asked Abraham, and this lesson comes late and painfully to Jocelin. The diagram of prayer is also "a diagram of the folly they don't know about"—the folly of sacrifice. Nor can man be sure that the folly he does is indeed done at God's will; Jocelin to the end is uncertain whether he has been moved by true vision, or by vanity, or by the witchcraft of a woman's beauty.

The narrative line—what Golding would probably call the *myth*—on which the emergent meanings of the symbol are developed is the process of building the spire. As the structure rises, a man is killed, and a woman dies in terrible childbirth, and both deaths stem from Jocelin's "dedicated will." Roger, the master mason, becomes a drunken wreck and attempts suicide. Old friendships end, the harmony of the cathedral chapter is broken. Even the social habits of the town and countryside around are altered; new roads lead to the new landmark, and new roads bring new people. Looking out from the tower, Jocelin sees these changes, and muses:

I thought it would be simple. I thought the spire would complete a stone bible, be the apocalypse in stone. I never guessed in my folly that there would be a new lesson at every level, and a new power.

The principal lesson is that for man there are no simple acts, that in his folly he cannot foresee the consequences of his actions. Because the spire is the work of man, it is built on blood and sin—"there is no innocent work," Jocelin thinks as he lies dying; nevertheless the spire stands, a gesture of assent, in spite of its dark foundations.

The Spire is a novel about vision; vision motivates Jocelin in his obsessive drive toward his goal, the goal itself a symbol in stone of man's capacity to make his visions actual. If the spire is a gesture of assent, it is assent to that proposition. But that assent is not reached easily. The novel is, as I have said, a novel of emergent meanings, not one of inspirational assertions. The meaning of vision develops in the novel, from Jocelin's first joyous confidence in God's imperative to his final complex comprehension.

Vision is simple while it is spiritual; when man tries to transform it into matter, with human hands, vision becomes complex. The principal complexity, as Jocelin learns, is the human cost; the dynamic tension in the novel is drawn in just these terms: *vision* against *cost*, what man wills against what he can endure. The cost for Jocelin is the willful sacrifice of persons he loves to the vision that he wills.

Golding has dealt before with the immorality of *using* human beings: both Pincher Martin and Sammy Mountjoy are guilty of this sin. Jocelin, in his obsession, uses two men and their women, and destroys them; surely this is evil. Yet out of this crime against humanity rises the spire, an act of faith. The point is not simple, but perhaps a consideration of Jocelin's last two thoughts will make it clearer (Golding has emphasized these sentences by setting them in italics): *"There is no innocent work. God knows where God may be"* and *"It's like the appletree."* The latter sentence requires a gloss. Jocelin had earlier described the complication of his vision in terms of a growing plant—"a single green shoot at first, then clinging tendrils, then branches . . ." Later he goes out into the spring sunshine, and sees an appletree:

There was a cloud of angels flashing in the sunlight, they were pink and gold and white; and they were uttering this sweet scent for joy of the light and the air. They brought with them a scatter of clear leaves, and among the leaves a long, black springing thing. His head swam with the angels, and suddenly he understood there was more to the appletree than one branch. It was there beyond the wall, bursting up with cloud and scatter, laying hold of the earth and the air, a fountain, a marvel, an appletree; and this made him weep in a childish way so that he could not tell whether he was glad or sorry.

It's like the appletree: that is, the spire that Jocelin has built has more to it than one miraculous thrust; it touches earth and air, men and angels, corruption and faith. And perhaps the gesture of assent that it makes is simply an assent to this proposition about the mixed nature of man's works, even in praise of God.

If this *is* the moral of *The Spire,* it is neither heterodox nor startling; it emerges naturally and inevitably from the nature of the mythic material, and in this respect makes a more organic novel than was *Free Fall,* with its didactic moral pointing. But this organicism, based as it is on one entirely dominant symbol, has its limiting features too.

The Spire seems a particularly extreme case of Golding's
characteristic mythmaking method—it is, of all the novels,
the one that most clearly began with a symbol to be explored. What can the building of a cathedral spire *mean?*
The novel is a complex answer to that question. Consequently the spire remains throughout the novel the most
vivid presence, as it is in Jocelin's mind.

All of the distinctive formal properties of the novel
derive from this fact. There is, first of all, a diminished
sense of the actuality of the novel's physical world; the
construction of the spire is often treated in meticulous detail, but the men who build it are dim shadows, performing dim actions in undefined space. Characters are drawn
largely through their relation to the spire, rather than to
each other. There are few strong scenes, and those that are
potentially powerful—the tormenting and murder of the
verger in the fourth chapter, for example, and the death of
his wife in the seventh—are treated sketchily, as if seen by
a man with a mind closed by obsession. And indeed that is
the mind that sees them; but Golding, by choosing to imitate obsessive preoccupation, has weakened everything in
his novel that is not tower or builder—the symbol and the
man who learns it.

Each of these judgments would be an indication of
serious weakness if applied to a conventional novel, and a
novel with all of these limitations would, one might con-
clude, be a certain failure. But few critical principles are
prescriptive; a novel without strong characterization and
without effective scenes of interacting personalities lacks
two valuable fictional elements, but it may have other
compensations. *The Spire* has a magnificent symbol, which
grows and accretes meaning and composes in its rela-

tionship with its builder a sufficient human meaning. One might say that there is one further symbolic meaning to be added to the meanings already ascribed to the cathedral spire: it is a symbol of the novel that contains it, because though it lacks sufficient fictional foundations, yet it stands.

Golding has testified to his belief that there is no point in repeating old inventions, and each of his novels has been a new kind of verbal contraption. The first five, however, share a common allegorical (or fabulous or mythical) form; the sixth disturbs this pleasing uniformity. To the reader familiar with Golding's other novels, *The Pyramid* will astonish by what it is not. It is not a fable, it does not contain evident allegory, it is not set in a simplified or remote world. It belongs to another, more commonplace tradition of English fiction; it is a low-keyed, realistic novel of growing up in a small town—the sort of book H. G Wells might have written if he had been more attentive to his style.

The book is made of three separate episodes in the life of Oliver, son of a dispenser in a provincial town; the dates are from the 1920s to the late 1940s, the locale is Wiltshire (though Golding adopts Trollopian place names, as he did in *The Spire*). The first episode is a traditional one in the fiction of adolescence: young Oliver discovers sex with the daughter of the Town Crier. In the second he reluctantly participates in a farcical amateur performance of the town operatic society. The third—also traditional— is the mature man's return to the town, and his recollections of the spinster who had taught him music.

Among these three episodes there are certain connections of character and scene, but these do not make for a very tightly or very elaborately structured book. The principal unifying element is the theme suggested by the epigraph: "If thou be among people make for thyself love, the beginning and end of the heart." In each episode Oliver is involved with a person who needs, and reaches out for love: Evie, the Town Crier's promiscuous daughter, Mr. De Tracy, the effeminate director of the musical show, and Miss Dawlish, the music teacher. But in each case he fails; he uses Evie, he laughs at De Tracy, and he admits, over Miss Dawlish's grave, that he is glad she is dead. Among people, he has made nothing.

This is a familiar theme in Golding's work: it is the principal argument of the last three novels, and particularly of *Pincher Martin* and *Free Fall*. The method seems at first glance a new departure. However, if one looks back at Golding's earlier work, one can see that his imagination has always had this other, less flashy side. Piggy, in *Lord of the Flies*, is kin to Mr. Polly, and there are realistic episodes and commonplace characters in the other books (excepting, of course, *The Inheritors*). In those novels, Golding had subordinated his realistic imagination to his allegorizing ends, but actuality would thrust itself pushily forward; and it may be, if one reexamines those books in the light of the latest novel, that they will appear less diagrammatic than one thought, and that Golding's critics will have to revise their critical vocabularies.

The Pyramid is set in the twentieth century, but Golding has never been much concerned with the immediate present, except occasionally to deplore it, and he certainly seems to have no feelings that the present moment in human history is unique. His classical training, and his amateur interests in Egyptology and archaeology have en-

couraged him to see man's story as an evolving one, and
have fed that quality of his mind that is most individual,
and that makes him irreplaceable—his sense of the human
species. His humanity reaches back beyond history, and
finds us there; he is an anthropologist of the imagination.
He is primarily interested in the cruxes in the evolution of
consciousness, and the childhood of individuals or the
childhood of races serves him equally well, providing
those points at which a mind opens imaginatively to
knowledge, learns to use fire or to impose discipline,
learns evil or love or the nature of death. His courage in attempting such subjects is admirable, and when he has
failed, he has failed courageously.

   The Scorpion God, Golding's latest book (as of 1975),
is not a major work, but it is nevertheless a pure example
of Golding's gift, and it will help, perhaps, to fix the nature
of that gift. It consists of three long stories, of which one,
"Envoy Extraordinary," is something of a makeweight (it
was first published in 1956, and was later dramatized as
The Brass Butterfly). The title story is from Golding's
Egyptological side; set in ancient Egypt (exactly how ancient other Egyptologists will know), it turns on the moment when a man, by a leap of imagination, chooses to
become a God. The best text for further elucidation is
Golding's essay, "Egypt from My Inside," in which
he describes what he calls "the heart of my Egypt": "It is
to be at once alive and dead: to suggest mysteries with no
solution, to mix the strange, the gruesome and the beautiful; to use all the resources of life to ensure that this left-
over from living and its container shall stand outside
change and bring the wheel to a full stop." By treating the
unfamiliar with familiarity, explaining nothing, he teases

the reader into the strange world of the story. It is as brilliant a tour de force as *The Inheritors,* if on a smaller scale.

The other story, "Clonk Clonk," is somewhat less satisfying. It is one of Golding's "childhood of the species" stories, set apparently in Africa (there are rhinos and chimpanzees), at a date that the last paragraph suggests was at least a hundred thousand years ago. In this stage men, appropriately, are childish and polymorphously perverse; women, however, are women—knowing, material, and wisely deceitful. As a fable of the relations between the sexes the story is clumsy; as a fable of a growth of consciousness it scarcely works. One must judge it one of the honorable failures.

"Envoy Extraordinary" will be familiar to Golding's admirers from its first appearance in the collection titled *Sometime, Never* and, in dramatic form, in *The Brass Butterfly.* It is unique among Golding's writings in that it is witty and amusing, and quite lacking in the solemnity that rather weighs down his other work. Though classical in setting, it plays with anachronisms in a cheerful, unserious way—though the story has its Goldingesque point about civilization and its discontents.

Golding has said that he wrote *The Inheritors* to refute Wells's *Outline of History,* and one can see that between the two writers there is a certain filial relation, though strained, as such relations often are. They share the fascination with past and future, the extraordinary capacity to move imaginatively to remote points in time, the fabulizing impulse, the need to moralize. There are even similarities in style. And surely now, when Wells's reputation as a great writer is beginning to take form, it will be understood as high praise of Golding if one says that he is our

Wells, as good in his own individual way as Wells was in his.

It would also be appropriate praise to say that Golding has something of Wells's gift for variety of invention. In his essay, "The Crest of the Wave," Golding has written feelingly of the need "for the novel which tries to look at life anew, in a word, for intransigence," and each of his books has been one more example of Golding's own intransigence—his refusal to make concessions to our expectations, or to do again what we know he can do. Every book is a radical attempt to "look at life anew," and each has altered our sense of the meaning of his work as a whole. As long as Golding goes on writing, this intransigence will go on, and final critical judgments of his achievement must wait. Even an assessment of the last term in the series must be understood as conditional upon the next novel, and the next. For like all truly original imaginations, his goes on surprising us.

JOHN UNTERECKER

Lawrence Durrell

Lawrence Durrell is a man of infinite variety. But he's a man of marble constancy as well. The forms in which he has worked embrace the whole range of literary possibility. Yet the themes he has dealt with—even the images which carry those themes—display a simple kind of shining directness, mark out a clear path for his developing but remarkably consistent point of view. He is consequently one of our most protean writers and at the same time one of our most predictable ones.

It is variety, however, that immediately strikes anyone who does no more than glance through a stack of Durrell's collected works. (Getting that stack together is, as Durrell's bibliographers have pointed out, no easy task; for private publication, out-of-the-way publication—Shanghai and Cairo are among the exotic addresses of Durrell's publishers—and the book-destroying accidents of war have made Durrell's early works collector's rarities.) Even if one limits one's glance to works currently in print, something of Durrell's enormous range is bound to be suggested. He is author, for instance, of the espionage thriller

White Eagles over Serbia (described by Durrell's American publisher as a book "for young persons"); of intricate poems (among them the sonnet of sonnets, "A Soliloquy of Hamlet") and bawdy ballads (Dylan Thomas's favorite being "A Ballad of the Good Lord Nelson"); of a trilogy of "travel books" which should perhaps more accurately be called island portraits (*Prospero's Cell, Reflections on a Marine Venus,* and *Bitter Lemons*); of the lovely, casual collection of letters, poems, essays, and paintings, *Spirit of Place;* of three poetic dramas, startlingly different in tone—though not in theme; of the "solipsistic," raw fictional account of prewar London, *The Black Book;* of comic interludes about life in the diplomatic corps (*Esprit de Corps* and *Stiff Upper Lip*); of *The Dark Labyrinth,* a novel which Durrell accurately described to Henry Miller as "an extended morality, but written artlessly in the style of the detective story"; of literary criticism (*A Key to Modern British Poetry*); and—by far his most popular work—of the extraordinarily complex, expanding study of the emotional education of a hero and his friends, *The Alexandria Quartet.* He has also in his time turned out public relations copy, newspaper columns, and—presumably unavailable to the public—a whole series of confidential reports, the bulky stuffing of diplomats' bags and Home Office files. He has published some of his letters to Henry Miller and a smaller group of letters (to Alfred Perlès) about Henry Miller. He has acted as translator of prose (Emmanuel Royidis' novel *Pope Joan*) and poetry (Constantine Cavafy, not only in the body of *The Alexandria Quartet,* but elsewhere), anthologist, and magazine editor. He was for a while one of the principal script writers for the motion picture *Cleopatra*—and once, in his youth, a would-be composer-lyricist of popular songs. For years after the completion of *The Alexandria Quartet* he was reported as being engaged in work on "an enormous Rabelaisian comic novel," some of which may have surfaced in the double-decker novels *Tunc* (1968) and *Nunquam* (1970) and more still of which may have appeared in the fictional exploration of the nature of "reality," *Monsieur* (1974).

His variety is, in fact, so spectacular that one suspects that, consciously or unconsciously, somewhere along the line Durrell must have toyed with the idea of being literature's Leonardo—the master of each literary form. So far as I know he has not as yet written the libretto of an opera—but give him time.

Give him time enough—and space—and you will have set up the space-time continuum that, from very early in his career until the present moment, operates for Durrell as a kind of subterranean metaphor—a metaphor for a literary structure that does not significantly change from work to work and on which he has draped all of the superficial variety of poems, novels, essays, plays.

But before examining the details of that metaphor, we should perhaps explore a little of the clock time and the yardstick space which lie far behind his present work but which help account for the present writer. For though Durrell is quite careful to avoid "autobiographical" fiction, poetry, and even letters, some at least of the "facts" of his life do touch on his work.

Most of those facts are, of course, the sort recorded on public documents: place of birth, age, marital status, etc. Durrell's proper efforts to keep his private life private set him—as he recognizes—in odd contrast to his friend Henry Miller, whose stance and method are determinedly autobiographical. Durrell hesitated, for example, to allow his half of the Durrell-Miller correspondence to get into print—"I have tender feelings about my private affairs and private life and don't want to exhibit my sore spots to a wondering world"—and was only won over to the publication scheme after Miller had assured him:

there's hardly ever anything very personal in your letters. I'm the one who blurts things out; you're discreet, reserved, veiled. The reader will hardly know whether you're talking about a wife, a mistress or one of the characters in your books. Your personal life is bound up with places, fauna and flora, archaeology, the planets, mythology. You're always "heraldic."

If we take Durrell at his own word and at Miller's and find him "always 'heraldic,' " and if we go on to construct for him a kind of heraldic shield, one indispensable element on it will have to be a snow-covered mountain peak. For as Durrell points out in "Cities, Plains and People," a poem which in its early versions was accompanied by a geographical-biographical gloss, the "mortal boy" who is the subject of the poem had his beginning in India, that area of India bordering Tibet where each day of his childhood he could see "the Himalayas like lambs there / Stir their huge joints." Going to school in that high country until he was eleven produced for him, as he was eventually to tell Miller, "the most wonderful memories, a brief dream of Tibet." But chief among those memories of "the soft klaxons crying," of "pure lakes," of the "the prayerwheel" was the overwhelming memory of the snowcovered peaks themselves. ("White white the Himalayas from the dormitory windows. . . . I wanted to go one summer into the passes. They promised to take me. But I left

without going—alamort—it is a kind of unreasoning disease when I think of it.") The visual echo of those snow-
covered peaks crops up as incidental obsessive imagery in
almost everything Durrell has written. Often, as we might
expect, the peaks are associated with an "innocent beginning" not altogether unlike the one that took place at one
A.M. on February 27, 1912, when Durrell was born. But
Durrell is too much of an artist to make all of his peaks
Tibetan. In *The Dark Labyrinth* they surround a high Cre-
tan mountain valley, the "Roof of the World," cutting it off
completely from the rest of the island and turning it, for
one couple who accidentally find its isolated splendor,
into a miracle of rediscovered innocence, a twentieth-century Garden of Eden. In Durrell's third play, *An Irish
Faustus*, the hero—after a descent into the elemental darkness of a private Hades—withdraws at the end to a mountain inn, where comfortably blocked in by winter snows,
he can join three old friends for a game of cards, there to
look out—isolated from it—at the panorama of a white and
distant world. In *White Eagles over Serbia*, the mountains
are Yugoslavian, but the journey up out of the corruption
of Belgrade, along one mountain stream after another,
always carrying the narrator higher and higher, brings him
finally—predictably—onto "the roof of the mountains," a
land where "only the shepherds with their flocks ever ven-
tured," a land where "there were no roads to tempt a traveller," a land itself capped by the rough beauty of the
Janco Stone, a "great obelisk" of stone which rises above
all of the "clusters of peaks and canyons" and which in the
novel marks the trysting place of a loyal group of heroic
anti-Communist guerrillas. Peaks of this sort are easy
enough to locate in Durrell's texts, the isolated peak "fitter

for the eagle than for men," for instance, which dominates
an uninhabited island in the Sporades and onto which
Phaon—in Durrell's play about her, Sappho's most elo-
quent, most ardent, and most honest lover—retires to seek
private peace in a warring world; or, in *Nunquam,* the
little skier's hut high in the Alps where, looking down on
an "empty . . . cold world" the narrator and Julian, the
director of the world "firm" that controls him yet permits
him to function, discuss the nature of nature itself and the
" 'signatures' of things" that both determine the structure
of society's "culture" and, through the intrusion of men of
genius, permit its transformation: "What we call genius
occurs when a gifted man sees a relation between two or
more fields of thought which had up till then been believed to be irreconcilable. He joins the contradictory
fields in an act of intellectual harmony and the chain
begins to hold once more. The so-called genius of the matter is merely the intuitive act of joining irreconcilables."
Less obvious but no less important are the metaphoric
snow-capped peaks—like that peak Durrell's Sappho herself, finally, in the imagination of old age, "after so very
long," climbs, a peak of the emotions only from which she
hopes she can observe the world with an Olympian detachment: "So at last, after so very long, / I have climbed
up here / On this icy peak of my indifference." These invented peaks, the peaks which "the artist at his papers,"
say, inhabits, "Up there alone, upon the alps of night,"
show up—as in this example from Durrell's poem "Alexandria"—in all sorts of sea-level places. For these are the
peaks which rear behind a writer's literal subject and
which provide—sometimes consciously, sometimes half

consciously, sometimes wholly unconsciously—a metaphoric unity in his diverse subject matter.

If Durrell's early childhood contributed to his work, as
I strongly suspect it did, not just imagery of innocence but
a locale for the good life, the rest of Durrell's childhood
seems to have offered him, in England, imagery tied to the
experience of corruption and a vision not so much of evil
as of hypocrisy, a major ingredient of the "English death"
which is the subject of *The Black Book*. For when Durrell
at the age of eleven left the College of St. Joseph in Dar-
jeeling and set sail down the "long sad river" of his adolescence, his westward path took him not toward literal
but toward metaphoric death. He went westward only "To
the prudish cliffs and the sad green home / Of Pudding
Island o'er the Victorian foam." Here in England, eventually enrolled in St. Edmund's School, Canterbury, young
Durrell watched "the business witches in their bowlers,"
and concluded, if we can trust "Cities, Plains and People,"
that London could at best be nothing more than "a
promise-giving kingdom."

Though England's citizens may have seemed to Durrell "good crafty men," its libraries were well stocked with
sturdier men of the world, dead in the flesh but for an omnivorous reader altogether vital in spirit. And Durrell consumed not only passionate Englishmen—from Bede to
Blake, from Shakespeare to the Brontës, from Keats to
Lawrence—but as much of continental literature as he
could get under his belt. He read Church Fathers and philosophers—St. Augustine, Jerome, Descartes—and, glanc-
ing into "the great sickroom, Europe," Dante and Homer.

Though his biographer will undoubtedly find in that

period the roots of all of Durrell's subsequent accomplishment, his adolescence is one phase of Durrell's life which is, so far as I can see, only marginally touched on in Durrell's printed work. There are passing references to Durrell's brother Gerald—the writer whose own recollections of childhood give us brief and affectionate glimpses of the entire Durrell family and whose graceful, open accounts of his work as a collector of wild animals seem, in their casual structure, altogether antithetical to his brother's careful constructions. But the rest of Durrell's family—his widowed mother, his brother Leslie, his sister Margaret— and all of Durrell's school experiences are bundled into a privacy which catapults Lawrence Durrell, in those few reminiscences about his youth which he has published, from eleven-year-old schoolboy to precocious young writer. For in the intervening years, he later told Miller, England, "that mean, shabby little island," was chiefly responsible for frustration rather than for the kind of education Durrell felt he needed. England "wrung my guts out of me and tried to destroy anything singular and unique in me. My so-called upbringing was quite an uproar. I have always broken stable when I was unhappy. The list of schools I've been to would be a yard long. I failed every known civil service exam." And though Durrell—twenty-four years old at the time of the letter from which I have quoted—was obviously indulging in a good deal of self-dramatization for the older writer whom he had not yet met, he was also, I suspect, getting as quickly as possible past a part of his life that he has never very much wanted to draw on. For all the variety of his subject matter, there are precious few children in Durrell's collected work, and those who are present—Justine's child,

for example—are never allowed introspective voices. Even
the young men in Durrell's works—those in *The Black
Book,* especially—have an almost middle-aged self-consciousness. They are superb at understanding—or, if need
be, misunderstanding—their present predicaments; but
they are not much inclined to dip back to adolescence for
source material. It's as if they accept themselves—without
much question—as types; and certainly the narrators and
inner-narrators who examine them see them also as types.

Perhaps, of course, Durrell is here reflecting only his
admiration for Freud, a writer he studied carefully and
who found, as Durrell notes, "the nuclear structure of all
anxiety" in "the sexual preoccupation of childhood." For it
is the childhood of infancy and preadolescence that is for
Freud most illuminating, and it is precisely to this territory
of childhood that Durrell, when he deals at all with childhood experience, turns.

If Durrell seems carefully to skirt the years of adolescence both in reminiscence and in the adaptation of reminiscence to fiction, he obviously draws very heavily on
the years of his first literary activity, a hectic time spent
chiefly in and near London. "I hymned and whored in
London," he told Miller, "playing jazz in a night-club,
composing jazz songs, working in real estate. Never really
starved, but I wonder whether thin rations are not another
degree of starvation." Here, accidentally gathering material for *The Black Book,* Durrell met Nancy Myers, who, in
1935, was to become his first wife: ". . . we struck up an
incongruous partnership: a dream of broken bottles, spu-
tum, tinned food, rancid meat, urinals, the smell of the
lock hospitals. . . . Ran a photographic studio together. It

crashed. Tried posters, short stories, journalism, everything short of selling our bottoms to a clergyman. I wrote a
cheap novel. Sold it."

Durrell's "cheap novel," *Pied Piper of Lovers*, turned
out, in spite of its account of bohemian Bloomsbury, to be
neither an artistic nor a financial success; but it did lead to
his producing two years later a second commercial novel,
Panic Spring, "A Romance by Charles Norden," Durrell
having been persuaded by the editors at Faber and Faber,
who published the book, that a pseudonym might be a
likely method of dissociating himself from his unsuccessful first book.

Soon after the publication of *Pied Piper of Lovers*,
however, and well before his second novel was printed,
two significant biographical events took place: Durrell
read Henry Miller's *Tropic of Cancer*, which had just been
published in Paris; and he succeeded in persuading his
mother to pull up stakes, to pack up bag, baggage, and all
three children, and to leave England. Though the two
events were undoubtedly only casually related, they certainly coalesced in the novel Durrell set himself to write
when he and his family finally found a place for themselves on Corfu, the island Durrell had forced his family to
select for his experiment in expatriation. For, like all of the
other expatriate novelists of our time—from James to Joyce
to Miller himself—Durrell had simply decided that the
only satisfactory way to deal with his country was to escape from it long enough to observe it dispassionately.
Miller's book offered him both a model and a technique:
"*Tropic* opened a pit in my brain," he confessed to Miller,
to whom he was soon writing:

It freed me immediately. . . . *Tropic* taught me . . . to write
about people I knew something about. Imagine it! I had this
collection of grotesques sitting inside and I hadn't written a line
about them—only about heroic Englishmen and dove-like girls,
etc. (7/6 a volume). The whole collection of men and women
opened up for me like a razor. I borrowed the historic present
and sat down to it.

The product of this discovery was, of course, *The Black
Book,* Durrell's first really serious literary enterprise.

Just how serious it was can perhaps be in part gathered from the "Dear Alan" letter at its heart, a letter that,
like Stephen Dedalus' declaration of intention in *A Portrait of the Artist as a Young Man,* has to be taken finally
as a statement of the author's point of view. Durrell's character speaks not altogether in his author's voice (the fictional character, for one thing, is permitted an enormously
inflated ego), but he speaks nevertheless very much to the
author's point. That there was in fact a living Alan (Alan
Thomas, one of Durrell's most faithful friends) is only of
passing interest. What is of lasting interest is the point
made in the fictional letter: that in order to rescue what is
best in his country, the artist must subject the country itself to the scorching analysis of satirical rejection.

This is the world which was implicit in our extravagant gust, our
laughter, our tears, our poems. That is why, when I tell you I
have rejected it, I want you to understand clearly the terms of
that rejection. That is an England I am going to kill, because by
giving it a quietus once and for all, *I can revive it!* . . . The important thing is this: if I succeed, and I will succeed, then I shall
become, in a sense, *the first Englishman.*

When, in 1960, the book was finally made widely available to an English-speaking audience (it had first been published in 1938 in Paris, from which place, "in plain wrappers," it seeped gradually into England and America), Durrell tried to reconstruct in his preface something of its private value. It had marked for him, he concluded, a dividing line. Before *The Black Book*, he had been through "a long period of despair and frustration"; his early work, "though well-contrived, was really derivative." But in *The Black Book*, he explained, "I first heard the sound of my own voice, lame and halting perhaps, but nevertheless my very own." The book, with whatever imperfections, was in this respect "the genuine article."

The writing of it was in an odd way both a consequence of spiritual agony and a labor of love. For Durrell had no expectation that any publisher would risk bringing out a book so savage in spirit and so uncompromising in language. It was, in this sense at least, the *purest* work Durrell was ever to do; it was a demonstration, principally for Lawrence Durrell's private benefit, that he had the potential of becoming a major writer.

Durrell worked hard at it, taking out only enough time to dash off Charles Norden's *Panic Spring* ("a cheap romance," he told Miller, "a leprous distillment"). Through much of 1936 and 1937, Durrell cut, revised, and rewrote. Miller, who had been allowed to examine one of the intermediate drafts, wrote from Paris wildly enthusiastic and extraordinarily perceptive comments—and also wrote letters so fiercely fulminating about an author's need for absolute integrity ("You stand firm and let the world come round") that Durrell was finally persuaded to reject Faber and Faber's tempting offer to bring out an expurgated English edition of his book.

When the uncut 1938 edition finally did appear, it was published as the first volume of the Villa Seurat Library, an enterprise invented and edited by Henry Miller, subsidized by Durrell's wife Nancy, and printed through the good offices of Jack Kahane of the Obelisk Press. (The Villa Seurat Library died shortly after its other two subsidized titles—Miller's *Max and the White Phagocytes* and Anaïs Nin's *Winter of Artifice*—were published.)

The six months at the end of 1937 and the beginning of 1938 that Durrell spent in Paris working on the final draft of his book and editing with Miller and Alfred Perlès that strangest of all strange publications, the official organ of the American Country Club of Paris, *The Booster*, must have been superb ones. Throughout the next twenty years of their correspondence, Durrell and Miller over and over turn back to what begin to seem golden prewar days. Even immediately after the end of the European campaign, in 1945, Durrell looks back to that earlier time as to an improbable and marvelous era light years in the past:

Ah Henry, Europe is so far upside down that it will take a few years to settle. I reckon we have five years before the atom war. Can't we all meet and create a little of the warmth and fury of the Villa Seurat days: a glass of wine and pleasant soft furry murder of typewriters going; Anais in her cloak and pointed ears; the letter to Nijinsky; Fred and Madame Kalf; Betty Ryan and Reichel. It is all fixed now inside like a kind of formal tapestry—you with the skylight open, typing in your hat, and little Joe unwrapping the cheese with delicate fingers murmuring "Ja Ja das ist gudt." And do you remember Mr. Chu? And the chiropodist whose legs you cut off before throwing her in the Seine in No. 2 of *The*

Booster. And Valaida Snow? Have you a set of *Boosters?* And Herbert Read in the black muffin of a hat giving his young son an ice at the Deux Magots, and how you insisted on paying Chez Henriette to the acutely British discomfort of same? And how furious you were when you tried to sell *Booster* No. 1 to some bastard in a bar and he was insulting about it? And those long icy walks by the Seine with Anais in her cloak through the garish sulphurous ruins of the Great Exhibition into the Latin quarter to find the little street where Dante wrapped his feet in straw and where you found only the suicide Max? And those strange evenings on La Belle Aurore with Moricand the astrologer? And walking in the Louvre like mad angels? And the sudden scream that Soutine gave one night? Had he discovered another painting? And Fred writing letters to himself in that little dog-leg room, starving to death. And Edgar talking talking talking talking, his noble pure face caught up in a tic of anguish like a curtain pulled back. It was a complete finished little epoch. I remember the particular smell of the *Tropic* typescript, and the early novel you showed me. And lovely black little Teresa Epstein at the Closerie des Lilas. Hell, what are we going to put up against all that now that the war is over?

For just as London had offered Durrell "grotesques" from which characters could be modeled, first Corfu, then Paris, and still later Alexandria would provide Durrell with the human material from which fictions could be produced. (Durrell's brother Gerald vividly recalled one specimen, an improbably bald countess who, shortly after the family had settled in on Corfu, arrived at Durrell's invitation for an extended visit. Defending not the countess but his invitation, Durrell explained to his mother: "Why, I hardly know her . . . can't stand the woman; but she's an interesting character and I wanted to study her at close hand.") What Durrell seems to extract from the characters he examines is, however, personality rather than appearance. His characters, erected on armatures of studied personality, are drawn from models more useful to Durrell for the ways in which they react to the world than for the way they look. And once his fictions get into action they lead lives very nearly independent of the lives lived by their human counterparts.

Even Durrell's nonfiction adjusts carefully the materials it draws from real life. In the long retrospective letter to Miller from which I have already quoted, Durrell tells a little about the human materials he drew on in constructing his portrait of life on Corfu, *Prospero's Cell*. Some of the figures were familiar to Miller, for in the summer and autumn of 1939, under the impending shadow of the big war yet to come, Miller had visited Durrell and his wife, first on Corfu and later in Greece. The book, Durrell explained to Miller, should

bring back many old memories, I hope, with its portraits. Theodore and Spiro, etc. Too bad you never met the great Zarian or old Dr. Palatioano, a fine mythological old man on whom I modelled the count. He had the skull of his mistress on a velvet square before him on the writing desk; liked holding it up to the light and talking to it.

Strangely enough, this extraordinary detail about the mistress's skull—perhaps privately crucial to Durrell's view of Dr. Palatioano—vanishes in *Prospero's Cell*. There, "Count D," the central figure of the latter half of the book, becomes a philosopher-host whose brilliant, speculative conversation creates an amalgam of wit, history, guesswork, and sentimental love-of-place. Of course, the count—as Durrell told Miller—is still very close to the real man; nevertheless, in the course of being modeled, the count loses that remarkable skull. He also begins to act as spokesman for some of Durrell's favorite ideas about life and art. He isn't independent of the man he is modeled on; but he isn't independent of his modeler either.

Even *Prospero's Cell* itself, set up as a day-to-day account of Durrell's 1937–38 life on the island, is far from the fact it pretends to be. It is, for example, written—as we learn from the letters and as we can guess from the epilogue—six years later than the events on which it is based, events that are recorded diary-fashion so freshly as to seem spur-of-the-minute jottings. But the freshness is the freshness of art rather than of nature: "I've done about half of a little historical book about Corfu," Durrell writes Miller in the spring of 1944; "tried writing in the style of a diary—you know the French anecdotal novel type of things."

By the time he publishes *Prospero's Cell*, Durrell has assembled not only a body of useful characters, he has, as well, begun, both in life and in art, to sketch in on the heraldic shield of his work an image to oppose the isolated snow-covered peak: he has begun to construct the image of an isolated island, Mediterranean, sun-washed, sea-stroked. As Durrell moves from place to place, the particular name of his island changes—from Corfu to Crete to Rhodes, and finally, for a few years in the fifties (1953–56), to Cyprus. But however it is used—as the subject of his trilogy of island portraits, say, or as the point of departure and return in *The Alexandria Quartet*—it retains its isolating, healing function. It becomes a place—even when it is war-torn Cyprus—for isolation from the cities in which the artist finds much of his material, a place in which the artist can compose his fragmented experience by linking it to a landscape soaked in the past, a landscape richer and older and more meaningful than his modern, chaotic one. For the Mediterranean world, "Where mythology walks in a wave / And the islands are," has entered Durrell's work in almost precisely the same way that his childhood memories of Tibet have entered it. It has given him more than a locale for his work; far more subtly—in imagery, in metaphor, in symbol—it has become an integral part of the living tissue of the work itself. It becomes in *The Black Book* the sea that drives up "night-long over one's dreams, washing, forever washing and breaking up into one's thoughts, purifying, healing, destroying," the sea that frees him from the "English death," his "pigmy history," so that he can enter at last the "heraldic universe" of art—"A latitude where even a lifeline is no good and the diving bell of the philosopher crumples with laughter." It becomes in the "Conversations with Brother Ass" chapter of *The Alexandria Quartet* the underlying metaphor which defines the artist, that artist who "finds himself growing gills and a tail, the better to swim against the currents of unenlightenment," the man who "unites the rushing, heedless stream of humanity to the still, tranquil, motionless, odourless, tasteless plenum from which its own motive essence is derived." And in *Clea* it reduces to that little spur of rock, at high tide submerged, Narouz's island, from which Clea must dive to swim among dead men, and where she must suffer that life-renewing wound that will not only transform her own art but will as well later free Darley, "on a blue day," to step into that "secret landscape," the "kingdom" of the artist's imagination.

Though we could perhaps justly say that everything in Durrell's career thrust him toward this secret landscape, it was most conspicuously in the years during and immediately after the war that Durrell began half-consciously assembling not just the imagery but the attitudes, the points of view, which were to find full development in *The Alexandria Quartet*.

For much of this time he held a series of positions which left him little chance to write. In 1939 and 1940 he was in Greece, teaching at the Institute of English Studies; early in 1941 he was in Crete; from April of 1941 until the summer of 1945 he was in Cairo and Alexandria, first as Foreign Press Service Officer and then as Press Attaché. Then came two years of work on Rhodes as Director of Public Relations of the Dodecanese Islands, a painful year's exile in Argentina as Director of the British Council Institute of Córdoba, and finally a grim two and a half years in Yugoslavia as Press Attaché in Belgrade. Even the time he spent in Cyprus as Director of Public Relations for the island government, though idyllic enough in the beginning, was, as he records in *Bitter Lemons*, more exhausting than restful; for in the years between 1953 and 1956 the island tumbled into that revolutionary violence which still troubles it.

Durrell's private life was also in these years a full, sometimes a chaotic, one. In 1940 his daughter Penelope Berengaria was born. In 1943, he was divorced from his first wife. In 1947, he married his second wife, Eve, whose recollections of Alexandria, Durrell told Miller, helped focus *Justine*. In 1955, four years after the birth of his second daughter, Sappho-Jane, Durrell and his wife were estranged. In this year, Durrell met Claude, a French writer who had also been in Alexandria and whom Durrell was to marry in the spring of 1961, and who, until the time of her tragic death on New Year's Day of 1967, was to be at the center of Durrell's life.

Durrell did, nevertheless, write—and copiously—in these years, producing island portraits, comic accounts of English and Yugoslavian diplomats, the body of his poetry (four substantial volumes), and two novels, a play, and a book of literary criticism. From one point of view, all of these were tentative trial runs—experiments with theme and technique—for the *Quartet* he would eventually produce.

The book of literary criticism—that *Key to Modern British Poetry* which Durrell assembled from his Argentine lectures—can be a helpful, though once in a while misleading, introduction to many of the most important themes he was later to develop, for in it he traces out the ideas that at the time of its 1952 publication seemed to him to be of dominant importance, not just to contemporary poetry but to contemporary man as well.

Durrell's image of reality as it is presented in his *Key* can be reduced, it seems to me, to two not altogether dissimilar landscapes—both of them founded on relativity principles—and to an implicit pattern behind both of them that may be a good deal more like an absolute.

The first of the two landscapes is, of course, the external one developed by Einstein and popularized by men like Eddington and Whitehead, a landscape oddly like Baudelaire's symbolist forest, where people watch trees watching people. For one important aspect of the relativity theory, the Principle of Indeterminacy, effectively cuts the ground out from under the neat causality of nineteenth-century science. The new physics, Durrell points out, "is founded upon the theory that we cannot observe the course of nature without disturbing it." Perhaps the most significant consequence of this theory is that it altogether changes the nature of knowledge. For when we can never

observe without to some extent corrupting the thing observed, we soon find we have to discard the notion of veri-
fiable truth. Truth, if it is to be ascertained at all, becomes
available only through a kind of intuition: we imagine
what things might be like if we weren't around observing;
we do our best to get rid of the observer's perspective!
"Under the terms of the new idea a precise knowledge of
the outer world becomes an impossibility. This is because
we and the outer world (subject and object) constitute a
whole." If we are part of a whole, Durrell insists, "we can
no longer objectify it successfully." Try as we will, we'll
never have the comfortable assurance that we see things as
they are!

The literary consequence of this notion, Durrell realizes, is momentous; for the relativity theory involves a
reorientation for the modern writer not only toward the
materials of his art but also toward himself, his audience,
his world. It shows up, Durrell contends, both in the
places in which it might be expected to appear—the plots,
say, of Joyce and Virginia Woolf, the characterization of
Gide, the poetic structure of Eliot's "Gerontion"—and also
in the places we are least likely to look for it: in symbol, in
metaphor, in incidental imagery, even in sentence structure.

Durrell works through a good deal of modern literature to document his point. But for us the most obvious
demonstration is in Durrell himself, who rather tentatively
in *The Black Book,* and then with great assurance in *The
Alexandria Quartet,* and finally in greatest intricacy in
Monsieur, creates a dense arrangement of constantly discovering, constantly qualifying observers, each of whom
distorts the scene he observes and is in turn distorted by

it. There is really no single "true" view of any of the
events offered. Only with total knowledge, Durrell darkly
suggests, could we approach such a view. With such
knowledge, of course, what we would see would be most
spectacular for, seeing everything, we would be spectators
of pure unadulterated process. Or so it would for a while
seem to us, the characters dancing through a frantic in-
terrelationship in much the same way that atoms in a bal-
loonful of hot air bound and rebound against one another.
But we would soon realize, if we were witty enough, that
the patterns we saw those atoms creating were—because
of our limited (and distorting) visions—patterns as much of
our own construction as of the atoms themselves. There
are therefore always in Durrell's fiction viewpoints casually mentioned but left tantalizingly unexplored, un-
digested "data" which, Durrell makes clear, could significantly change the "reality" of what we thought we had
finally grasped were we fully to assimilate that data. Durrell very nearly shatters the tight structures his novels
threaten always to fall into by tossing into his narrative—
preferably toward the end of a book—masses of what seem
to be irrelevant facts, characters who we are told are important but who are dismissed in a phrase, their important
actions deliberately undeveloped. A dozen pages from the
end of *The Black Book*, for instance, as the narrator explains his reasons for leaving London, a rushed paragraph
full of such data hints new arrangements of reality that had
been grasped by the narrator but that we are forbidden to
know:

I have entered into the personality of the external things, and am
sharing their influences. I skate along the borders of the daily
trivialities like a ghost, observing but withholding myself from

them. There are such things as the Banquet of the Sydenham
Cycling Club, for example, which I would write about if I were
less tired. There is Honeywoods and the vexed problem of the
drainage. There is Marney talking about getting married; and a
host of other data for which there is no room. There is Eustace,
going down, as he says, "into the valley of shadow" as his wife
has her fourth.

By the time he reaches *The Alexandria Quartet*, Durrell is
prepared to exploit information of this sort to the fullest,
drawing on it for the enigmatic "workpoints" that end *Justine* and *Balthazar*, showing us in following novels how
some of those workpoints could be developed, withholding workpoints conscientiously from "naturalistic" *Mountolive*, and giving us in *Clea* five final ones to chew upon.
Durrell uses these last workpoints, as he explains in his
general preface to *The Alexandria Quartet*, "only to
suggest that even if the group of books were extended in-
definitely the result would never become *roman-fleuve;* if,
that is to say, the axis of the work has been properly laid
down it should be possible to radiate from it in any direction without losing the strictness and congruity of its relation to 'a continuum.' "

For it is ultimately the "continuum" of Einsteinian
physics that is to act as a metaphor for the kind of art Durrell proposes for himself, the "word continuum" of *The
Alexandria Quartet* and certain of the poems reflecting not
just the way the characters of a work (its "particles") are affected by one another and by an observer, but more impor-
tantly how the events of a novel are deployed, not just in
space and not just in the "time-saturated" chronologies of
nineteenth-century fiction but in a new "space-time." For
time, Durrell believes, is "the measure of our death-con-

sciousness," and when our notions of time began to change, first under the impact of Darwin and then under the impact of Einstein, all of our ideas about life and death began to change too. Locating evidence of this change in such different works as Eliot's *Four Quartets*, Rilke's *Duinese Elegies*, and Joyce's *Ulysses*, Durrell decides that Einstein's treatment of time, not in serial fashion but rather as a pervasive aspect of the space-time continuum, forced onto our more perceptive writers a new view of life and a new form in which to express that view:

I do not think it is stretching a point too far to say that the work of Joyce and Proust, the poetry of Eliot and Rilke, is an attempt to present the material of human and supernatural affairs in the form of poetic continuum, where the language no less than the objects observed are impregnated with the new time. . . . In Proust and Joyce you see something like a slow-motion camera at work. Their books do not proceed along a straight line, but in a circular manner, coiling and uncoiling upon themselves, embedded in the stagnant flux and reflux of a medium which is always changing yet always the same. This attitude towards the material of the work has its effect on character also. Characters have a significance almost independent of the actions they engage in: they hang above the time-track which leads from birth to action, and from action to death; and, spreading out time in this manner, contribute a significance to everything about them. An article of clothing worn by a character becomes as significant as anything he does, or any drama he enacts. If there is any movement at all it is circular, cyclic, and significant only because it is repeated.

Writing these notions down in his *Key to Modern British Poetry*, Durrell blurred, as he later realized, Bergsonian time with the time-structure of modern physics. "I'm afraid I made a mistake there," he told one interviewer, "as a result of following Wyndham Lewis' *Time and Western Man* which first led me in the direction of this kind of thinking." Time in the space-time continuum was a good deal more complex than Bergson's fluid experiential time. "It only dawned on me years later," Durrell told Kenneth Young, "that time wedded to matter in the Einsteinian conjunction is not precisely Bergsonian time, because the notions of time between Plato and Bergson had not changed very much. Indeed Bergson (under whom Proust studied) said he could not understand Einsteinian time and that the continuum was an enigma to him."

The utility of the theory for the artist, however, is in its application to his work. And Durrell, at first trying to abolish time, then adapting experiential time for his purposes, and finally in *The Alexandria Quartet* "using the continuum as one of the most important cosmological formulations of the day to do a poetic dance upon, as it were," does his best to give to fiction the kind of enigmatic density that the day-to-day world has for those of us who live in it only. "If the experiment comes off," Durrell explained, "if you have all four books held in your cranium, you should get a notion of the continuum."

Durrell's progress toward the continuum of *The Alexandria Quartet* has, as I've suggested, evolved out of an initial rejection of time. *The Black Book* was written, Durrell told Miller, "to destroy time." First planned as volume one of a trilogy ("AN AGON, A PATHOS, AN ANAGNORISIS. If I write them they should be The Black Book, The Book of Miracles, The Book of the Dead"), the book turns tense into a weapon ("In order to destroy time I use the historic present a great deal, not to mention the gnomic aorist");

but its principal imagistic device to indicate the nature of
the world is precisely the one he had selected for his
"Cities, Plains and People" poem. For in that crucial later
work, "Time, the lovely and mysterious / . . . moves /
Through her swift degrees" as if those degrees were
spread out on a map. There, rivers and seas become the
"roads" on which we travel to avoid "The tidebound,
tepid, causeless / Continuum of terrors in the spirit." Dis-
tributing the time of his life over a globe similar to that
globe which balances on a man's shoulders, Durrell learns
to construct a "personal landscape," a "space" built out of
"feeling and idea" and "Within the Chinese circle's calm
embrace."

In *The Black Book*, somewhat more heavy-handedly
than in the poem, Durrell expands his "monologue of the
white road" with such a diligence that no reader is likely
to miss its symbolic importance—though many readers are
likely to have trouble calculating *what* it symbolizes. But
then, perhaps, like Yeats and Eliot, we should agree that
symbols are most meaningful when least allegorical. Having something to do with the "fatal world" which frames
itself in windows, "the long concrete road" seems always
doomed to have its snowy "pure white nap . . . gouged
and muddied by the rubber lips of the buses, the carts, the
feet of the ants." Many of the characters of the novel, as
Tarquin in these passages, look down that road in search
of other characters—in this instance the gigolo Claire—
only to see undesired figures, Lobo, for example, "in di-
minishing perspective on the roads."

Lobo, a Latin sensualist caught in mysterious London,
may be Durrell's most road-minded citizen. Perpetually
working over an "enormous parchment chart of South Lon-

don," Lobo dreams of Lima while "clambering his suburban girls like a powder monkey," dreams of Peru and finds
instead "dust, the eternal dust along the highroad." Like
Elizabethan dust, Lobo's highway dust has realms of secondary association: " 'I go along the road, pure as a Catholic, then I see a woman look at me and . . .' "

Lobo thinks his road is sensual. But to those who observe him it becomes something less neatly definable. One
of those observers is Gregory, a character who appears
conspicuously in *The Black Book*, but never in person.
Gregory, a character like many in *The Alexandria Quartet*,
Tunc, Nunquam, and *Monsieur*, survives in the pages of a
vanished person's "papers," in this instance a diary written in ominous green ink, though its subject is death and
though the narrator reads it in the dead of snow-draped
winter. To "Death Gregory," dedicated as he is to recording the spiritual deaths of those about him, the road, or at
least the railroad, has something to do with the way men
find themselves committed to paths frequently unconge-
nial and altogether arbitrary:

It is a fancy of mine that each of us contains many lives, potential
lives. They are laid up inside us, shall we say, like so many rows
of shining metals—railway lines. Riding along one set toward the
terminus, we can be aware of those other lines, alongside us, on
which we might have travelled—on which we might yet travel if
only we had the strength to change.

Gregory's observations lead in turn to those of the narrator, who neatly brings us back to Lobo's map:

If I reflect on our individual and collective funerals, here in the
Regina Hotel, running side by side in the snow in a chronology

which has nothing to do with time—for it has forfeited time for the living limbo—then I am forced back to a picture of Lobo sitting over his chart, his fingers busy, while Gregory watches from a chair. . . . As for the chart, it is the final symbol of this annihilation. . . . There is a transition from that place to this, where I sit and watch Lobo work at the map he will never finish. But it is immediate. The connecting links have snapped, or been burst into pieces. I live only in my imagination which is timeless. Therefore the location of this world which I am trying to hammer out for you on a blunt typewriter, over the Ionian, is the location of space merely. I can only fix it with any certainty *on the map.*

Other roads, however—if only briefly and at night—can free themselves from the map to carry the narrator not only out of London but out of his introspective agony. For, driving his car at a breakneck pace down the "great arterial road," he finds fragmented passionate instants of communion with the woman who waits for him on the snow-covered landscape: "Our lives stop here like a strip of cinema film. This is an eternal still life, in the snow, two crooked bodies, eating the second of midnight and sniveling."

But in spite of its release of passion, the "great arterial road" which leads out of London takes the narrator only a short way on those "immense journeys of discovery" which in his imagination he constructs, journeys which lead out from the day-to-day chaos of the world, a world which progressively "becomes less integral, less whole," toward something intangible, unattainable, toward something desperately desired, "toward the inaccessible absolute."

Travel on this plane, however, is accomplished, when it is, on an unmapped landscape. In most instances, that landscape seems to be the internal one explored by Freud and Jung and Adler, that landscape which Durrell sets up in the *Key to Modern British Poetry* as the private, internal complement to the public, external landscape of modern physics—both of them landscapes, Durrell arguing, similar in that their components are all caught in the interrelationships of a relativity scheme. Even the language with which we must discuss both landscapes demonstrates a kind of relativity: We measure good by evil, evil by good, "and the same with all the other opposites." Language itself, therefore, is for Durrell, as he explains in his *Key:*

built upon what seems to be a dualistic foundation. . . . If the opposites are identical then statement is a relative affair, not, as our great-grandfathers thought, an absolute affair. . . . This question of the inherent duality in things, and an acceptance of it as part of the human limitation, you will find both in the relativity-view and later when you come upon the term "ambivalence" in Freud.

For Freudian discoveries can offer us, as private citizens, "a new territory inside ourselves in which each one of us who is seeking to grow, to identify himself more fully with life, will feel like Columbus discovering America."

Most of Durrell's roads lead, therefore—as most good roads should—in two directions. His characters move vaguely forward along them in an almost meaningless clock-time; but simultaneously—unconsciously, sometimes half consciously—their minds drag them, over and over again, back along the paths they have walked, back toward that "innocent beginning" which each of them somewhere experienced. In *The Black Book*, Lobo returns nightly in his dreams to lost Peru, the narrator to a "Tibetan village" vivid, like that Tibetan village of "Cities, Plains and People," on its white mountain.

Balancing on the fulcrum of his two identities, man corrupts his internal landscape in much the same way that he corrupts his external one. Internally, however, the necessary distortions which he makes serve strangely to put him in touch with the world rather than to hold him off from it. The mountains, gates, and rivers of his obsessive dreams and daydreams arrange themselves into what Jung called archetypal patterns—man's secret means of ordering the accidental imagery of his life into a useful design. More satisfying than those he imposes on his external world, these internal patterns offer man roads on which he takes some of his longest journeys, those which lead him beyond the limits of self and into the mythical kingdom of the collective unconscious.

It is no accident, therefore, that the word *journey* echoes and re-echoes through *The Black Book,* and subsequently through everything Durrell writes. Certainly it is no accident that in the final pages of *The Black Book,* the internal and the external journeys—the one backward and the one forward, the physical and the mental ones— fall together. As the narrator sets off from London toward Greece, his mind rushes backward, defining the two directions in which his road runs:

This is the theme of travel whether the towns whirl by me under the moon, or whether I am at my deal desk in the Commercial School. Thule, ultima Thule. There is a stepping-off place—a little Tibetan village, stuck like a springboard in the side of the mountains. There are no friends to see us off: our banners, our catchwords, our heroism—these things are not understood here. The natives have other criteria. Beyond us the passes open like flowers in the setting sun, the delicate gates of the unknown country's body, the Yoni of the world, luteous, luteous, unbearably lonely. Is the journey plural or am I alone? It is a question only to be answered at the outposts. I will turn perhaps and find a shadow beside me. No tears can scald the snow, or the malevolence of the white peaks. I can invoke no help except the idiotic squeaking of the prayer wheel. We move softly down the white slopes, irresistible as a gathering landslide, toward the last gaunt limit of flesh. Now we have nothing in common but our clothes and our language. The priests have stolen the rest as gifts for God. The ice under our hoofs aches and screeches, murderous as the squeegee. This is the great beginning I planned for so long.

Geographers of landscapes significant as this one, Durrell's characters are perpetually setting off for adventures in mountains (*White Eagles*), in caves (*The Labyrinth*), and, most frequently of all, in mirrors (everywhere in Durrell, but most conspicuously in *The Alexandria Quartet* and the three novels that follow it).

Seeking reality in the relativity of the external and the internal worlds, many of these adventurers come to physical or spiritual grief. Reality, for them, is, in the echoing word of a central character in *Monsieur*, "precarious." Once in a while, however, by a never very carefully explained mystical leap, Durrell's characters find themselves suddenly swept beyond the limits of internal and external landscapes. Suddenly they confront a cosmology, the "heraldic universe," utterly unlike anything in the ego-dominated universe of modern physics or modern psychology; for this strange territory is trustworthy, not "relative," intangible, unalterable, perpetually valid. If it bears a likeness to any landscape of modern science, it may in some ways bear a likeness to that one described by Groddeck in *The Book of the It*. Groddeck, as Durrell points out in his

Key, has set up a theory about a pervasive but insubstantial life-force (the It) which not only antedates the ego but which, in fact, brings it into being. In Groddeck's scheme, this life-force It creates a fiction—the ego—which in turn, in order to explain itself, must invent the opposed fiction of an external intangible force, the It. "I am not concerned with your belief or disbelief in Groddeck's hypothesis," Durrell told the no doubt baffled Argentinian students of modern British poetry for whom he had written the lectures that became his *Key:*

I am concerned to show that so-called rational methods have finally led us to dethrone the "ego," to seek in it the source of our malorientation to the world of reality—the unknown It outside. . . . Groddeck's ego-It polarity is a brilliant rationalization of the Eastern mystic's position—who seeks to free himself from the opposites of being, and to emerge into Reality.

In search of this mystical reality—a reality behind that of the phenomenal world—Durrell's most valiant heroes set out on journeys more extraordinary even than those paced off by the giants of modern physics and modern psychology. "Above all there is the journey," Durrell's narrator of *The Black Book* observes. Recognizing that neither the journey across the face of the globe nor the journey into the face in the mirror is ultimately satisfying, he determines to set out "in the direction of the quest." His quest may be, he has to admit, "in the wrong direction." It is, in fact, literally directionless: "There is only trial and error on a journey like this, and no signposts." If it reaches a destination, that destination will have to be something beyond the ego, even beyond the world: "The end is somewhere beyond even Ethiopia or Tibet: the land where God is a yellow man, an old philosopher brooding over his swanpan." His quest—by way of art—will be into the heraldic universe that exists beyond time and space. For this man, the work of art becomes nothing more than an extraordinary springboard. From it he will be catapulted into a reality both extreme and universal: "Art must no longer exist to depict man, but to invoke God," the questor of *The Black Book* exclaims. "It is on the face of this chaos that I brood."

This theme of the quest, as Eve Zarin has brilliantly demonstrated, is at the core of most of Durrell's serious work. Like the medieval quests of Arthurian legend that underlie Eliot's *Waste Land,* Durrell's quests involve almost always a ritual journey across water either to or from a sick land ruled by an ailing monarch. (Piers, the character in *Monsieur* who finds both reality and existence itself precarious, had once begun a set of speculations about the nature of "his own coming death" by writing " 'A Water-biography' because he was astrologically a fish sign!") In many variants of the myth, the sickness is both physical and spiritual. When Durrell sets up his parallel designs, we should therefore expect him to fill out his picture with a whole host of wounded men and women, with medical doctors, with psychologically twisted characters, and with psychoanalysts. And, of course, he does. Wounds, in fact, both spiritual wounds and physical ones, bulk almost as large in Durrell's scheme of things as mountains, islands, and roads. Should we add them to our heraldic shield?

One of the functions of the wounded characters is redemptive. For the sight of wounded men can lift the self-centered hero out of his own solipsism and into com-

munion with other men. His flood of tender concern—
something altogether different from pity—can, in the long
run, save not only the wounded person he must deal with
but—both Durrell and ancient legends suggest—the
wounded land itself. In some of the medieval romances,
the quest ends in a question. (Medieval writers had no
more difficulty than we do in recognizing that the two
words spring from one common root.) The hero makes a
public sort of gesture; he asks the wounded man: "What's
wrong with you?" After the question has been asked, the
waste land can burst into bloom. Spring can defeat the
desolation of winter. Though in Durrell the question is
never so explicitly phrased, the implicit concern for others
does bring an end finally to the winter death of *The Black
Book* and to the private anguish of—to name only a few of
the most conspicuous figures from *The Alexandria
Quartet*—Darley, Clea, Balthazar, Nessim, Amaril, and
even, perhaps, Justine. And though the gestures of affection which end *Clea* can hardly be said to end World War
II, the end of that war is coincident with the "recovery" of
all of the principal characters. At its most extreme, compassion even for the artificial woman in *Nunquam*, a "living"
compound of plastic and wire and computerized "mind,"
helps heal the observing, manipulating scientists who
create her, believe in her, and finally are unable to control
her. The tender concern for the junk that once had been an
imitation woman forces, finally, Felix Charlock from the
solipsistic neurosis that had dominated him early in that
work and earlier yet in *Tunc*. Able in the end to love, he is
also able to realize that the "precarious" moment is every
moment. "So it will be either/or once again; it will be now
or never."

Most frequently, however, Durrell turns, not to a Parsifal-like figure, but to a model closer to home, a man considerably more of a questioner than a questor: Hamlet. Lurking in the background of *The Black Book* and very much in the foreground of " 'A Soliloquy of Hamlet,' " that long poem compounded from fourteen fourteen-line sections, Shakespeare's character may first have attracted Durrell because of those hesitations and doubts associated with his definition of that "undiscovered country from whose bourne no traveller returns," a country that—with the proper squint of an eye—fairly suggests a heraldic universe. But to understand how Hamlet approaches that country, or for that matter how his alter ego in Durrell's novel does, we must learn a travel technique spelled out by Durrell in his Hamlet poem: we must learn how to "Walk upon dreams, and pass behind the book." And to accomplish this dexterous passage, we must become adjusted to reading poems and novels that seem always to go in circles.

Durrell's Hamlet poem is a sterling example of such a circling thing. Setting up in the opening lines of the first of the fourteen sonnets an image of the spherical world ("the curve of the embalming winter"), Durrell carefully continues the line of his curve through section after section, until in the fourteenth and last one he can complete it by pointing out "I bend a sonnet like a begging-bowl." This earthly circle of world and art has, moreover, a heavenly counterpart—"the sweet spherical music" of the grand design itself. Nothing in Durrell is quite so simple, however, as any examining critic can make it. The everlasting circle is, for instance, bisected by a whole host of temporal verticals—the hands of a clock, candles and crosses, pens, finger bones, and phalli—all imagery appropriately associated not only with this mortal life but specifically with the various kinds of big and little deaths that in one way or another end it, and so send us catapulting back into natural process. Amused by such neat machinery, Durrell probably hoped we would notice that the opening words of a significant line in the third sonnet are "O I" and that the last two lines of the tenth sonnet and the first two lines of the eleventh begin respectively with O, I, I, and O. (And is it accident or a trick of memory or a deliberate echo that years later Durrell will nickname *Nunquam*'s artificial woman Io, and throughout that book play games with her name?)

But this is only machinery. The route by which each *I* escapes the *O* of this world, Durrell suggests, is through private pain ("This pain goes deeper than the fish's fathom"), a pain that acknowledges personal mortality ("I kneel at the keyhole of death's private room / To meet His eye, enormous in the keyhole") but that miraculously overcomes private death through human sympathy. Able finally "to dance upon the void," Durrell's Hamlet figure steps into the heraldic universe of "the fabulous lion," propelled perhaps by that "mercy" which he carries with him "like a berry bright."

But it is another figure that the Elizabethans had dredged up from a medieval world who provides Durrell his most conspicuously "heraldic" breakthrough. That figure is, of course, Marlowe's *Dr. Faustus*.

Durrell's version of the Faustus legend, *An Irish Faustus*, seems in its early scenes almost imitatively similar to its model. Marvelously ranting speeches pile on top of each other, and the sorts of materials Marlowe used so well—alchemical experiment, wonder-working magic spells, sinister forces of evil—are robustly employed by a group of larger-than-life grotesques: hermit, madwoman, priest; innocent, sinner, devil. (Durrell even tosses in a bloodsucking vampire!)

But Durrell's organizational scheme is really much closer to the one he had used in *The Alexandria Quartet* than it is to Marlowe's play, for Durrell projects his plot forward by a series of inventive reversals: in each of them we see a significantly different Faustus. Only by the end of the play do we become aware of the fact that Durrell's real object has been the demolition not just of Marlowe's medieval Faustus or even of the medieval world, but the demolition of the medieval frame of mind which had invented a Faustus in the first place.

Durrell achieves this end through irony rather than through direct assaults on our emotions. For Durrell's Faustus, we soon learn, differs most conspicuously from Marlowe's in that he is not really a practitioner of black magic at all—that sort of meddlesome activity has been given up years before the play opens—but rather an urbane moral philosopher, Margaret's gentle, good teacher. Even though he knows all of the dark texts and even though he has in his possession that very useful magical device, a ring of transmuted gold that could be used to bring him all knowledge, Faustus' only concern is to lead a simple, quiet life.

Carefully playing irony against irony, Durrell intrigues, teases, and surprises us as he contrasts what we know about the Faustus legend with what, he argues, we ought to know about the real, flowering world around us.

What seems to be the crowning irony is achieved after
Faustus' ring has been stolen and, with Mephisto's collaboration, recovered. Faustus, at last fully alerted to the
danger of its power, determines to destroy it. And in a
splendid scene, detail after detail meticulously reversing
the last act of *Dr. Faustus*, Durrell's Irish hero first tempts,
then tricks, and ultimately drags a protesting Mephisto
back into the fulminating, brimstone-belching jaws of that
hell of elemental process from which Mephisto had first
emerged! Even then, however, the ironies do not end. For
Faustus returns from what he had expected to be Hell, his
hair white and his clothes burned beyond recognition. But
he looks twenty years younger than on the evening before,
when, ring in one hand and Mephisto in the other, he had
entered the pit. Because more has been destroyed in those
elemental flames than clothing, a ring, and a cross that
Faustus had assumed would protect him against chthonic
powers. Faustus' illusions have also been destroyed. He
has been both purified and, to his surprise, educated. For
experiencing first fear and then despair, he had in that
throbbing world found himself at last suddenly transported beyond such private emotions to an acceptance of
the design of things: "I found myself laughing. / For the
first time I knew I was in reality." And though Durrell's
Faustus does not use the term *heraldic universe,* we who
are adjusted to it in the rest of Durrell's work should have
no difficulty in realizing that it is that universe which has
opened up before him:

                                                    I saw
    The whole Universe, this great mine of forms
    For what it is—simply a great hint. . . .

> Yes, I saw it all so clearly for the first time from
> There.
>
>   .   .
>
> I have never felt so happy, such relief.
> It's as if my whole life had become a sort of vestige.
> Somehow I must refresh it and renew it.
> You know, I think I shall go on a long journey.
> I want to see the world again through these new eyes.

His journey, as he explains to a character in the penultimate scene, is to be "Anywhere. Nowhere." He is, he says, "taking a long journey / In any direction at all." But as I have already indicated earlier, and as we could with no difficulty have guessed from the context of Durrell's other work, his journey is to be vertical rather than horizontal. He travels up a winding road into the snow-covered mountains, there to join three old friends—Matthew, his teacher; Martin, a manufacturer of fake relics; and Mephisto, who, wearing a mask feature for feature identical to Faustus' face, reports that snow has blocked all of the passes. Comfortably provided for in Matthew's log hut, the four friends settle down to a game of cards before the long winter sets in.

Each of these friends, we suspect, has come to a vision similar to Faustus', but it is Matthew, once teacher and now hermit, a man prepared to face that death which he knows will overtake him before another spring, who helps Faustus understand precisely what had happened in Hades. For what had happened was "nothing, absolutely nothing." And that Faustus realizes the significance of that non-event is, Matthew makes clear, the culmination of his education:

. . . for when nothing begins to happen at long last Everything
Begins to cohere, the dance of the pure forms begins.

No man comes quickly to knowledge of this sort. For
years, Matthew explains:

> The central plan eluded me.
> From my own vantage-point in time,
> I saw it only as a man might imagine
> Joining a quiet company of holy fishermen,
> Dotting a river-bank—each one intent
> To spool out time and capture the great
> Leviathan, eternity; what I did not know
> Is just how busy all this nothingness can be.

It is Faustus' arrival exactly when he is needed—in the
winter of the old man's death—that helps Matthew see
"with wonder"

> the circle slowly being completed,
> The unhurried curvature of process.

Driven by the grand design itself—"the moments fused
and intersected suddenly"—Faustus comes on the scene
when he must, just in time to pick up from his old master
"the slender thread" of wisdom. For in the design of
things "the order is invariable"; nature "knows what it is
doing."

Though *An Irish Faustus,* published in 1964, seems in
some ways the neatest summary of the images and themes
that dominate the uncollected works of Lawrence Durrell,
the fullest development of those images and themes is, of

course, in *The Alexandria Quartet*. And though all of their rich interrelationships cannot be demonstrated, something at least of their structure can be hinted.

When I had earlier tried to compress *The Alexandria Quartet* into a phrase by describing it as the extraordinarily complex, expanding study of the emotional education of a hero and his friends, I was not so much attempting to define the novel as to insist on some of its most basic elements.

Its complexity is, I suppose, obvious; and, as Durrell makes clear in his headnote, it is deliberate. The work is laid out carefully in Durrell's up-to-date geometry, the first three sections constructing for us a three-dimensional "solid" Alexandria, while the fourth, adding the dimension of time, should enable us to see the book—if we are willing to see in such a fashion—as a kind of "objective correlative" for the experience of a space-time continuum.

Durrell is careful to keep this structure constantly before his readers; and he is equally careful to keep before them the similar relativity-pattern discovered by modern psychoanalysis. We are therefore always aware in Durrell's book that both external and internal "truth" is constantly being modified by its observer (who is in turn modified by it).

Durrell is sometimes heavy-handed in his treatment of these relativity motifs. (Mirrors and masks obtrude so much as to be conspicuous; and the letter-writing device, as Miller pointed out in a long letter to Durrell—itself perhaps the most penetrating critical comment yet delivered on the *Quartet*—threatens sometimes to get out of control.) But it may be that in order to enjoy later subtleties, later delicacies, we need the heavy-handedness. You could write a whole book on the importance of the obvious! Yet the obvious and its importance are sometimes missed by supersubtle minor novelists and major critics. Durrell never makes this mistake. He realizes, for example, that many of the early intrusive remarks of *Justine*—glaringly functional in a second reading of the *Quartet*—serve, the first time round, as absolutely necessary guideposts for the reader who otherwise might well be bewildered by the structure of the world he is about to enter. Less than a dozen pages into the first book and barely introduced as a character, Justine spells out for that reader what he must not miss. She sits in front of a dressmaker's "multiple mirrors" and speculates on the art of the novel: " 'Look! five different pictures of the same subject. Now if I wrote I would try for a multi-dimensional effect in character, a sort of prism-sightedness. Why should not people show more than one profile at a time?' " This is clearly a case of author forcing dogma into the mouth of one of his characters. Nevertheless we must have explicit statement of this sort if later we are to be able to accept the brilliant variants Durrell's characters will play upon it. We need, for example, to have precisely this statement somewhere in the backs of our minds if we are properly to respond to Darley's reflections on the nature of reality in the second book of the *Quartet*. Trying to piece together the meaning of Balthazar's interlinear, Darley calls into question the nature and the utility of truth itself:

The really horrible thing is that the compulsive passion which Justine lit in me was quite as valuable as it would have been had it been "real"; Melissa's gift was no less an enigma—what could she have offered me, in truth, this pale waif of the Alexandrian littoral? Was Clea enriched or beggared by her relations with Jus-

tine? Enriched—immeasurably enriched, I should say. Are we
then nourished only by fictions, by lies? I recall the words Balthazar wrote down somewhere in his tall grammarian's handwriting: "We live by selected fictions" . . .

We need both Justine's early statement and this one of
Darley's to coalesce back there in our unconscious if a casual remark of Justine's in the last book, Clea, is properly to
achieve its literary function. In that book mirrored images
from Justine transform themselves gracefully into Balthazar's fictions. Justine is once again speaking to Darley:
"We are after all totally ignorant of one another, presenting selected fictions to each other! I suppose we all observe each other with the same immense ignorance." For
none of the millions of mirrors of the world—or the millions of possible points of view available to a writer—
present truth, though all mirrors and all points of view
present reality of a kind. Truth, as this world knows it, is
finally, Darley realizes, something which can be discovered only in relationship:

I . . . saw that lover and loved, observer and observed, throw
down a field about each other. . . . Then they infer the properties of their love, judging it from this narrow field with its huge
margins of unknown. . . . I had only been attesting, in all I had
written, to the power of an image which I had created involuntarily by the mere act of seeing Justine. There was no question of
true or false. Nymph? Goddess? Vampire? Yes, she was all of
these and none of them. She was, like every woman, everything
that the mind of a man . . . wished to imagine. She was there forever, and she had never existed! Under all these masks there was
only another woman, every woman, like a lay figure in a dressmaker's shop, waiting for the poet to clothe her, breathe life into
her.

If mirrors present to us distorted images of a single face, that single face presents its own distortion to the mirrors. And when it moves away from mirrors, it freezes into something fixed, immobile, deceptive. Reality, in Durrell's major work, becomes in fact something very much like a masked ball—with the masks nothing less than our own false faces and those false faces we project onto the faces of all men and women around us. The difficult trick for the novelist in this sort of carnival atmosphere is to find a way of revealing the kinds of "realities" each of his major characters observes—and also as many as possible of the "selected fictions" which that major character uses to disguise the poverty of his irresolute and private self.

Durrell's solution is a little like Gide's in *The Counterfeiters* or Faulkner's in *Absalom, Absalom!:* a storyteller finds variant accounts of what ought to be a single story. Later on, in *Monsieur,* a novel as much about the nature of fiction as it is about the nature of reality, so many characters are other character's "fictions" that Durrell amuses himself and some of his readers by tacking on at the end of the book a genealogy of its fictionalizers, himself, presumably, the D. who heads the list: "So D./ begat/ Blanford (who begat Tu and Sam and Livia)/ who begat/ Sutcliffe/ who begat/ Bloshford . . ." etc., etc., etc. In *The Alexandria Quartet,* Darley's initial version of a set of events is corrected by Arnauti's *Moeurs* and by the diaries of Nessim and the false diaries of Justine; these versions are in turn corrected by Balthazar's interlinear; that interlinear is corrected by the objective history of events in *Mountolive* and by a number of sets of letters, most significant of which are those between Leila and Mountolive, Pursewarden and Mountolive, and Pursewarden and Liza.

Finally, time itself offers a shifted perspective; and in *Clea*, the one novel that moves forward in time, each of the central characters is allowed the opportunity to reexamine and reevaluate his past and the pasts of the group of wounded survivors from the first three books.

For just as *Justine* is most conspicuously the book of mirrors, *Balthazar* the book of masks, and *Mountolive* the book of intrigue—the first two volumes offering private false faces and the third offering the public false faces of political action—*Clea* must take its place, it seems to me, as Durrell's book of wounds, the damaging but in a way life-giving wounds that strike through all of the false faces to the quick body beneath and that can be healed only by proper questions, proper concerns for others, such as those we find displayed in the tenderness of human affection. There are of course wounds, as there are mirrors, masks, and intrigues, through all four books; in one way or another, hardly a character in the *Quartet* escapes disfigurement or death. (Think of the crowds of blind or half-blind figures alone: from one-eyed Hamid, through one-eyed Scobie, one-eyed Capodistria, and one-eyed Nessim, to totally blind Liza and the whole host of minor figures—blind servants, sheiks, and priests—who fumble through the novel.) But in *Clea*, the education of the hero and his friends begins to bring rewards as well as penalties. Proper questions (not: "What can you do for me?" but instead: "What can I do for you?") begin to accomplish nearly miraculous cures, and some, at least, of the wounded are not only restored to health but actually transformed—given a new and fuller life—thanks to apparent disaster. The virtuous Semira, complete with the nose designed for her by Clea and fashioned for her by Amaril, dances triumphantly before the affectionate assembled Alexandrians; and Clea herself—cured by Amaril of her troublesome virginity—is freed, tenderly, to cure not just anyone but the bankrupt and broken doctor, Balthazar, who must finally wound her and, aiding Darley, bring her with rough tenderness back to life. Minor characters also experience a similar transformation: the journalist Keats turns into a Greek god when he questions the nature of war and discovers simultaneously that " 'Even the dead are overwhelming us all the time with kindnesses.' " And who is not pleased to discover that Scobie, though battered to death in his Dolly Varden, is tenderly ("How much the city misses him") elevated to sainthood and then, thanks to Nimrod's delicate, ironic hint, saluted by his murderers, "the boys of H.M.S. Milton," with a fine display of naval fireworks.

For it is, in the long run, only tenderness that illuminates for an instant the solipsistic darkness, that lonely, terrible darkness that had dominated *The Black Book* and into which all of the major characters of *The Dark Labyrinth* had briefly, at least, plunged. Yet it is also onto this darkness that the more perceptive of Durrell's major characters see projected the crucial figures of a private "heraldic universe." It is no accident, therefore, that Darley discovers his limitations as an artist precisely when he discovers the illusory nature of the universe he must attempt to represent. ("It was life itself that was a fiction— we were all saying it in our different ways, each understanding it according to his nature and gift.") And it is also no accident that at this painful moment fictive Clea, "all tenderness," drops the mask of her reserve to step out of her fictional world and, in a transparent interval, join Darley in that bright world where, restored, he will be able to function. It is here, too, in the last book, that the reader, if he has been attentive, will recall that passage from *Baltha-zar* in which Pursewarden has set down for Clea the plan for his own "last volume":

I feel I want to sound a note of . . . affirmation—though not in the specific terms of a philosophy of religion. It should have the curvature of an embrace, the wordlessness of a lover's code. It should convey some feeling that the world we live in is founded in something too simple to be overdescribed as cosmic law—but as easy to grasp as, say, an act of tenderness, simple tenderness in the primal relation between animal and plant, rain and soil, seed and trees, man and God.

If tenderness—an "utterly merciless" tenderness res-cued from sentimentality by the distancing power of irony—is the primary lesson in the "emotional education" the questing central characters experience, they learn their lesson most frequently from painters and from writers, also wounded—and some of them healed—in their efforts to transmit a vision of the elemental processes, those pro-cesses that constitutute the very design of life.

The book, in fact, is overrun with artists of one kind or another. For in addition to the professional writers and painters—Arnauti, Pursewarden, Darley, Keats, and Clea—there is a battalion of casual diarists and Sunday painters, most conspicuous among them Nessim, Mount-olive, and Justine. And behind all the fictional characters are the flesh-and-blood writers and painters of the flesh-and-blood world. For not only does Durrell allow Purse-warden to give a quick two-page survey of English litera-ture, he also has the audacity to set him corresponding

with D. H. Lawrence! Some of the characters in the novel
have also known Cavafy, the poet whose poems about
Alexandria provided Durrell parallels important to the action of the novels, subtle, ingenious, and psychologically
accurate. And Sir Louis, Mountolive's senior in Moscow, is
permitted, after his retirement to Italy, both to meet Claudel and to pass on to Mountolive one of Claudel's diplomatic stories! Like the living landscape, living and recently deceased "real" writers ground the book in reality
and feed their truths to the fictional artists and writers who
live only in the novel.

　　And the artists and writers in the novel feed on each
other, identify with each other, merge into each other.

　　By offering us this collection of interrelated artists and
writers, Durrell has left himself open to the sort of criticism reviewers are fond of making: Durrell becomes his
own protagonist. The problem, however, is more complex
than that; for not only does Durrell play games with his
reader by assigning his own initials to Darley, but he also
goes on to assign his own ideas to several of the other
writers and painters. Reviewers, easily confused, find this
confusing. And to some extent they are justified in being
confused. Pursewarden, for example, seems, in some ways,
the real author-identification figure. He is by far the most
intelligent person in the book; and he is even made the
author of a novel famous for an asterisk that refers to a
blank page! He seems, therefore, just right as "author" of
Justine, for in the one-volume edition of the *Quartet* Durrell carefully places an asterisk in the next to the last sentence of the body of the text ("Does not everything* depend on our interpretation of the silence around us? So
that . . ."), and then in his note ("See page 196") refers

the reader to the only blank page of the book. Shades of *Tristram Shandy!* Yet Pursewarden, for all his likelihood as "author" of *Justine*, is unfortunately killed off halfway through the *Quartet*, and Darley himself survives until the last page where, putting pen to paper, he writes, "Once upon a time."

But I think we should not really be misled by Pursewarden's inventive asterisk, and I think we should not be seriously troubled by the whole problem of author-identification. (An author is, I suppose, never one of his characters but rather the sum of them. And so far as Pursewarden is concerned, if a model need be found for his ideas, that model is as likely to resemble Henry Miller as it is to resemble Lawrence Durrell.) Within the novel, Pursewarden's function seems obviously to be less author-spokesman than teacher. Like Faustus' teacher in Durrell's play, Pursewarden passes on the "slender thread" of wisdom to Darley. He also has much the same function that another one of the *Quartet*'s teachers, Clea, has: he shows Darley not just how to see, but what to see; and he suggests one method—the ironist's—for capturing those figures of the "heraldic universe" who, like Capodistria's homunculi, scramble, desperate for love, out of their life-sustaining fluids into the thin air of the artist's "real" world.

For love, as Pursewarden explains in his long ironic, "imaginary" dialogue with Darley, is finally what makes— the only thing that makes—the world go round. And the great book—when it is written—"will be characterized," he goes on to say, "by a *total lack of codpiece.*" It will strip us, if not to the bone, to the flesh that drives the bone and it will present, without editorializing, the enormous variety of love: "I mean the *whole bloody range*—from the little greenstick fractures of the human heart right up to its higher spiritual connivance with the . . . well, the absolute ways of nature, if you like." Such a book, Pursewarden argues, might allow us to "rediscover in sex the key to a metaphysical search which is our *raison d'être* here below."

And though the *Quartet* is not quite the book Pursewarden visualizes—perhaps Miller's two trilogies come close to it—it is a book that does explore in the right way the right territory. For its range is very wide: from rape to homosexual passion, from child prostitution to narcissistic masturbation, from the unrequited love of Narouz for Clea to the tender exchanges of Clea and Darley, from the random skirt-chasing of Pombal to the intricate incestuous relationships of Liza and Pursewarden, and the suppressed, but just as real, incestuous quadrangle set up by Leila and Nessim, Mountolive and his mother. Durrell's project is, if you want, mere presentation, not judgment. And it has for that reason perhaps incensed those readers who feel clear lines always must be drawn between what for each of them is "good" and what for each of them is "evil" and that the novelist's lines must be their lines of demarcation. Durrell's scheme of course forbids this sort of public moralizing. But yet his unjudging presentation does achieve a kind of moral end: if it neither praises nor condemns, it does reveal to us significant landscapes of the human heart.

So ambitious a project, though it may eventually reduce the world, as Pursewarden suggests, to boy-meets-girl, involves, before that reduction is accomplished, each of the world's boys and girls in extraordinarily complex designs of affection. To turn again to the physicist's metaphor, it involves each figure of the novel in a "field" of emotional entanglement. This field, radiating out from each character, in intricate ways distorts the "fields" set up around each of the other characters. No figure, therefore, is uncomplicated. Justine, for example, is caught in a tangle of loves—wife of Nessim, former wife of Arnauti, mistress of Darley and Pursewarden, lover of Clea; she is also obsessed by her childhood experience of Capodistria's rape and by her passionate desire to recover her child. Yet she experiences sexual passion only when it can be coupled with political intrigue! Virginal Clea is in some ways more complex still; for, involved in the affair with Justine, she is loved by Narouz, loves Amaril, is freed by him to love Darley, and is loved by Keats. Melissa, given so little personality as to seem at times merely an object, is nevertheless involved in her own tangle of love: for, mistress to Cohen and to Darley, she sells herself for one night to Pursewarden and bears a child by Nessim. Yet each of these lovers—pair them up as we will—sees not even the false face his beloved presents to him! He sees only something he projects onto that false face: "If you can't do the trick with the one you've got," Pursewarden tells Justine, "why,—shut your eyes and imagine the one you can't get. Who knows? It's perfectly legal and secret. It's the marriage of true minds!"

Yet, if in Durrell's world *everything* admits impediment to the marriage of true minds, Durrell does suggest in his imagery of interacting fields of personality, a world not strictly private, a world which, though misunderstood by each person in it, can be understood by an outsider in terms of the interactions of those persons. And beyond persons, the impersonal operations of the "fields"—internal and external—seem not altogether unlike that process which is the busy happening of "nothing" within the liberating cosmology of the heraldic universe!

Sometimes the machinery of Durrell's huge novel creaks. Clea's reading lips through a telescope seems to me farfetched. And I think Durrell is guilty of a failure in invention in the last book, when he has to have Scobie imitated by three different characters. Yet in spite of occasional gasps and grunts, the machinery does finally present us a landscape essentially believable, a believable landscape on which believable characters, mired in time, struggle—not only with each other but as well with themselves—toward a tender acceptance of things as they are.

"It is not peace we seek but meaning," Durell writes halfway through "The Reckoning," a poem composed about ten years after the *Quartet* was published. In the last line, however, he qualifies that aphoristic truth: "It is not meaning that we need but sight." "Precarious," truth—like reality—balances opposites and miraculously reconciles them. Sight and insight, at least in Durrell's fiction, become conjoined.

RUBIN RABINOVITZ

Iris Murdoch

Iris Murdoch writes fiction and teaches philosophy. A category—philosophical novelist—seems ready-made for her, but Murdoch does not feel that she is a philosophical novelist in the sense that a writer like Sartre is. Her aim, she says, is to keep academic philosophical concerns from intruding on her novel writing; she is certain that her books would suffer in quality if they became merely fictional illustrations of philosophical principles.

Nonetheless, ideas do creep into Iris Murdoch's novels. One of Murdoch's greatest interests, in the classroom as well as in her philosophical articles, is ethics; and ethics is certainly the legitimate concern even of the non-philosophical novelist. Her fictional characters often find themselves in moral dilemmas, hard put to discover a solution because they are believers in faulty ideologies. These ideologies, which include the ethical aspects of most contemporary philosophical schools, are subjected to a more formal attack in Murdoch's philosophical articles. This, then, is the most obvious link between the artistic and academic sides of her career.

Iris Murdoch's academic career, both as student and as instructor, brought her to Oxford. She first came there in 1938, after finishing secondary school. She studied classics at Somerville College and in 1942 took a First in "Greats." In the next four years she worked for the British Treasury and for the United Nations Relief and Rehabilitation Administration; here she had a chance to do active work with war refugees. She won a scholarship for study in the United States in 1946, but was denied a visa as an ex-Communist; instead she spent the year in London, reading philosophy, and won a studentship to Newnham College, Cambridge, where she continued her studies in philosophy. In 1948 she returned to Oxford as a fellow of St. Anne's College and a tutor in philosophy; she kept this position until 1963 when she became an honorary fellow of St. Anne's and a lecturer at the Royal College of Art. She still lives in a small village outside of Oxford with her husband, John Bayley, an English literature don at New College.

Many of these experiences have been incorporated into Iris Murdoch's novels: the UNRRA work, for example, provided some of the background for her second novel. Perhaps because she is Irish (she was born in Dublin in 1919), her only novel with a historical setting, *The Red and the Green,* describes the Irish rebellion which occurred just before her birth. Though many other details which reflect her life and interests crop up in her novels, she has, in the novels she has published so far, avoided writing a university novel or even using an extensive academic setting which might suggest her life at Oxford. This is possibly still another aspect of her resolve to keep her novel writing apart from her interest in academic philosophy.

Murdoch's first published book was not a novel but a philosophical study, *Sartre, Romantic Rationalist* (1953). This work, intended as an introduction to Sartre's thought, deals with his novels and political writings as well as with his philosophy. Though she feels that Sartre is a philosopher of great importance, especially because of his influence among contemporary thinkers, the most interesting parts of Murdoch's book—and those which tell the most about her own ideas—are the objections she put forward to some aspects of Sartre's philosophy.

Sartre, Murdoch says, derives many of his ideas from Descartes and Hegel; this, perhaps, is a reason why she calls him a romantic rationalist. Sartre and his fictional heroes, says Murdoch, begin in the tradition of Descartes who, suspecting the reality of all objects he perceived in the universe, found that only the truth of his own existence could not be challenged. But unlike Descartes, Sartre does not believe in the dualism of mind and body, nor does he accept Descartes's metaphysical arguments leading to a proof in the existence of God. At this point Sartre, with a monistic, historical outlook, comes closer to being a follower of Hegel. An emphasis on the factors of isolation and utter dependence on self, Murdoch feels, has caused a strong tendency toward subjectivity in the philosophical followers of Descartes because of a concentration on the Cartesian *cogito ergo sum.*

The problem with *cogito ergo sum* is that the man who utters it becomes too obsessed by the *sum* of the formula. Sartre, according to Murdoch, carries this strain of subjectivity to the point where he is almost solipsistic. This inordinate preoccupation with self causes the Sartrean man to abstain from contacts with things outside of himself. The greatest loss for the Sartrean hero, Murdoch feels, is the diminished effectiveness of his contact with other human beings.

Sartre's idea of interpersonal relationships, says Murdoch, is a more subjective version of the "master and slave" situation in Hegel's *Phenomenology*. A lover, according to Sartre, constantly speculates about his beloved's attitude toward him; the result of this sort of speculation is torment. Each lover demands that he be imaginatively contemplated by the other; but because of human loneliness and the poverty of the human imagination these needs cannot be satisfied and the result is continual frustration. Such a description may have a certain amount of psychological veracity, but ultimately it is incomplete. It denies the day-to-day experience of being in love; it is no more, says Murdoch, "than a battle between two hypnotists in a closed room."

From her analysis of Sartre's views Iris Murdoch's own philosophical position begins to emerge: she has a more objective view of the universe than the Sartrean existentialist and, indeed, distrusts the Cartesian *cogito* precisely because it can undermine a position which insists on the reality of things outside the self. Objectivity is also the key to Murdoch's idea of love: it is in the suppression of subjectivity and through the recognition of the objective existence of other people that love begins. Sartre's ideas on extensive moral self-analysis lead to still another danger of subjectivity: too much self-examination can end in total preoccupation with oneself. The idea recurs in

Murdoch's novels: moral excellence and love come with the observation of others, moral shallowness and neurosis are the result of self-attention. She would disagree most with a point like the one Sartre makes in *Huis-Clos:* "l'enfer, c'est les autres." People are hell to one another only when they refuse to observe and love one another.

Her comments on Sartre are similar to Murdoch's criticisms of existentialism in general. Only a few of the religious existentialists have managed to avoid the weaknesses of Sartre's position: she mentions Simone Weil and Gabriel Marcel, and one could probably safely add Martin Buber to this list. These philosophers, it may be noted, do not stress the subjective element which Murdoch feels is implicit in the Cartesian *cogito*. At the same time they would be more reluctant than Sartre or a Hegelian thinker to reject dualistic or metaphysical ideas. As will be seen, Simone Weil especially has been a great influence on Murdoch, even in her fiction.

Iris Murdoch's objections to existentialism and her affiliation with Oxford have led some critics to assume— wrongly—that she is a follower of the English linguistic analysts. In fact, Murdoch has often criticized the ideas of her colleagues. The linguistic analysts, she feels, hold too mechanistic a view of human behavior; this brings them close to determinism. The method of the linguistic analysts is based on a careful logical examination of statements; error, they feel, creeps into language when meaningless, illogical, or indefinable concepts are unwittingly used. To avoid error, it is necessary for each speaker to examine the statements he hears or utters and weed out these meaningless concepts. This means, says Murdoch, that the primary responsibility for determining the reality of the events which occur around him rests with the individual person and that the individual person (and not the outside world) is the primary center of reality. This encourages a subjectivity in the method of the linguistic analysts which Murdoch feels is similar to the weakness of the existentialists who stress the Cartesian *cogito;* both schools, she says, share "a terror of anything which encloses the agent or threatens his supremacy as a center of significance. In this sense both philosophies tend toward solipsism."

An even more serious charge which Murdoch levels against logical analysis is that it has been especially weak in the area of ethics. As she explains in a recent philosophical work, *The Sovereignty of Good* (1970), one of the words which the linguistic analysts feel is indefinable is "good"; G. E. Moore called the attempt to define the word "good" the "naturalistic fallacy." Moore's followers were unable to develop a meaningful ethical system based on linguistic analysis; they were satisfied with admonitions about sincerity and everyday reasonableness. This is a mediocre ethical position, in Murdoch's view.

Because of their weaknesses in formulating an ethical position, neither the English nor the French philosophical school, Iris Murdoch feels, has developed a valid ideological approach to politics. After a brief period as a Marxist, Murdoch left communism in the Stalinist era and now describes her position as unilateralist, liberal, and pro-Labour—a position which might be inferred from a careful reading of her novels. She is aware that many existentialists and linguistic analysts share her political views, but she is unhappy that these views are held more as individual opinions than as the logical outgrowth of a philosophical system.

Iris Murdoch had reached a philosophical position from which she could discern the shortcomings both of logical analysis and of existentialism by 1953, when she published her book on Sartre. Before this, however, she had been somewhat attracted to existentialism. Though the logical analysts were very influential at Oxford when she studied there, Murdoch seems never to have been particularly sympathetic to their views. It was while working in Brussels for UNRRA immediately after World War II that she first became interested in contemporary French philosophy. Later, visits to Paris heightened that interest: discussions in sidewalk cafés, the songs of left-bank nightclub singers, the appearance of the city itself—all seemed to enhance the purely philosophical aspects of existentialism. Murdoch even met Sartre, whom she remembers for his patience with youthful questioners.

For Murdoch, the rejection of existentialism seemed like part of the maturing process; she once said afterward that she had outgrown existentialism. Moreover, she was growing at the same time as a creative writer. Before publishing any fiction, Murdoch had written and destroyed five novels. The sixth novel she wrote, *Under the Net*, was the first she felt was worth preserving, and it was published in 1954.

Jake Donaghue, the hero of *Under the Net*, is similar to the protagonist of a *Bildungsroman:* the novel gives the details of Jake's spiritual education. Moreover, his path to maturity is marked by experiences which give the novel an autobiographical tinge. Jake is a former member of the

Young Communist League turned Labourite; a judo expert; an Irishman who has seen little of Ireland; an experienced London pub-crawler; and a frequent visitor of Paris.
All of these elements recall details from Murdoch's own
history. Jake, after doing translations of Jean Pierre Breteuil, decides to become a creative writer; this is reminiscent of Murdoch's own early work on Jean-Paul Sartre and
her later decision to publish her novels.

Murdoch's main interest in Sartre was as a philosopher; Jake, however, appears in the opening pages of the
novel as one who has much in common with the heroes of
Sartre's novels. He is self-involved and subjective, even
solipsistic: on the third page of the novel Jake says of a
friend, "I count Finn as an inhabitant of my universe, and
cannot conceive that he has one containing me." This, as
Murdoch certainly knows, is very close to the classical
statement of the solipsist. Just as Roquentin, the hero of
Sartre's *Nausea,* is disgusted by the meaninglessness he
observes in his walks around Bouville, Jake finds that the
contingency in some parts of London is nauseating. Sartre
also hates contingency; Murdoch has translated Sartre's
concept of nausea as "horror of the contingent."

There are other hints of Sartre in *Under the Net.* Breteuil, whose novels Jake translates, is an echo of the names
of the principal characters in *The Age of Reason:* Brunet,
Mathieu, Daniel. Jake is in love with a girl who sings in
Parisian nightclubs, like a Sartrean *chanteuse;* her name,
Anna Quentin, recalls the hero of *Nausea,* Antoine
Roquentin. Jake's quest for Anna throughout the novel is
perhaps symbolic of his emulation of Sartre's heroes. Like
those heroes, he avoids binding relationships with other
people in an attempt to preserve his freedom; ponders the

differences between self-explanation and self-dramatization; and even receives messages in Parisian cafés. As A. S. Byatt has shown in her book on Iris Murdoch, the last scene in *Under the Net*, when Jake outlines the details of his coming life as a creative writer after hearing Anna sing on the radio, is parallel to the last episode in *Nausea*. There, Roquentin makes a similar decision after listening to a jazz singer. By the end of *Under the Net*, however, Jake has learned to accept contingency; his maturity consists in the renunciation of the subjective, Sartrean elements in his character and the acceptance of an artistic discipline. This is again parallel to the beginning of Murdoch's period of artistic maturity, coming as it did after her infatuation with existentialism.

In addition to the material relating to Sartre, there are other elements in *Under the Net* which have philosophical overtones. The most obvious of these is the portrayal of Dave Gellman, a teacher of philosophy. Dave is a linguistic analyst: he places a high premium on oral communication, weeds out Jake's "nonsense" statements, and believes that clear, practical rules are of more value in morality than lofty abstract notions. As Dave types an article for *Mind*, a philosophical journal, he glances in a mirror and examines his hands. One critic, Peter Wolfe, says that this is an allusion to G. E. Moore, who in "Proof of an External World" described a similar process; Anthony Quinton, however, thinks that Murdoch's reference is to an article by her friend D. F. Pears. In either case, contemporary English philosophy is no more Jake's cup of tea than it is his author's; Dave is a friend of Jake's, but not an intellectual influence.

The character whom Jake finds most influential is

Hugo Belfounder, the pacifistic son of a munitions maker, who manufactures fireworks and produces movies. Jake is impressed by Hugo's insatiable desire to learn the theory behind particular processes and his refusal to attempt to find an underlying general theory which would unite these particular theories. For example, Hugo can spend hours questioning Jake about the problems of a translator; but he is unwilling even to discuss the possibility of applying what he has learned to a more general theory of thought or of existence; he refuses absolutely to associate himself with any philosophical school. This is in opposition to the position of the Sartrean hero, who, nauseated by the formlessness of reality, seeks to discover some underlying rational principle to alleviate the messiness of existence.

Hugo is also interested in the problems of human communication. When people speak, he feels, most of what they say is in some way a falsification of reality; the few truthful statements which may slip through are so pale and undramatic in comparison to the lies that the truths are rarely noticed. The Sartrean hero, in this situation, burrows deeper into himself, attempting to discover the reality which he has falsified; the linguistic analyst goes through sentence after sentence weeding out the tautologies and nonsense statements. Hugo's solution is simpler, if more drastic: he will be silent. People talk too much anyway, he feels, and he experiments with fireworks and silent movies.

Hugo's ideas about silence, as Iris Murdoch herself has disclosed, come in part from Ludwig Wittgenstein's *Tractatus Logico-philosophicus*. The *Tractatus* is divided into seven sections, and the seventh consists of only a single sentence: "What we cannot speak about we must pass over in silence." Wittgenstein regarded the *Tractatus*—and perhaps philosophical discussion in general— as a necessary evil, as something to be dispensed with once an understanding of reality has been achieved. His propositions, he said, would be understood as nonsensical by one who used them to attain a higher understanding of reality; at that point they could be disregarded. Wittgenstein also uses the image of the net, or mesh; the net, he says, represents the picture of reality we construct to describe the world. Each different system for describing the world (like, say, a mechanistic system) could be represented by a particularly patterned net (having, for example, a triangular pattern) which enclosed the same surface as any other net. This image is used by Hugo when (in the role of Annandine, a character in a philosophical dialogue) he says that in the analysis of any single human decision all attempts at theorizing and generalization are essentially falsifications of the particular, individualistic nature of that decision. Theorizing—ideas, concepts, language—constitutes an impassable net, barring us from understanding the essential reality of a single human situation. Each situation, Hugo says, is "unutterably particular"; however hard we may try, we can never "crawl under the net."

In addition to ideas, Hugo has many personal characteristics which resemble Wittgenstein's. Arriving at Cambridge just after Wittgenstein had left, Iris Murdoch must have found him a mysterious and elusive character; Hugo is portrayed in similar fashion. Just as Wittgenstein's disciples often garbled his philosophy, Jake's book *The Silencer* and Anna Quentin's mime theater are both imperfect attempts at translating Hugo's ideas. Hugo, like Wittgenstein, has an honest, forceful personality coupled with a quiet kindliness. Both had worked as mechanics, lived with sparse furniture, gave away great sums of money, tamed birds, and had an omnivorous appetite for diverse types of information. As Murdoch once said in an interview, she admires an expression Wittgenstein often used: "Let's see," an expression not just of curiosity, but of love. A similar expression of willingness to examine each particular situation without theorizing symbolizes Jake's maturity at the end of *Under the Net*. Speaking about his future plans to Mrs. Tinckham, Jake says, "Well, we'll see." The oracular Mrs. Tinckham replies, "That's always the best thing to say, isn't it, dear?" Jake has grown up and accepted the contingent world.

In addition to the elements in the novel reminiscent of the *Bildungsroman*, *Under the Net* is in some ways in the tradition of the picaresque novel. This is not because, as some critics have suggested, Iris Murdoch has an affinity for her contemporaries, Kingsley Amis and John Wain. As Murdoch has acknowledged, Jake is modeled after Samuel Beckett's Murphy and Raymond Queneau's Pierrot; two books of Jake's that are mentioned early in the novel are *Murphy* and *Pierrot mon ami*. Jake's adventures with the canine film star, Mr. Mars, recall Pierrot's animal friends, especially Mésange, an ape. His name may also allude to Jupiter, a dog in Queneau's first novel, *Le Chiendent*. Jake, like Murphy, has an enjoyable time working as a hospital orderly; the hospitals in both novels are described in terms of church architecture; the people who work in Jake's hospital, "the Pid" and Stitch, are reminiscent of Bim Clinch and other hospital workers in *Murphy*.

Each of these novels has wildly humorous scenes arising from grotesque or improbable situations.

Despite Iris Murdoch's literary and philosophical borrowings, *Under the Net* is an extremely original novel. All of the allusive elements are subservient to the general framework of the book. Most of the novel deals with Jake's mistakes about people. He thinks that Sadie loves Hugo, that Hugo loves Anna, that Breteuil will never write a good book, that Finn will never return to Ireland. In every case, the opposite turns out to be true. People try to tell Jake how they feel, but he imposes his own theories on their comments; he refuses to listen, to see people as they are. Jake's errors lead to the comical situations which, along with concise, accurate characterizations and amusing background descriptions, are the most successful elements in *Under the Net*.

An inability or a refusal to see people as they really are is a trait of many of the characters in Iris Murdoch's second published novel, *The Flight from the Enchanter;* but here the misunderstandings lead to tragic rather than humorous consequences. In this novel Murdoch deals with refugees—with people who are spiritually as well as geographically uprooted. In addition to drawing on her firsthand experiences with refugees as an UNRRA worker after World War II, Murdoch shows the influence of Simone Weil in this novel.

One of the important themes in Simone Weil's books is that suffering and uprootedness do not necessarily ennoble the afflicted person. It takes a Christlike saintliness to rise above one's suffering; most of the victims of affliction sink into spiritual lethargy; afterward they become afflicted with self-hatred and even participate in their own degradation. Simone Weil says in *The Need for Roots* that uprootedness is the most dangerous malady threatening human society because it is self-perpetuating; if the uprooted person does not succumb to his own lethargy he becomes an active agent in the uprooting of others. Slaves, war refugees, and assembly-line factory workers are some of Simone Weil's examples of uprooted people.

The war refugees who appear in *The Flight from the Enchanter* are uprooted in Simone Weil's sense. Jan and Stefan Lusiewicz (who work in a factory) victimize others, notably Rosa Keepe, one of the few Londoners who befriend them. This illustrates another idea of Simone Weil's: that the uprooted often strike out first at those who attempt to reduce their suffering. A dressmaker, Nina, and the mother of the Lusiewicz brothers are two refugees who represent the other alternative Simone Weil mentions, spiritual lethargy; Nina finally commits suicide, and her thoughts before death echo Simone Weil's comments on the state of mind of the uprooted.

The chief cause of uprootedness is power, usually military, financial, or bureaucratic. In *Gravity and Grace*, Simone Weil says that the rich and powerful man cannot recognize his own wickedness toward those whom he oppresses, since both he and his victims begin to believe that power makes the oppressor superior to the oppressed. "The powerful," she says, "if they carry oppression beyond a certain point, necessarily end by making themselves *adored* by their slaves." Since the thought of being the absolute plaything of another human being is horrible for the slave, he substitutes devotion for obedience, he pretends he does willingly what he has been forced to do. This fawning state corrupts the soul of the slave and also fools the master, who thinks that the devotion is genuine.

Freedom from slavery, rather than freedom in an abstract or philosophical sense, is an important theme in *The Flight from the Enchanter*. Mischa Fox, a rich and powerful man, is the enchanter of the title; like Circe, he captures and transforms those whom he enchants. Almost every important character in the novel is in some way in Mischa's power; Nina and Calvin Blick are his absolute slaves. Like Nina, Calvin is a victim of spiritual annihilation; Mischa, he says, killed him years ago. Calvin spends his time doing Mischa's dirty work. Blackmail is his specialty; he is one of the uprooted who uproots others. Nina, in Weil's sense, adores Mischa, as do the other women in the novel who willingly make themselves his slaves.

In the exercise of power, the master suffers as well as the slave. Simone Weil points out that the man with a lust for power can never achieve that for which he longs the most: to dominate other humans completely. The knowledge that his domination is only partial causes him to seek to extend his power and increase the number of the people he has enslaved; but since the master cannot wholly dominate his new slaves, he is again frustrated, setting up a destructive cycle in which master and slaves are both victims. In the story of a power struggle (Simone Weil mentions the *Iliad* and Shakespeare's history plays) the true villain is power itself. This may explain why, in *The Flight from the Enchanter,* Mischa is presented not as a villain but as one who pities those who suffer and even suffers himself.

Power is a dominant theme in this novel. Factory workers are an "enslaved group of machine minders"; the Lusiewicz brothers, first Rosa's slaves, enslave her; Annette Cockeyne puts herself into her brother's power, but gets a sense of freedom from the knowledge that others (like Nina, the dressmaker) must work for her. Rainborough joins SELIB, an UNRRA-type organization for the rehabilitation of war refugees, because he thinks he will soon be in a powerful position; instead he becomes the pawn of his secretary. The result of all of these struggles is affliction, and only the word "suffering" is more recurrent than the words "power," "master," and "slave."

Many of the slaves in the novel enter into servitude voluntarily; seeking love or affection, they readily submit to domination. Iris Murdoch uses the word "enchantment" to describe the process by which potential slaves fool themselves into thinking they seek love and not domination. The Lusiewicz brothers cast a spell over Rosa as they sit in a bedframe which is an enchanted enclosure. Hunter, Rosa's brother, and Annette are also victims of spells. The great enchanter in the novel is of course Mischa, and Murdoch constantly uses images of magic and enchantment in describing him.

Another set of images used in association with Mischa comes from the legend of the Minotaur. This theme begins on the first page of the novel: Annette dislikes the passage in Dante's *Inferno* where the Minotaur is shown suffering in hell; it was not his fault, she feels, that he was born a monster. Here Murdoch introduces the idea of innocent suffering which is so important throughout the novel. Later Mischa emerges as a Minos figure: a rich and cruel king, demanding the annual sacrifice of lads and maidens to avenge an old grievance. His sprawling London house is like the palace of Minos at Knossos: underneath the resplendent main story is a dark labyrinth. In its heart is the

Minotaur, Calvin, developing dirty pictures to be used for even dirtier purposes. The candidate for Theseus in the novel is the appropriately named Hunter. But Murdoch is not a writer to be bound by myths; when Hunter confronts Calvin in the darkroom it is without the help of an Ariadne, and it is Hunter, not Calvin, who is defeated.

The person who could perhaps have helped Hunter, and from whom many other characters in the novel seek help, is Rosa Keepe. At first it seems as if she is a true humanitarian. Like Simone Weil, who worked in the Renault factory, Rosa takes a factory job because, as Hunter puts it, "she wants to be in touch with the People." Rosa is a namesake of Rosa Luxemburg, a founder of the German Communist Party who was murdered in 1919; in *Oppression and Liberty* Simone Weil cites Rosa Luxemburg as one of the sources of the "aimless merry-go-round" idea, the idea that oppressor and oppressed are both enslaved by a power greater than themselves which sets up a destructive, frustrating cycle.

Rosa Keepe, then, seems to have the credentials of a liberator, and many of the characters in the novel who are about to fall under Mischa's spell look to her for help. Murdoch makes it clear that it is possible to elude Mischa: the women on the board of *Artemis*, a liberal magazine edited by Hunter, resist Mischa's takeover attempt; and Rosa herself, once in love with Mischa, managed to free herself. Throughout the novel, however, Rosa fails to help those who appeal to her.

Iris Murdoch sees Rosa's weakness as a failure of love. Love, according to Murdoch, is a human relationship in which one person apprehends his fellow as an equal; by intently focusing his attention on another person, the lover

begins to understand that all of the individuality, complexity, reality which he feels he possesses himself similarly
exist in another person. Love is imperfect when this equal-
ity is absent; if the lover sees himself as being either
above or below the object of his love, the result is a
master-slave relationship. One achieves balanced love
through attention, a term Murdoch borrows from Simone
Weil. Attention consists of the accurate apprehension of
another person's reality; this is why the word "see" is so
often important in Iris Murdoch's fiction. Opposed to attention, as slavery is opposed to love, is fantasy, an imperfect type of observation in which a person imposes his
own preconceived image of the beloved on the real one.
One who fantasizes falls in love, not with a real person,
but with an imaginary person whom he himself has created, with a part of himself; fantasy, then, is a form of self-
love. A person who wishes to enslave another is adept at
encouraging fantasies; he tailors himself to fit the fantasies
of the potential slave until he achieves domination. This is
enchantment; the slave is trapped by his own fantasies as
well as by the spell cast by the enchanter.

   Calvin Blick sums up Rosa's state of enchantment at
the end of the novel. "You will never know the truth, and
you will read the signs in accordance with your deepest
wishes," he says, "I have done nothing for you and your
brother but provide you with rather grotesque pretexts for
doing what you really want to do. The truth lies deeper,
deeper." His remark is similar to a comment of Simone
Weil's in *Gravity and Grace:* "If we go down into ourselves we find that we possess exactly what we desire."
This is Rosa's problem, as it was Jake's in *Under the Net;*
she creates the false reality she desires through fantasy

and can never perceive the deeper truth. Moreover, Rosa enjoys having a sense of power over those who love her, like Peter Saward and the Lusiewicz brothers; with those who appeal to her for help she is inattentive. Immersed in herself, she realizes only when it is too late that both Hunter and Annette needed her help. The immediate cause of Nina's suicide is her fear of being deported from England. Her problem is one that Rosa could probably have solved; yet on three different occasions Rosa carelessly refuses to hear Nina out. It is with justice that Calvin implies that Rosa is partly responsible for Nina's death.

Rosa's great weakness, an unwillingness to observe the people around her, is again a fault of a number of the characters in Iris Murdoch's next novel, *The Sandcastle*. Published in 1957, a year after her marriage to John Bayley, and dedicated to him, the novel appropriately deals with the problems of married life. *The Sandcastle*, however, is not autobiographical: the married couple in the book, Bill and Nan Mor, have two teenage children. The marriage is on the verge of disintegration; Mor submits too easily to his wife's domination and Nan, unobservant, underestimates Mor's capabilities. Here, on a more modest scale than in her other novels, Murdoch returns to the themes of insufficient attention and the master-slave relationship.

Nan, according to her husband, does not bother to understand that other people might be very different from herself. This is certainly true, but Mor has a similar flaw. Nan, having gained the upper hand in the marriage, forces Mor to crawl back to her after they quarrel; she begins to respect him less and less. Mor is strong in other spheres, however; as the most popular and respected teacher in a secondary school with a weak headmaster, Mor also enjoys wielding power.

As might be expected, the Mors feel their children drifting away from them and are at a loss to explain the reasons. As they go their separate ways, the children indulge in seemingly harmless pursuits which are frightening to their parents and harmful to themselves. Donald Mor likes mountain climbing; he perceives that risking his life is a way of attracting his parents' attention. In a crucial scene in the novel he hangs perilously from the spire of the school where he is a student and Mor a master. This act is both a rebuke to his parents and a plea for love. It is significant that Donald is saved because of the quick thinking of a student whom Mor had previously underestimated. Felicity, Donald's sister, is left by herself for a good deal of time; she has imaginary conversations with supernatural creatures and comes to believe that she is psychic. Magic, as in *The Flight from the Enchanter,* can be destructive; Felicity's fantasies help to make her more self-involved and unloving.

The action in *The Sandcastle* begins with the arrival of Rain Carter, a portrait painter. She has been commissioned to do a portrait of Demoyte, the retired headmaster of the school, whom Mor admires, unlike his weak successor. Mor, a frequent visitor at Demoyte's home, gets to know Rain, and eventually they fall in love. Rain is sympathetically portrayed. Though she is encouraged by both Mor and Demoyte to feel scorn for Everard, the inept headmaster, she perceives his kindly qualities as a human being. Similarly, she refuses to be rushed in her painting; the truthful quality of a portrait, she feels, can only emerge after long and patient observation. Her portrait is, in this respect, a success: looking at the painting Mor feels as if he is seeing Demoyte for the first time. The accuracy and truth of the portrait enable Mor to see Demoyte with a new compassion.

Accurate, objective observation, then, is as important in a work of art as it is in a human relationship. Rain says to Mor, while she sketches him, "Exactly as you are is how I want you." This idea is echoed by Bledyard, the school's art master. The great painter, he says, is one who can humble himself enough in the presence of the object which he paints to show that object as it really is.

This approach to art, an aesthetic counterpart to her ideas about ethics, is one which Murdoch has often expressed in her philosophical writings. In "The Sublime and the Beautiful Revisited," for example, she discusses the problems of the novelist in the same terms that Bledyard and Rain Carter explain the role of the painter. For a novelist, says Iris Murdoch, the greatest test is the extent to which he shows an awareness of others; he must portray his characters without permitting his own personality to intrude on the objective description he attempts to present. "Art is not an expression of personality," says Murdoch, "it is a question rather of the continual expelling of oneself from the matter in hand." Great art must be completely impersonal; that artist who manages best to eliminate his personality from his works is the one we admire the most.

Murdoch does not care much for romantic art; it is almost always too self-involved. The great nineteenth-century novelists, however, were more objective; writers like Jane Austen and George Eliot have truly permitted their characters an independent existence. The very best

writers—Murdoch mentions Homer, Shakespeare, and
Tolstoy—have managed to eliminate themselves entirely
from their works; as a result their characters emerge with a
vividness, a clarity that no other writers can match. This
view, incidentally, is shared by John Bayley, Iris Murdoch's husband; in his critical study *The Character of
Love*, Bayley praises the nineteenth-century novelists
whose memorable characters are the result of an objective,
loving approach.

Twentieth-century fiction, Murdoch feels, has de-
clined because it has produced few characters who are
portrayed as well as those of the nineteenth-century novelists. Murdoch has divided modern fiction into two groups,
the crystalline and the journalistic novels. Crystalline
novels are quasi-allegorical, often poetic, and deal with
general human truths rather than with specific characters;
The Stranger of Camus is an example. The journalistic
novel is quasi-documentary, large, shapeless, and usually
deals with a contemporary institution or a historical topic;
Simone de Beauvoir's *The Mandarins* is such a novel. The
crystalline novel is too neurotic, solipsistic, and isolated.
The journalistic novel lacks creative vitality and is too concerned with masses of people, as opposed to individuals.
Though Murdoch feels that crystalline novels are somewhat superior to journalistic novels, both categories produce fiction that is inferior to that of the last century.

Murdoch's emphasis on the importance of the portrayal of characters in fiction is of course related to her
willingness to link ethics with aesthetics, the good with
the beautiful. In "The Sublime and the Beautiful Revisited" she begins with a critique of Kant's aesthetic ideas.
Murdoch dislikes Kant's idea of the sublime and the beau-

tiful because it reveals a horror of the raw, messy, contingent aspects of nature and yearns for an underlying perfection, for formal order. This need for perfection is also a
weakness in romantic as well as in Symbolist art. As Jake
learned in *Under the Net,* one must give up theorizing and
pattern-seeking and accept contingency. Murdoch does ap-
prove, however, of Kant's idea that the beautiful is somehow analogous to the good.

The desire to connect art and ethics, especially when
it is expressed in the dictum that literature must be moral,
is a prevalent tendency in modern English aesthetic
theory. Murdoch does not go so far as critics like T. S.
Eliot and F. R. Leavis, however; she does not insist on an
overt moral core in a work of art. Too much emphasis on
morality in art can lead to didactic art, and didactic art,
aside from being dull and uninspired, is art which begins
with a pattern and does not present a contingent view of
reality. The link between art and morality, for Murdoch, is
more subtle and metaphysical: a writer must love his characters and cause the reader to love and understand them
too. A reader who has observed this process in a novel will
then be able to cultivate an analogous apprehension of
people in his daily life.

It is a weakness of Murdoch's theory that it can be
applied successfully to tragedy and fiction and not so well
to comedy and poetry. Murdoch anticipates this objection
with a claim that tragedy and nineteenth-century fiction
are the high points of Western literature. When applied to
painting, her aesthetic ideas (like Plato's theory of art) are
far less satisfactory; one may insist on loving apprehension
in a portrait, but how is loving apprehension to be distinguished from photographic realism in a still life or land-

scape? There is no use in even attempting to apply Murdoch's ideas to abstract painting or to music, and, wisely, she is silent on these topics. Murdoch also spends too little time explaining why writers who are extremely self-involved—Joyce, Proust, Dostoevsky—manage to succeed in spite of their subjectivity. Using Murdoch's own fiction as an example, one would expect *The Sandcastle*, containing fewer autobiographical elements than either *Under the Net* or *The Flight from the Enchanter*, to be the best novel of the three. But this book lacks the intensity and vividness of her first two novels, and a lack of subjective elements may even be one of the causes of the failure of *The Sandcastle* to involve the reader.

The ultimate resolution of these problems may be in remembering that Murdoch dislikes airtight, logical theories; since she is a metaphysician she may feel that there is no need to define what is essentially inexpressible. She cites with approval Tolstoy's comment that art is the religious perception of the age. If religion can be defined as a rational set of principles which appeal in the end to metaphysical or transcendent ideas, then Iris Murdoch can be called a religious novelist in this sense as well as in Tolstoy's more metaphorical sense. As she said recently, the attempt to look compassionately at another human being gives one a sense of transcendence, a feeling that "there is more than this." This transcendent feeling must remain a tiny spark of insight, if it is not to be corrupted by "some sort of quasi-theological finality." The transcendent spark of insight is the same, she says, as the feeling we have when we stand before a great work of art.

As can be inferred from her comment about quasi-theological finality, Iris Murdoch does not care for religion in any formal or organized sense. The function of religion, she feels, is to provide a sort of middle ground between morality and a mystical belief in transcendent goodness. The failure of modern religion lies in its failure to fulfill this role. Theology has been debased in various ways: by those who become overly involved in dogma and useless precepts; by those who present an overly mundane and unmystical picture of transcendent reality; and of course by those rationalists who have completely eliminated all traces of mysticism from their theologies.

Iris Murdoch, raised as a Protestant, now calls herself a Christian fellow-traveler; she is sympathetic to many ideas in Christianity but unable to accept it in its complete and formal version. Unlike so many philosophers who believe in a transcendent reality, she stresses this belief without insisting on the existence of God. If there is a God, she has said, He is transcendent, perfect, nonrepresentable, and, as the chief source of goodness, a focal point for human attention. "God, if He exists, is good because He delights in the existence of something other than Himself." Here one can see, in addition to the influence of Plato and Simone Weil, the recurrence of Murdoch's central concept of attention and love for others. Unlike Simone Weil, Iris Murdoch stresses goodness more than religion; the question of God's existence may be left to the individual believer. If God does exist, however, one of His chief functions is to act as an epitome of that sort of goodness which resides in the love of beings outside oneself.

Iris Murdoch deals with many of these religious questions in *The Bell* (1958), a novel about the disintegration of a lay religious community, Imber Court. The community

has been founded by Michael Meade on his family estate,
which adjoins an Anglican-Benedictine convent; Meade
and the others at Imber hope to make it a retreat from secular life which will draw spiritual nourishment from the
nearby convent.

The collective failure of the community is made up of
a series of failures on the part of its members. These failures, as the wise Abbess of the convent remarks, are all
failures of love; and on a greater scale, in the world at
large, they are analogous to the failure of most established
religious systems. Two great enemies of love, Murdoch
says, are convention and neurosis, and many of the people
at Imber suffer from one or the other. Mrs. Mark Strafford
illustrates convention in its lowest sense: constantly fuss-
ing about rules and about what is correct, she has mis-
taken propriety for holiness. James Taypor Pace, formerly
a military officer, lives by the rules in a different way. Morality for him is like a series of orders which must be followed without question or compromise, and for a while
this seems to be a successful approach. Finally, however,
the inflexibility of the rules proves to be a barrier to love:
after Michael Meade is involved in a homosexual incident,
Pace speaks to him without the compassion which might
prevent further mishaps. Meade is an offender; he has broken one of the rules.

Michael Meade represents the other barrier to love,
neurosis. Neurosis, in Iris Murdoch's terms, is an excessive involvement with oneself which heightens any tendency toward inner sickness; and it does this while mas-
querading as a cure. Michael is given to self-questioning
and self-exploration; he nurses his guilty feelings; in a ser-
mon he delivers to the community he urges the residents

of Imber to become more immersed in themselves. This self-involvement prevents Michael from looking outside himself to those who appeal to him for love. Michael's difficulties are compounded because of his sense of destiny— a rejection of the contingent. Again and again, as Michael is about to make a decision, his destiny seemingly interferes, causing him to choose the more attractive, if morally inferior, alternative. By the end of the novel Michael finally learns that his sense of pattern and destiny is a product of, as he puts it, his "romantic imagination." A. S. Byatt, who similarly interprets Michael Meade and James Taypor Pace as representatives of neurosis and convention, goes a step further: Michael, says Byatt, is similar to the neurotic Sartrean hero and James lives by the ordinary moral rules of the logical empiricists. This certainly seems plausible, and the moral failures of these two characters are related to what Murdoch feels are the failures of the respective ideologies they represent.

The failure of love is a problem of the other characters at Imber Court. Catherine Fawley, in love with Michael, confuses him with Christ and decides to become a nun; her repressed sexual feelings blossom into religious hysteria. A convent is no place for Catherine, and at the end of the novel she is still recuperating in a hospital. Her brother, Nick Fawley, is a victim, one of the afflicted in Simone Weil's sense. As the Abbess says, Michael, with the right sort of love, could help Nick; but Nick (like Nina in *The Flight from the Enchanter*), after countless appeals to Michael go unanswered, commits suicide.

Along with these permanent residents at Imber are a few recent arrivals. Toby Gashe, a young engineering student, wants to spend the summer at Imber before entering

Oxford; protected by his youthful innocence, he survives the collapse of the community. Paul and Dora Greenfield come to Imber because Paul, an art historian, is interested in some medieval manuscripts there. Dora arrives after Paul: his violent, assertive character frightens her, and she had already left him for a while before the action of the novel began. When she returns to him at Imber, Paul's tyranny again undermines their love; at one point he tells Dora that he is in love with her, but doesn't respect her. This, in the light of Murdoch's definition of love, is a flat contradiction.

In conventional terms, Dora is a very ordinary person: not overly brilliant, attractive, holy, or even neurotic; most of the residents of Imber ignore her or view her superciliously—Mrs. Mark Strafford, for example. But early in the novel Dora shows her innate goodness; in rescuing a butterfly trapped in her carriage of a train, she loses her suitcase. She has forgotten about herself, her possessions; turned her attention to another living thing; and in doing this defied convention. Her husband views this incident as a typical example of her stupidity. Dora's simple goodness presents a contrast to Michael's involuted quest for spirituality, and she emerges, with Michael, as one of the central characters in the book.

With so many in the novel actively engaged in spiritual searches, Dora, without seeking, is the only one to have a true mystical experience. It is significant that she has this experience when she is away from Imber: at the National Gallery, looking at pictures she knows well, she sees them suddenly on a higher plane, with respect, understanding their reality and perfection. When she articulates the idea that the pictures are something real outside herself, the "dreary trance-like solipsism" of her earlier mood disappears and tears come to her eyes. This experience is a fictional counterpart of the glimpse of transcendental reality which Iris Murdoch says, in her philosophical writings, is to be found in great art. Dora feels spiritually rejuvenated afterward; but, on her return to the stifling atmosphere of Imber, this feeling is dissipated.

The spiritual strength of the nuns in the abbey is based on the same quality of loving respect which Dora learns, but the nuns, much wiser than Dora, have much more strength. Occasionally they reach out to help the people at Imber, as when Mother Clare helps to save Catherine from drowning or when the abbess advises Michael. But Michael rarely heeds the advice he receives, and Catherine, saved from suicide, suffers a mental breakdown afterward. The last time that the Abbess appears in the novel she tells Michael that she cannot help him. The point seems to be that while cloistered, formal religious life may provide a few believers with a strong spiritual foundation, not everyone is capable of submitting to such a discipline, nor can those in the cloister always provide the means to salvation for those on the outside.

Though few of the people at Imber heed the signs, the path to salvation is constantly indicated in *The Bell:* the path of love. Above the door of Imber, Dora, when she arrives, reads the inscription *Amor via mea.* The sunken bell has a similar inscription, *Vox ego sum Amoris. Gabriel vocor.* Though a number of symbolic meanings can be attached to the bell, it must first be understood as few of the people at Imber understand it, on its most simple and literal level. It is the voice of love. In various places in the novel the characters speak about bells; each interpretation of the symbolic meaning of the bell is in reality a summary of the speaker's own neurotic or conventional ethical code—which has no relationship at all to the bell except to give a clue to the speaker's incapacity for love. For James Taypor Pace (who was a great success as a youth worker) the bell is a symbol of innocence, and this is the key to his great moral failure in the book: loving the innocent he abhors the wicked; he cannot show compassion to a homosexual. Michael sees the bell as an invitation to self-analysis, his most neurotic tendency. The bell reminds Catherine of the legend of an impure nun; the ringing bell is a signal to Catherine that her buried sexual feelings have been discovered.

There are two bells in the novel, and both are named Gabriel, a fitting name since Gabriel will sound the note that indicates the coming of eternity. The bells also indicate eternity, on both the aesthetic and the ethical level. The sunken bell is an art object: it has a majestic tone and on its side appear scenes from the life of Christ. The bell inspires in Dora a feeling of reverence similar to her experience before the paintings in the National Gallery. In ethical terms the bell, sounded, is a call to prayer and the voice of love. In each case it can be an indicator of eternal, transcendental reality to those who are not too preoccupied with themselves to listen and look.

Preoccupation with oneself is a theme which carries over to Iris Murdoch's next novel, *A Severed Head;* here this theme emerges as a consideration of the value of psychoanalysis. As one reads the novel it soon becomes clear that Murdoch, though she respects some of Freud's ideas, does not feel that psychoanalysis provides a universal solution for the problems of neurosis. The cause for this feeling lies in the fact that the psychoanalyst encourages his neurotic patient to engage in extensive self-analysis. Murdoch feels that such introspection may increase the neurosis by seemingly magnifying its importance; the patient also becomes less willing to look outside himself at other people.

In a critique of contemporary English ethical philosophy, Murdoch mentions Stuart Hampshire's use of psychoanalysis as an ultimate arbiter in moral questions; she objects in particular to Hampshire's setting up of the analyst as a God-like figure. An analyst, she says, is not fit for such a role; "psychoanalysis is a muddled embryonic science." Palmer Anderson, the analyst in A Severed Head, makes himself the moral arbiter in the life of Martin Lynch-Gibbon, the novel's central character. After stealing away Martin's wife, Palmer solidifies his Godlike position by becoming Martin's father figure. Ever on the move, he next turns up in bed with his own half-sister; he is last seen boarding an airplane with Martin's old mistress.

From psychoanalysis Palmer has developed a notion of permissiveness by means of which he hopes to free his patients. This is a reversal of Kant's idea that freedom resides in respect for moral law. Ultimately Palmer's teaching is summed up in a single phrase: all is permitted. As both his ideas and his actions show, Palmer's version of psychoanalysis leads to utter moral anarchy.

Moral anarchy is a contagious disease. The major characters of the novel indulge in lying, hypocrisy, adultery, incest, but always with a warm smile and a sincere wish for the rapid recovery of the victim. There are, mathematically, nine heterosexual relationships possible between the three men and three women in the novel; eight of these liaisons occur. The lack of the ninth is offset by a hint of homosexuality in the relationship of Palmer and Martin. Rather than acting as a moral arbiter, Palmer, with the help of psychoanalytic jargon and his privileged position, is one of the chief instigators in this continual shift of sexual partners. If Stuart Hampshire feels that the analyst has an important role in determining ethical behavior, Murdoch seems to be saying, here is just one example of how this scheme can go wrong.

Iris Murdoch does not object so much to Freud's ideas themselves; Freud, she feels, made great discoveries about the human mind and still remains the greatest scientist in his field. But his picture of man is pessimistic; according to Freud the psyche seems quasi-mechanical, hard to control, confused by fantasies, a constant source of selfishness. Freud's aim is to make man workable, while the moral philosopher's goal is human goodness. This is still one more reason why a metaphysical, rather than a scientific, approach is necessary in moral philosophy.

As Jacques Souvage and a number of others have shown, Iris Murdoch makes use of a variety of Freudian ideas in *A Severed Head*. Martin's immaturity, his marriage to Antonia, an older woman, betray latent Oedipal feelings. Even more important here is Freud's interpretation of the Medusa legend; Murdoch also mentions this idea in her book on Sartre. Freud, in his papers "Medusa's Head" and "The Infantile Genital Organization," says that the male infant assumes that females have genitals similar to his own. Upon first seeing female genitals, the male refuses to believe that the penis is missing; later he imagines that it is gone because the female has been castrated. The chopping off of the Medusa's snaky head is a symbolic expression of this castration and of all the fears associated with it. The title of the novel, like the many symbolic decapitations in A *Severed Head,* is an allusion to Freud's interpretation of the Medusa story. The males in the novel, especially Martin, are sexually immature and still retain an infantile fear of female genitals; when Honor Klein says to Martin, "I am a severed head," she recognizes that she is both repugnant and fascinating, a fearsome castration symbol and a desired female symbol. Martin's ability, at the end of the novel, to love Honor indicates his new sexual maturity.

Martin's failure to attain a mature sort of love throughout the novel can also be attributed to his excessive dependence on rationality and his tendency to care more for inanimate objects than for humans. His love of the rational, symbolized by his great interest in the eighteenth century, is strong enough so that a plea to be rational will cause him to sanction almost any bit of irrationality at hand. He first falls in love with his mistress when he sees her bed; about to lose his wife, he first mourns the imminent loss of his furniture. In his final encounter with Honor, Martin has learned to see people instead of objects: as they declare their love for one another, the words "look" and "see" are continually used.

It is clear why Martin should love Honor; with her he has arrived at emotional and sexual maturity after two less satisfactory relationships. Why Honor should care for Martin, however, is more enigmatic. Murdoch gives Honor too many roles: anthropologist, Medusa symbol, incestuous sister, Martin's beloved, and an expert in Iris Murdoch's own hobbies, jujitsu and the Japanese sword. It is difficult to reconcile Honor as the Medusa and incestuous sister with the role she has as the one character in the novel who does not need to be taught to respect other human beings. When Martin asks Honor why she has accepted him she responds by telling the story of Gyges and Candaules: as Gyges saw Candaules' wife naked, Martin has seen Honor in bed with Palmer; hence Martin is next in line to occupy her bed. This is contrived and unsatisfactory. As Murdoch once said to Frank Kermode in an interview, in A *Severed Head* she has given in to myth. Still, the novel has wit, fascination, and a sprightly pace; while inferior to Murdoch's first two novels, it is still more lively and interesting than *The Sandcastle*.

In *An Unofficial Rose* (1962) Iris Murdoch returns to a number of problems which were central in her earlier books: freedom, slavery, contingency, and enchantment. The novel is complex: each of these themes is explored from the points of view of a number of characters; the reader is given a number of alternatives, a number of possible solutions to each problem. Many of the characters feel free at the beginning of the novel, for example. Examining various ideas of freedom, Murdoch shows in the end that these initial feelings are illusory.

In the opening scene of the novel, Hugh Peronett feels free because his wife, Fanny, is dead; years before, because of his wife, he had suppressed his love for Emma Sands. Emma never married, and with his wife dead Hugh hopes to return to Emma. Hugh's son Randall resembles his father. He is tired of his wife Ann and in love with Lindsay Rimmer, the secretary of the woman whom his father loves, Emma Sands. Randall stayed with his wife while his mother was alive, but now all he lacks for his freedom is enough money to run off with Lindsay. Father and son, moreover, are certain that the women they love lead lives that are free. Even young Penn Graham, the son of a Peronett girl who has settled in Australia, thinks he is free because he is away from his parents' authority while visiting England.

Iris Murdoch's own idea of freedom is quite different from these. In "The Sublime and the Good," an article she wrote a few years before this novel, Murdoch says that freedom consists in our ability to imagine the being of others. Freedom, then, is implied by love. If love is the actual recognition of otherness, freedom is one's capacity for this recognition.

Freedom is exercised in the confrontation by each other . . . of two irreducibly dissimilar individuals. Love is the imaginative recognition of, that is respect for, this otherness.

Her idea of freedom, says Murdoch, is close to Kant's concept of *Achtung*. Another idea which derives from Kant is the Romantic concept of freedom: here the individual is solitary and all-important. The Romantic hero assumes that since the world is a place of solitary individuals he may as well cut superficial ties to others in his quest for freedom. This idea of freedom, which many modern novelists (especially existentialists) have taken up, is one which Iris Murdoch opposes.

It is now possible to see why the many quests for freedom in *An Unofficial Rose* fail. Randall thinks that by leaving home, wife, and country he can find freedom; instead he becomes the slave of Lindsay Rimmer. Lindsay, herself for many years a slave of Emma's, enjoys her new role of master. Neither Emma nor Lindsay is really free for, as Simone Weil says, a master must give up his own freedom to ensure the captivity of his slave. Penn Graham, uprooted from his homeland and full of courtly, romantic delusions, becomes the victim of his cousin Miranda, a young but frighteningly efficient enchantress. Only Hugh Peronett—dear slow old Hugh, whom no one credits with much intelligence—manages at the end of the novel to have any real freedom. In recognizing that his life with his dead wife had been a good one, in recalling her dignity and kindness, Hugh sees Fanny as he had never seen her when she was alive. For Hugh, thinking of his dead wife is a process of freedom which ends in renewed love; this brings him to a level of understanding which no other character in the novel really attains. He sees that his early idea of freedom, freedom with Emma, is illusory. He rejects Emma, and in doing so avoids slavery.

As they fail to achieve love or freedom these characters, especially Randall, again illustrate the strain in modern life and literature which Iris Murdoch calls neurotic: isolation from others, self-involvement, solipsism. The opposing and equally bad tendency, it will be recalled, is what Murdoch has named the conventional: a willingness to accept the opinions of others, to conform to social niceties, in lieu of a deeper moral code based on love. Ann Peronett, Randall's wife, is conventional in this sense. Her stubborn, unthinking allegiance to Anglicanism causes her to refuse to believe her marriage is over even long after Randall has run off with Lindsay. Marriage, she feels, is based on habit, convenience, and religious law; it does not depend on love. Douglas Swann, the village pastor, tries to show her that she is wrong and stresses the importance of love. But Swann, though married, is in love with Ann himself, and, an interested party, he cannot really persuade

Ann to change her views. A great source of trouble in her marriage had been that Ann, an observer of the rules, constantly irritated Randall, who felt that freedom was synonymous with breaking rules. When Randall leaves her, Ann is courted by Felix Meecham, a career officer who is in his way as conventional as Ann. Ann refuses Felix; the opposition of her daughter and her own conventional morality are enough to discourage Felix. Ann's subsequent suffering, the result of a refusal to understand and to receive love, is something she has brought on herself. Ann and Randall both suffer for an additional reason: they seek patterns and refuse to accept a contingent view of reality. The cultivated roses in the novel are symbols of this determinism, of a human desire to impose order on nature; opposed to the cultivated rose is the unofficial rose of the title: wild, less symmetrical, and contingent.

A minor theme in this novel is Penn's romantic notion that, as a sort of modern courtly lover, he can win the affection of Miranda. There is a similar theme in *The Bell;* Toby Gashe tries to play the role of knight—his quest is the raising of the bell and Dora is his lady. In *The Unicorn* (1963) this medieval theme becomes dominant. A number of Iris Murdoch's articles contain attacks on the Romantic movement; usually in her novels such attacks have been in the form of parodies of the modern neurotic novel, showing the shortcomings of self-involved characters who resemble the heroes of writers like Sartre. *The Unicorn,* however, is filled with allusions to writers of two different periods: the medieval writers of romances and later writers who used these medieval romances as a basis for their own works.

Structurally, *The Unicorn* bears a resemblance to Jane

Austen's parody of the Gothic novel, *Northanger Abbey*. Marion Taylor, Murdoch's heroine, arrives at Gaze Castle, where the medieval atmosphere promises a varied assortment of gothic excesses. Unlike the heroine in *Northanger Abbey*, however, Marian is less under the influence of a medieval spell than the other inhabitants of Gaze. Hannah Crean-Smith, the wife of Gaze Castle's absent owner, attempts to mold her life to various legends: she is an Iseult, an enchanted princess of the castle. Her maimed husband, Peter, is represented as a sick fisher-king; perhaps Denis Nolan, who attempts to live the pure life, is the young knight who will replace him. With her husband away, Hannah has two courtly suitors: Pip Lejour, a neighbor, and Effingham Cooper, who in his visits to Gaze attempts to woo Hannah according to the rules set down by Andreas Capellanus.

The Unicorn also has many allusions to nineteenth-century fiction. Murdoch's book is similar in mood to the novels of Thomas Hardy and the Brontës, especially *Wuthering Heights*. In describing the vampire-like qualities of Hannah, Murdoch drew on "Carmilla," by Sheridan Le Fanu, a Victorian writer of ghost stories in the tradition of the Gothic novel.

Iris Murdoch uses all of these allusions to provide an atmosphere of fantasy and enchantment. The characters in *The Unicorn* attempt to live out roles, to govern their lives by myths, till they are prisoners of their own fantasies. To live according to a myth destroys contingency; if one is deluded by fantasies it is impossible to see, and to love, others.

Hannah's suffering provides another central theme in *The Unicorn*. Filled with guilt after attempting to murder her husband, Hannah has locked herself into Gaze, hoping that her suffering will purify her. In delineating Hannah's attempt at self-purification, Murdoch again shows her debt to Simone Weil, who in *Gravity and Grace* says that suffering usually leads to self-hatred or to violence. Echoing this idea, Murdoch said in a recent paper that suffering, in the context of self-examination, can masquerade as purification. This sort of suffering is in reality a form of self-involvement and leads to more evil. Hannah exemplifies this idea: instead of purification, the fruits of her suffering are at first excessive self-involvement and finally violence.

A related concept is the idea of Até, the transfer of suffering from one victim to the next, which Max Lejour explains in the twelfth chapter of *The Unicorn*. According to this idea, an evil act does not end after a single person has been victimized; the victim finds his own victim and passes the evil on, so that a long chain of evil is created. Max attributes the idea to the Greeks, but it is likely that another source for this concept is Simone Weil, who frequently mentions it. An understanding of Até goes a long way in explaining some of the puzzling events in *The Unicorn*. As each character is mistreated or humiliated he thrashes out indiscriminately at someone else: in his need to pass on his suffering, a victim is seldom rational in the choice of a new victim. As Max explains to Effingham, the chain of suffering grows in length and magnitude until it encounters a truly good person, who suffers quietly without attempting to pass the evil on. Effingham asks whether Hannah is such a person, and Max says he doesn't know; but toward the end of the book the answer is clear. Hannah is certainly not a good person in this sense. Her suffering is a form of self-involvement, and she does pass it on to others. Indeed, no character in the novel has enough goodness to absorb all the evil into himself so as to prevent the destruction which comes at the end of the novel.

The illusion and naïveté, which go along with too strong a belief in courtly romances, so important in *The Unicorn*, are treated again by Murdoch in *The Italian Girl* (1964), though only on a minor scale. The hero, Edmund Narraway, is compared to Sir Galahad and Edward the Confessor. There are echoes from Murdoch's other novels as well. Like Martin Lynch-Gibbon of *A Severed Head*, Edmund suffers from an Oedipus complex; to overcome it he must learn to accept the femininity of Maggie, the Italian servant girl. In a scene in which Maggie's hair is cut off, the reader is reminded of *A Severed Head* in a number of ways: the scene is reminiscent of Georgie's loss of her hair in the earlier novel; Freud's interpretation of the Medusa story is again used; one is even reminded of the title when Murdoch refers to Maggie's "severed hair." Like one of the Lusiewicz brothers in *The Flight from the Enchanter*, David Levkin is a foreigner who preys on others; his sister Elsa is a victim, uprooted and afflicted. Like *An Unofficial Rose*, *The Italian Girl* begins with the death of a matriarch and contains a scene where two lovers go off to Rome. A number of critics have found that this is one of Murdoch's less successful novels, and these repetitive elements may provide one of the reasons why this is so; as these themes are repeated they are presented in a less exciting and vital manner than they were the first time.

The central issue in this novel is again Murdoch's favorite problem: the self-involvement which prevents a person from looking objectively at another, which impedes love. Edmund Narraway, in his quest to be courtly and saintly, succeeds only in being prissy; *Narr,* the German word for fool, is the first part of his family name. Edmund, like the others in his family, does not look at the people who surround him. The Narraways, over the years, have had a series of Italian servant girls working for them. They forget the names and personalities of each of these girls as one servant replaces the next; they amalgamate the entire series into one mythical figure, whom they call "the Italian Girl." When they call the present Italian girl by name it is "Maggie": an Anglicized version of Maria Magistretti, a refusal to take notice of the real person that is there. The events of the novel force them to look, however, and Edmund likes what he sees. He goes off with Maria, having gained an understanding of love and lost an Oedipus complex simultaneously.

It may be that after this novel Iris Murdoch felt that she should move off in a different direction. *The Red and the Green* (1965), her first historical novel, deals with Dublin as it was in the time when her parents lived there. The red and green of the title are symbols of the opposition of the English and Irish; the climax of the novel is the Irish uprising which occurred at Eastertime in 1916. The Anglo-Irish family described in the novel has members who are involved on either side: Pat and Cathal Dumay are fiercely devoted to the Irish cause; Andrew Chase-White wears his English uniform somewhat reluctantly, mainly because he is a cavalryman who hates horses. The idea of cousins fighting gives the rebellion an overtone of family feud; even more pervasive is the air of incest in the novel, since all the characters in the book are, even if distantly, related.

Despite a certain amount of talk about Irish politics,

the historical setting is not of prime importance in *The Red and the Green;* with a few changes in background the novel could have been set in the time of the American Civil War, or the Bolshevik Revolution. The personalities of the characters, similar to those in Murdoch's other novels, are most important here. Andrew Chase-White, the English soldier, is naïve and inexperienced; his attractive aunt Millie, who had once seduced his father, undertakes the task of educating him. Millie, a sort of Circe figure, uses her beauty for power. She contributes to Andrew's downfall much as she had once ensnared Barney Drumm, at that time about to go into the priesthood. Millie's treatment of Barney, along with his own weak personality, caused him to become her slave; years ago a promising scholar, he now keeps a diary in which he distorts reality so as to vindicate his own actions. Millie herself is trapped, in this chain of Até, by Christopher Bellman, who uses his wealth as Millie had used her sexual attractiveness.

Along with sex and money, Murdoch shows a third means by which human relationships are often undermined: political fanaticism. Pat Dumay's patriotic fervor has caused him to value human beings only insofar as they could be of possible help to his cause. He finds himself in a position where he must choose between his strongest human attachment, his love for his younger brother, and his revolutionary activities. His final choice is a compromise, but one which favors politics over human relationships.

The one character who seems capable of love is Frances Bellman, Christopher's daughter and Andrew's fiancée. The only one who shows affection to the afflicted Barney, she almost helps him to rise above his enslaved state. Frances's own life is confused because she falls in love with Pat Dumay, a love which she conceals, probably because she is certain that Pat is too involved with the cause of Irish freedom to have room for any other emotions. At the end of the novel Murdoch makes it clear that she has condemned Millie, Barney, and Christopher for the ways in which they permitted outside values to wreck human lives. Her feelings about Pat Dumay and the cause he symbolizes are less conclusive, however. In its futility, in its inability to accomplish its set goals, a revolution is romantic and silly; but the revolutionary who is wholly devoted to the cause of human freedom is worthy of respect.

In *The Time of the Angels* (1966) Iris Murdoch returns to the theme which had occupied her in *The Bell* and other earlier novels, the problem of ethical behavior as it is influenced by modern religious and philosophical ideas. Unlike *The Bell*, this book has no characters to provide it with a moral center, which helps to account for its depressing and pessimistic quality.

The two ethical alternatives offered by the book are Satanism and weak atheistic humanism. The second category can again be subdivided into the various forms it takes as it is represented by different characters in *The Time of the Angels*. Marcus Fisher, the headmaster of a secondary school, has taken a leave to write a book which he has provisionally entitled *Morality in a World without God*. The morality of his friend Norah Shadox-Brown is based on a belief in decency and ordinary rules of human behavior; in this sense she resembles the English empirical analysts. An Anglican bishop with whom the two dine plays down the need for the belief in a personal God.

The Satanic alternative is represented by Carel Fisher, Marcus's brother and a fallen Anglican priest. Uncontent merely to theorize, Carel practices what he preaches: pride, slavery, incest; finally he commits suicide. His downfall can be attributed to his fascination with the dark side of German existentialism; he is particularly interested in the writings of Nietzsche and Heidegger. As Murdoch said in a recent paper, most existentialist thinking seems to her either optimistic romancing (a reference probably to French existentialism) or else something positively Luciferian. "Possibly," she says, "Heidegger is Lucifer in person." In the same paper she outlined the moral dichotomy she presents in this novel; the two modern ethical alternatives, she says, are "on the one hand a Luciferian philosophy of adventures of the will, and on the other natural science." Carel, in the novel, has a copy of Heidegger's *Sein und Zeit,* and Pattie, his servant, trips over it, a symbol for the action which is to come. The long quotation at the opening of chapter fifteen of *The Time of the Angels,* unidentified in the novel, is also from *Sein und Zeit* (p. 289 of the Macquarrie and Robinson translation). The word "angels" in the title is a reference to Carel's idea that, with the death of God, the dark angels have been liberated; the word "time," however, may again be an allusion to *Sein und Zeit.*

On the most elementary level, Iris Murdoch is opposed to Heidegger because his continuation in the tradition of Nietzschean nihilism poses a great threat to any ethical system based on an idea of goodness; Heidegger's idea of nothingness introduces a moral vacuum from which Carel never emerges. Specifically, Murdoch objects to Heidegger's phenomenology, which, unlike traditional phenomenology, does not offer a positive expression of the idea of being but begins instead with negative ideas, like nothingness and death. These negative ideas help to determine the concept which is at the center of Heidegger's phenomenology, the *Dasein*, the being-there quality of every existent thing. The human *Dasein*, confronted with its own eventual nonbeing in death, must respond to its own inner voice which constantly underlines its finitude. There can be no appeal outward to a transcendental being; the *Dasein* must turn back to itself and the inner voice which proclaims its limited existence. This is another version of the self-involvement which Iris Murdoch abhors, and in Carel's case it leads to self-deification, perhaps his most obnoxious sin. By a process of Até, similar to that of the earlier novels, Carel's evil spreads until his entire household is corrupted. Among Carel's victims is his niece, whom he keeps in a trancelike, enchanted state; a Negro servant whom he enslaves; and a refugee, an indirect victim, who resembles the refugees in Murdoch's other novels.

Among those characters who attempt to oppose Carel's evil, the most interesting is Marcus Fisher. At first he believes that the idea of moral goodness need not be regarded as a metaphysical concept, but later he comes to feel that perfection implies the idea of absolute values and moves toward a belief in metaphysics along Platonic lines. At the climax of the novel he begins to understand love; in the case of love, he feels, the ontological proof would work. "Is Love One?" he wonders, that is, is Love the one absolute metaphysical concept which can provide a basis for an ethical system? Norah Shadox-Brown, who hears this query, thinks he is taking leave of his senses; she represents the linguistic analyst who thinks that metaphysical questions are nonsense.

On the last pages of the book it seems that Marcus, though he has come close to an understanding of this idea of love, will not take the final steps in developing the idea: he abandons the book he is writing and resolves to think at some later time about the philosophical questions that had concerned him. Probably he will never return to them, for he is portrayed in the novel as a weak person who, despite his intuitions about love, was unable to prevent the destructive effects of Carel's evil. "The truly good," Murdoch has written, "is not a friendly tyrant to the bad, it is its deadly foe." Perhaps Marcus's mistake in the novel was his attempt to be friendly toward his brother; because of Carel's evil, Marcus should have treated him as a foe. Marcus, as an unsympathetic character who nevertheless expresses a number of ideas somewhat like Murdoch's, is similar to Bledyard in *The Sandcastle* and Douglas Swann in *An Unofficial Rose*. It may be that Murdoch, in an effort not to be too dogmatic, is careful to relegate any character who might become her spokesman to a relatively insignificant place in her novels.

In *The Nice and the Good* (1968) Murdoch abandons the dark mood of *The Time of the Angels*. One character, Joseph Radeechy, does seem left over from the earlier novel: he performs black masses in an abandoned air raid shelter. Murdoch wisely has him commit suicide in the opening paragraph and the result is a cheerful and entertaining book, more optimistic than most of her recent novels.

Since Radeechy's suicide takes place in his Whitehall office, it seems at first as if Iris Murdoch has taken up the official-intrigue-cum-spy-story genre so fashionable in contemporary popular fiction. John Ducane, the legal adviser to a Whitehall bureau chief, is assigned to investigate the suicide; he uncovers enough elements of sex scandal, deviant behavior, and blackmail to satisfy a James Bond fan. Ducane, however, begins a second inquiry which is of greater interest to Murdoch: an ethical self-examination which leads him to just moral choices, and from a plateau of conventional niceness to a higher plane of goodness.

Many of the characters in *The Nice and the Good* are nice in this sense; they conform to the "ordinary morality" of the linguistic analysts; are kind, cheerful, happy, and benignly unaware that beyond their niceness is an ethical level more nearly perfect and more painfully achieved. At first, Ducane is involved with the nice Kate Gray; his moral transition is symbolized by his eventual love for Mary Clothier whose concern for other people demonstrates her innate goodness.

There are many other characters and subplots in *The Nice and the Good;* Murdoch has chosen here to paint on a broad canvas. This approach is successful partly because Murdoch often eliminates dead matter: characterizations are deftly succinct, conversations often allude to events left undescribed so that the reader is forced to imagine them. This succinctness, however, has its drawbacks. Motivation, especially for characters as they fall in and out of love, is often missing or too briefly explained. Here again

the reader may feel puzzled or begin to suspect that the
author is withholding information to provide a surprise,
especially when events are also based on unexplained
philosophical considerations.

Bruno's Dream (1969) is also filled with surprises.
Most of these have to do with love affairs, as one character
after another grows bored with his current companion and
begins to covet his neighbor's. Iris Murdoch, like a square-
dance caller, insists on rapid movement and frequent
changes of partners. For example: Danby has grown tired
of Adelaide, whom he employs as his maid and enjoys as
his mistress. He flirts with Diana, his sister-in-law, but
soon discovers that he prefers Diana's sister, Lisa. Lisa unfortunately is more interested in Miles, who happens to be
married to Diana. And so on, until each of the seven participants in this intricate figure has had affairs with at least
two other members.

The instability of these relationships is based on a
problem Murdoch often describes: her characters are so
egotistical they become victims of their own subjectivity.
They project fantasies onto their lovers' personalities, and
the revelation of objective reality always brings disappointment. Until they understand this process, and their
own selfishness, each new disappointment leads them towards a new liaison in which they repeat their mistakes.

At the unmoving center of the lovers' circle is Bruno:
bedridden, dying, a momento mori the busy lovers try to
ignore. Bruno devotes himself to stamp-collecting, studying spiders, and brooding about the past. He recalls his in-
justices to his son, his marital infidelities, his meanness
and bigotry. Odious before his illness, he has become odif-
erous as well: his flesh gives off a repulsive odor which in-

sures that his visitors never overstay their welcome. Bruno
functions in the novel as a litmus test for compassion: the
moral stature of his friends is measured by their willingness to befriend him.

Bruno is cared for by Nigel, a male nurse. At first
Nigel seems capable of perceiving others in a selfless, loving fashion. But Nigel, oppressed, is only attempting to
compensate for his powerlessness. His pleasantness is a
cover for opportunism; his loving attention is actually
voyeurism. Slowly he accumulates power and begins to
manipulate the characters around him; this he does with
such success that he begins to think he is a god. Eventually, however, he repents, gives up his wicked ways, and
goes off to India to work for the Save the Children Fund.

This miracle is one of many. Adelaide—the maid who
was spurned by Danby—in a paragraph is transformed into
Lady Boase, wife of one of England's best-known actors.
Auntie, an almost senile old woman who keeps a boarding
house turns out to be a Russian aristocrat; her memoirs are
published to great acclaim. Many of the other characters,
seemingly paragons of self-absorption, contribute to the
happy ending by suddenly becoming capable of selfless
love. These rapid metamorphoses undermine and finally
erode the novel's small store of verisimilitude. By the end
of the novel the reader believes neither in the characters
nor in their abrupt transformations.

A Fairly Honourable Defeat (1971) again relies too
much on sudden turns of plot and melodramatic devices. A
broken telephone, a car that will not start, and a stolen letter: a crisis hinges on each of these.

The villain—a genuine old-fashioned villain—is Julius
King, who ruins the lives of his friends just for the fun of

it. Toward the end of the novel we learn that Julius is a survivor of Belsen; the evil he suffered in the concentration camp has transformed him into a power-seeker who must control and destroy others. Julius resembles Mischa Fox, the manipulative enchanter of *The Flight from the Enchanter*. An overwhelming need to be destructive indicates that Julius is involved in the Até process: the evil he once suffered has transformed him into a perpetrator of new evil.

According to Simone Weil, only a Christ-like person, capable of absorbing evil, can end the Até cycle. The most likely candidate for this role at first seems to be Rupert Foster, an amateur philosopher who has written a treatise on virtue. In this work, Rupert attempts to modernize Plato's ethical doctrine by eliminating its metaphysical aspects. But Plato's concept of Ideas, the very foundation of his philosophy, is a metaphysical concept; Platonic ethics without metaphysics is as likely as an omelette without eggs. Rupert turns out to be a disappointment not only as a theoretician of ethics but also as a practitioner.

A more successful moralist is Tallis Browne, who (like Murdoch) does not divorce metaphysics from ethics. Victimized by life, Tallis continues to perform good works; constantly tested, he retains his faith. He is an archetypal holy fool: though he is hounded by failure he nevertheless can help others to understand the ethical priorities in a muddled situation. He is juxtaposed against more worldly characters who try to undermine his religious faith; but in the end he is vindicated. Named after Thomas Tallis, a composer of lamentations, Tallis Browne emerges as a Job-like figure, and the failures of his would-be comforters are revealed.

Julius plays Satan to Tallis' Job. He believes in evil and delights in demonstrating its superiority to goodness. In a scene reminiscent of Satan persuading God to test Job, Julius wagers that he can corrupt anyone he chooses, and offers to use his friends as guinea pigs. This is Julius relaxing; his work is to develop a new strain of anthrax for use in biological weapons. The idea that he may have a hand in the eventual annihilation of humanity keeps him interested in his profession.

At the end of the book Tallis is still unhappy, Julius unrepentant and unpunished. The narrator, describing the situation blandly, refuses to moralize; the reader's indignation must serve as a commentary. There are no easy victories for goodness: this concluding idea provides the novel with an ending that is both subtle and powerful.

An Accidental Man (1971) centers on the story of Ludwig Leferrier, a young American who is called up for military service while he is studying in England. Knowing he will be forced to fight in Vietnam, he refuses to return, despite the pleas of his parents. They feel that he has a duty to serve his country or, if he believes that its laws are unjust, to confront those laws by standing trial as a dissenter and accepting a prison sentence.

While Ludwig ponders this issue he falls in with a group of Murdochian eccentrics. These include Austin Gibson Grey, an alcoholic whose failures deepen his neurotic self-absorption; Diana, Austin's estranged wife, trapped in an "enchanted" state; and Austin's brother Matthew, a charming intriguer who likes to manipulate his friends. Ludwig may be meeting these people for the first time, but devoted Murdoch enthusiasts will recognize them as old friends.

Still, *An Accidental Man* does have a number of shrewd and original characterizations. One example is the portrayal of a minor character, a schoolboy who, even in the throes of a grand and tragic passion (he loves another schoolboy), can speak of his feelings with wit and charm.

After much agonizing (and the usual backdrop of couplings, switches, and derailments) Ludwig is persuaded by his parents' arguments. He gives up the comforts of England and returns home to be jailed as a war resister. Ludwig's exile has been so comfortable that it seems he can only exonerate himself with martyrdom; but it is never made clear why prison should be the only ethical choice open to a committed dissident.

Ethical questions like this one are often treated as if they had simple or self-evident answers. This sometimes leads to perfunctory analyses of complicated ethical or psychological situations in Iris Murdoch's fiction. In this novel, for example, Austin's neurotic suffering is understood as a result of his egoism and his inability to love others. But certainly to some extent such a failure of love can be considered a symptom of the neurosis rather than its cause.

Murdoch often gives short shrift to characters who are immoral, damning them to a limbo of imperfect characterization. Her emphasis on ethics and distrust of psychology lead into this flaw; psychology stresses understanding, where ethics is concerned with making judgments. In fiction an overemphasis on ethics can too easily degenerate into authorial vindictiveness.

The Black Prince (1973) does show a concern with the psychology of its central characters; this is a clue to its quality. The narrator and protagonist, Bradley Pearson, is an unsuccessful writer somewhat hampered by his romantic view of the role of the artist. For years he has been engaged in a debate about the craft of writing with a friend and rival, Arnold Baffin, who publishes a new novel every year. Baffin is famous and can live off his best-sellers; Pearson, a painstaking craftsman, feels Baffin is satisfied with easy mediocrity and chides him for seeking popular success.

The debate between Pearson and Baffin deals in direct fashion with a question that has concerned a number of Iris Murdoch's critics over the last decade: the quality and intelligence of her writing make it evident that she wants to be thought of as a serious novelist; but some of her weaknesses—like plot manipulation and melodramatic effects—seem like a bid for easy popularity. It may be that Murdoch is using the quarrel between Pearson and Baffin to articulate an inner conflict of her own. Baffin, after one of Pearson's attacks on his careless artistry, defends himself this way:

> The years pass and one has only one life. If one has a thing at all one must do it and keep on and on and on trying to do it better. And an aspect of this is that any artist has to *decide* how fast to work. I do not believe that I would improve if I wrote less. The only result of that would be that there would be less of whatever there is.

This may be Murdoch's apology to her critics, many of whom have attributed a decline in the quality of her writing to her copious production (she has published sixteen novels, two plays, and numerous essays in twenty years).

The debate between Pearson and Baffin is never settled and of course never can be; but their remarks give interesting insights into how an artist thinks about his craft. And, as so often occurs in works about writers, Murdoch's descriptions of the novelists as they speak about their art have an authentic ring.

Bradley Pearson says that his story—which initially seems to be about art and creativity—is actually about love; and at the center of the novel is a description of his feelings for Christian Baffin, Arnold's young daughter. Bradley is too old for Christian; they have little in common; he knows he will be unhappy if he pursues her. But he is a romantic, and he succumbs to his passion. Helplessly he watches as his reserve, self-control, and integrity are swept away by the force of his love. Even as one part of him is cut loose, another part stands aside and muses on the powerful forces which have set him adrift. This sardonic note is a perfect companion to Pearson's rapturous descriptions of his passionate feelings; and these passages contain some of Murdoch's most effective and moving writing.

Pearson knows he will come to a bad end; this is a reason his story is so powerful. But after a series of complicated events—unlikely individually, unbelievable consecutively—Bradley finds himself in jail, unjustly convicted of committing a murder. Once again Murdoch succeeds in establishing the authenticity of an emotional experience only to throw it away with a tricky twist of the plot.

In 1973 Iris Murdoch published two plays which had been produced earlier, *The Three Arrows* and *The Servants and the Snow*. The plays have a good deal in common: a concern with the ethics of a political problem; an exotic setting; and an aristocratic protagonist whose life is in danger because he is trapped in a mansion or a palace.

The Servants and the Snow, first produced in 1970, deals with a landowner's attempts to govern his estate with justice and compassion. Upon the death of his father he arrives, filled with benevolent zeal, at his ancestral home. His father was a despot, an adulterer, and a murderer; the protagonist, Basil, is determined not to repeat his father's mistakes.

But like the characters in *The Flight from the Enchanter,* Basil finds that slaves who are corrupted by a bad master are not so easily liberated. His servants do not welcome Basil's reforms, and even his wife is openly contemptuous of them. The freedom he grants his servants gives them an opportunity to plot: they are urged to kill Basil by the son of the man his father murdered.

Basil's appeals to justice, reason, and decency are futile. The situation deteriorates; his bailiff leaves, and Basil, snowbound, realizes that he is trapped in his own mansion. A bad adviser persuades him to spend the night with his father's old mistress; this will help him reestablish his authority. Basil seems surprised when this plan backfires. At the end of the play he is murdered, though not, as one would expect, by the son of his father's victim.

Basil barely has time to breathe his last when his brother-in-law, General Klein, enters. Klein has the military strength to restore order to the chaotic situation. Had he arrived a few moments earlier, he might have prevented Basil's death; but alas, he did not arrive a few moments earlier. Like a latter-day Fortinbras, Klein supervises the mopping-up detail as the final curtain falls.

The play has other details reminiscent of tragedy, seems to hope to become a tragedy, but it never does. Basil lacks the stature of a tragic hero; his motivation is poorly defined; his actions are improbable. None of the people on stage have any reason to mourn his death, nor do the members of the audience.

The Three Arrows (first produced in 1972) is set in medieval Japan. A revolutionary leader, Prince Yorimitsu, is a prisoner in the Imperial Palace. He was captured in a battle with the Emperor's followers, but now these followers are divided into two rival factions. The leaders of both factions want Yorimitsu dead, but are afraid to kill him: each leader fears that the revolutionaries will join with the opposing faction to avenge Yorimitsu.

Adored by his followers, Prince Yorimitsu also commands the audience's respect: he is attractive, courageous, and intelligent. Making clever use of anachronism, Iris Murdoch demonstrates her hero's political acumen by having him suggest reforms based on modern social thought.

At the climax of the play, Yorimitsu is forced into a classic folkloric situation: he enters a contest where he must choose one of three arrows. The wrong choice means death; the right one, the hand of a princess who (conveniently) has fallen in love with him. The contest is of course rigged: the two contending factions have collaborated in a stratagem to get Yorimitsu out of the way without stirring up his followers.

But this is not to be. Surprise works well in this play when the charming, effete Emperor shows that he is capable of taking action and overruling the plotters around him. The events afterward lead to an unexpected and not entirely satisfactory conclusion; but the play is saved by entertaining dialogue, well-integrated ideas, and convincing characterizations.

Like *The Sandcastle, The Sacred and Profane Love*

Machine (1974) tells the story of an adulterous love affair. As in the earlier novel, a middle-aged husband falls in love with a younger woman; in each case the emotional stability of the children involved is threatened. Both books are set in the countryside near London. In both books the wife supports her husband's plans to change careers, and the mistress opposes them. In *The Sandcastle* the husband was a schoolteacher and the mistress a painter; here the wife is a former painter, the mistress a former schoolteacher. In each book the one person who can speak honestly in an emotionally charged situation is a scholar whom the other characters find a bit ridiculous. The abandoned wives both are pursued by suitors who deal with their children compassionately. It was Tolstoy who said that happy families are all alike; it may be that Murdoch wants to demonstrate that the same is true for unhappy families.

The unfaithful husband in *The Sacred and Profane Love Machine* is Blaise Gavender, whose chief characteristics are egoism and untruthfulness. He works as a psychiatrist, though it is difficult to understand why he ever became one: he is devoid of any self-knowledge, empathy, or responsibility. He is without the vaguest sense of the sort of speech or action one might expect from a member of his profession. He is not even particularly clever; in need of an alibi to explain his nights away from home, he goes to a neighbor—formerly a patient—for help. Gavender finally degenerates into a familiar stereotype, the psychiatrist who should see a good psychiatrist.

Gavender spends most of the novel trying to decide whether to remain with his wife (kind but aging) or to go off with his mistress (young but nagging). For most of the story he vacillates: distracted by the lies, cries, and sighs of his unhappy companions he finds it difficult to concentrate. At last his wife leaves him and (conveniently) is killed by terrorists in an airport massacre. After a short interval of mourning Gavender throws caution to the winds and marries his mistress. Again, melodrama combines with a need to tie up loose ends and produces an unlikely turn of the plot.

In Iris Murdoch's first novel as well as in her essays she has persuasively argued that the world is not orderly or determined, but contingent. Ironically, it is a lack of contingency which undermines Murdoch's later fiction; fragile plots and thinly disguised moralizing convey a sense, not of accident, but of authorial manipulation.

Murdoch, in her earlier philosophical writing, discusses the effect of injecting moral ideas into literature and insists that a work need not be didactic because it is ethical. Art and ethics have a similar basis, a "loving" discovery of reality; hence, art which is moral need not teach a lesson if it discovers the underlying truths of things. But often Murdoch goes beyond this limit and does try to instruct the reader.

In almost all of her novels the reader is encouraged to sympathize with characters who later turn out to be incompetent or immoral; when these deficiencies are fully revealed the reader is urged to take the lesson to heart. However one feels about the possibility of writing moral novels which are not didactic, the question here is superfluous; especially when philosophical ideas are involved, Murdoch cannot resist the impulse to moralize.

Her fiction often has this quality: an uncertainty about whether to include philosophical ideas or to withhold them. Because of her interest in ideas, especially moral ideas, and her conviction that the best fiction has a strong moral undercurrent, there is an impetus to include certain philosophical concepts. But the dangers of mythologizing, of didacticism, or of *la littérature engagée* check the impulse to include ideas. Murdoch's compromise is to introduce the ideas in subtle forms, to provide alternatives for the ideas, to introduce her own ideas through a minor or unsympathetic character, and even to leave the reader with problems that cannot be solved rationally, a sort of mysticism in fiction. Very often this is an unsatisfactory compromise. The intelligent reader of Murdoch's fiction who has not read her philosophical articles often finishes one of her novels with a puzzled feeling: an uncertainty about the moral positions represented in the novel or a feeling that somehow all of the significance of the action has not been grasped.

The reader who attempts to end this puzzled feeling and begins to read Murdoch's philosophical articles soon finds that it is also necessary to have an understanding of Simone Weil's books. Other philosophers are helpful: a good deal of the thinking of both Weil and Murdoch is based on Platonic ideas. Murdoch's critiques of Kant, Hegel, Sartre, and the linguistic philosophers have already been noted. To these one might add Kierkegaard, perhaps because he has not removed the idea of the mystery of religion from the universe of the isolated individual, unlike the more atheistic existentialists. Martin Buber's "I and Thou" concept is close to Murdoch's love idea; even more important is Gabriel Marcel's connection of phenomenological and ontological questions with the idea of love (as in *The Mystery of Being*, Vol. II). Marcus, it will be remembered, makes a similar connection in *The Time of the Angels*. The English philosopher J. L. Austen is praised by Murdoch for his opposition to the empirical idea of the sense-impression; but usually Murdoch's greatest use of English philosophy (especially of G. E. Moore and Stuart Hampshire) is to provide the background for a character whose "ordinary morality" cannot stand up in an extreme moral crisis. Discussions of love, power, suffering, enchantment, psychology, religion—and Iris Murdoch's novels are full of such discussions—usually contain allusions to some of the above-mentioned philosophers. The futility of Murdoch's masking of the ideas in her novels, of her denials in interviews that she is a philosophical novelist, should be obvious to the reader who has managed to get through the necessary background material. Murdoch is as involved with ideas as Conrad was with the sea.

The reason for these denials is perhaps that Murdoch has a fear of her own tendency to be dogmatic. In her philosophical articles, for example, she often overlooks gaps in her theories and possible objections to them. The fact that she does not attempt to apply her aesthetic ideas to abstract art or to music has already been noted. In addition, one might criticize Murdoch's idea of love because of its implication that those who are most concerned with the affairs of other people are the most loving. The quality of the concern is important, and here Murdoch often introduces a tautology: loving concern is necessary to achieve love. Murdoch offers too few distinctions between loving concern and mere curiosity to define her ideas accurately.

Another weak point is Murdoch's constant emphasis on the dangers of subjectivity. Certainly, some degree of self-knowledge is needed to achieve morality or love; a person must have a good idea of his moral strengths and weaknesses to be able to overcome the vicissitudes of a moral crisis. But Murdoch argues as if all swimming should be outlawed because swimmers sometimes drown; any introspection, she seems to feel, is a step on the dangerous path toward solipsism. She displays the same attitudes in her criticisms of literature: writers are praised or rejected mainly because of the degree to which they eliminate themselves from their works. Hence, Tolstoy succeeds, Dostoevsky does not. A thoughtful analysis of literature needs more critical tests than the few which Murdoch applies. Rather than attempting to conceal the ideas in her fiction, Murdoch might avoid didacticism better if these ideas were more overtly expressed and a better case were made for opposing ideas.

As a novelist, despite the qualities that make her one of England's foremost writers, Iris Murdoch somehow misses being of the first rank. To some extent this can be attributed to her own modest ambitions; she does not seem to want to write the great novel which deals with universal themes, perhaps because she does not want to risk the great failure. In addition she is hindered by a number of other faults: the puzzling quality already mentioned which at times is more irritating than intriguing; a drabness which permeates some of her inferior novels, like *The Sandcastle;* and a desire to fool the reader with sudden and unexpected twists of plot, as in *A Severed Head.* This explains, perhaps, why *Under the Net* is such a good novel: though the reader is surprised and amused by the incidents in the book, fantastic incidents are presented for the sake of humor and not of plot; moreover, whether he understands the philosophical overtones of the novel or not, the reader feels at the end of the novel that Jake has somehow gone on to a better life, learned something and improved. The reader puts down the novel with a sense of satisfaction and not irritation.

If Iris Murdoch is not in the first rank of novelists, however, she certainly belongs in the next. For her thoughtful characterizations, for her unpredictable inventiveness, and for her intelligent and compassionate ideas she deserves the reader's attention and respect.

Selected Bibliographies

GRAHAM GREENE

NOTE: *Only the first English and American editions are listed, except where later editions appeared under changed titles. A Collected Edition of Graham Greene's writings, with introductions by the author, is in progress, published by Bodley Head (in conjunction with Heinemann), London; and many titles are available in paperback editions published mainly by Penguin in Britain and by Compass (Viking) and Bantam in the United States.*

Principal Works

The Man Within. London, Heinemann, 1929; Garden City, N.Y., Doubleday, Doran, 1929.

The Name of Action. London, Heinemann, 1930; Garden City, N.Y., Doubleday, 1931.

Rumour at Nightfall. London, Heinemann, 1931; Garden City, N.Y., Doubleday, 1932.

Stamboul Train. London, Heinemann, 1932; Garden City, N.Y., Doubleday, 1933 (under the title Orient Express).

It's a Battlefield. London, Heinemann, 1934; Garden City, N.Y., Doubleday, 1934.

England Made Me. London, Heinemann, 1935; Garden City, N.Y., Doubleday, 1935. Reissued: New York, Viking, 1953 (under the title The Shipwrecked).

Journey Without Maps. London, Heinemann, 1936; Garden City, N.Y., Doubleday, 1936.

A Gun for Sale. London, Heinemann, 1936; Garden City, N.Y., Doubleday, 1936 (under the title This Gun for Hire).

Brighton Rock. London, Heinemann, 1938; New York, Viking, 1938.

The Lawless Roads. London, Longmans, Green, 1939; New York, Viking, 1939 (under the title Another Mexico).

The Confidential Agent. London, Heinemann, 1939; New York, Viking, 1939.

The Power and the Glory. London, Heinemann, 1940; New York, Viking, 1940 (under the title The Labyrinthine Ways). Reissued: New York, Viking, 1946 (under the original title).

The Ministry of Fear. London, Heinemann, 1943; New York, Viking, 1943.

Nineteen Stories. London, Heinemann, 1947; New York, Viking, 1949 (with one story changed). Reissued, as Twenty-one Stories (with three stories added and one omitted): London, Heinemann, 1954; New York, Viking, 1962.

The Heart of the Matter. London, Heinemann, 1948; New York, Viking, 1948.

Why Do I Write? An exchange of views between Elizabeth Bowen, Graham Greene, and V. S. Pritchett. London, Marshall, 1948.

The Third Man. London, Heinemann, 1950; New York, Viking, 1950.

The Lost Childhood and Other Essays. London, Eyre & Spottiswoode, 1951; New York, Viking, 1952.

The End of the Affair. London, Heinemann, 1951; New York, Viking, 1951.

The Living Room. London, Heinemann, 1953; New York, Viking, 1954.

Loser Takes All. London, Heinemann, 1955; New York, Viking, 1957.

The Quiet American. London, Heinemann, 1955; New York, Viking, 1956.

The Potting Shed. New York, Viking, 1957; London, Heinemann, 1958.

Our Man in Havana. London, Heinemann, 1958; New York, Viking, 1958.

The Complaisant Lover. London, Heinemann, 1959; New York, Viking, 1960.

A Burnt-Out Case. London, Heinemann, 1961; New York, Viking, 1961.

In Search of a Character: Two African Journals. London, Bodley Head, 1961; New York, Viking, 1962.

A Sense of Reality. London, Bodley Head, 1963; New York, Viking, 1963.

The Comedians. London, Bodley Head, 1966; New York, Viking, 1966.

May We Borrow Your Husband? and Other Comedies of the Sexual Life. London, Bodley Head, 1967; New York, Viking, 1967.

Collected Essays. London, Bodley Head, 1969; New York, Viking, 1969.
Travels with My Aunt. London, Bodley Head, 1969; New York, Viking, 1970.
A Sort of Life. London, Bodley Head, 1971; New York, Simon & Schuster, 1971.
The Pleasure Dome: Collected Film Criticism. Ed. John Russell Taylor. London, Secker & Warburg, 1972; New York, Simon & Schuster, 1972 (under the title Graham Greene on Film: Collected Film Criticism).
Collected Short Stories. London, Bodley Head, 1972; New York, Viking, 1973.
The Honorary Consul. London, Bodley Head, 1973; New York, Simon & Schuster, 1973.
Lord Rochester's Monkey. London, Bodley Head, 1974; New York, Viking, 1974.

Critical Works and Commentary

Allott, Kenneth, and Miriam Farris. The Art of Graham Greene. London, Hamish Hamilton, 1951.
Atkins, John. Graham Greene. London, Calder, 1957.
DeVitis, A. A. Graham Greene. New York, Twayne, 1964.
Evans, Robert O., ed. Graham Greene: Some Critical Considerations. Lexington, University of Kentucky Press, 1963.
Hoggart, Richard. "The Force of Caricature: Aspects of the Art of Graham Greene with Particular Reference to The Power and the Glory," Essays in Criticism, III (1953), 447–62.
Hynes, S. L., ed. Graham Greene: A Collection of Critical Essays. Englewood Cliffs, N.J., Prentice-Hall, 1973.
Kermode, Frank. "Mr Greene's Eggs and Crosses," in Puzzles and Epiphanies. London, Routledge, 1962, pp. 176–87.
Kunkel, Francis L. The Labyrinthine Ways of Graham Greene. New York, Sheed & Ward, 1960.
Lees, F. N. "Graham Greene: A Comment," Scrutiny, XIX (1952), 31–42.
Lewis, R. W. B. "Graham Greene: The Religious Affair," in The Picaresque Saint. Philadelphia, J. B. Lippincott, 1959, pp. 220–74.
Mesnet, Marie-Beatrice. Graham Greene and the Heart of the Matter. London, Cresset, 1954.
Modern Fiction Studies, Graham Greene Special Number, III (1957).
O'Donnell, Donat. "Graham Greene: The Anatomy of Pity," in Maria Cross. New York, Oxford University Press, 1952, pp. 63–94.
Phillips, Gene D. Graham Greene: The Films of His Fiction. New York, Teachers College Press, 1974.

Pryce-Jones, David. Graham Greene. Edinburgh, Oliver & Boyd, 1963.
Sewell, Elizabeth. "Graham Greene," Dublin Review, CVIII (1954), 12–21.
Stratford, Philip. "Unlocking the Potting Shed," Kenyon Review, XXIV (1962), 129–43.
—— Faith and Fiction: Creative Process in Greene and Mauriac. Notre Dame, University of Notre Dame Press, 1964.
Vann, J. Don. Graham Greene: A Checklist of Criticism. Kent, Ohio, Kent State University Press, 1970.
Wyndham, Francis. Graham Greene. London, Longmans, Green, 1955.
Zabel, Morton D. "Graham Greene: The Best and the Worst," in Craft and Character in Modern Fiction. New York, Viking, 1957, pp. 276–96.

C. P. SNOW

Principal Works

Death under Sail. London, Heinemann, 1932; revised edition, 1939.
New Lives for Old. Published anonymously, London, Gollancz, 1933.
The Search. London, Gollancz, 1934; Indianapolis and New York, Bobbs-Merrill, 1935. Revised edition with preface, London, Macmillan, 1958; New York, Scribner's, 1958.
Strangers and Brothers. London, Faber & Faber, 1940; New York, Scribner's, 1960. Paperback edition: London, Penguin, 1962.
The Light and the Dark. London, Faber & Faber, 1947; New York, Macmillan, 1948.
Time of Hope. London, Faber & Faber, 1949; New York, Macmillan, 1950. Paperback edition: New York, Harper Torchbooks, 1961.
The Masters. London, Macmillan, 1951; New York, Macmillan, 1951. Paperback editions: London, Penguin, 1956; New York, Anchor (Doubleday), 1959.
The New Men. London, Macmillan, 1954; New York, Scribner's, 1954. Paperback editions: London, Penguin, 1959; New York, Scribner's, 1961.
Homecomings. London, Macmillan, 1956; (titled Homecoming) New York, Scribner's, 1956.
The Conscience of the Rich. London, Macmillan, 1958; New York, Scribner's, 1958. Paperback editions: New York, Scribner Library, 1960; London, Penguin, 1961.

The Two Cultures and The Scientific Revolution: The Rede Lecture. London, Cambridge University Press, 1959.

The Affair. London, Macmillan, 1960; New York, Scribner's, 1960. Paperback edition: London, Penguin, 1962.

Science and Government: Harvard University Godkin Lecture. Cambridge, Mass., Harvard University Press, 1961; London, Oxford University Press, 1961.

Appendix to Science and Government. Cambridge, Mass., Harvard University Press, 1962.

C. P. Snow: A Spectrum. Ed. Stanley Weintraub. New York, Scribner's, 1963. (An anthology of selections from Snow's novels, speeches, and writings for periodicals.)

The Corridors of Power. London, Macmillan, 1964; New York, Scribner's, 1964.

The Sleep of Reason. London, Macmillan, 1968; New York, Scribner's, 1968.

Last Things. London, Macmillan, 1970; New York, Scribner's, 1970.

The Malcontents. London, Macmillan, 1972; New York, Scribner's, 1972.

In Their Wisdom. London, Macmillan, 1974; New York, Scribner's, 1974.

Critical Works and Commentary

"Afterthoughts by C. P. Snow," Encounter, XIV (February, 1960), 64–68. (A reply to the series of articles "The Two Cultures: A Discussion of C. P. Snow's Views.")

Bergonzi, Bernard. "The World of Lewis Eliot," Twentieth Century, CLXVII (February, 1960), 214–25.

Cooper, William. C. P. Snow. Writers and Their Work, Number 115. London and New York, Longmans, Green, 1959.

Cornelius, David K., and Edwin St. Vincent, eds. Cultures in Conflict: Perspectives on the Snow-Leavis Controversy. Chicago, Scott, Foresman and Co., 1964.

Fison, Peter. "A Reply to Bernard Bergonzi's 'World of Lewis Eliot,'" Twentieth Century, CLXVII (June, 1960), 568–71.

Graves, Nora Calhoun. The Two Culture Theory in C. P. Snow's Novels. Hattiesburg, Miss., The University and College Press of Mississippi, 1971.

Greacen, Robert. The World of C. P. Snow. New York, London House and Maxwell, 1963.

Green, Martin. "A Literary Defense of the Two Cultures," Kenyon Review (Autumn, 1962), 735–36.

Johnson, Pamela Hansford. "Three Novelists and the Drawing of Character (C. P. Snow, Joyce Cary and Ivy Compton-Burnett)," *Essays and Studies*, 1950, vol. 3 of the new series.
Karl, Frederick. C. P. Snow: The Politics of Conscience. Carbondale, Southern Illinois University Press, 1963.
Kermode, Frank. "Beckett, Snow and Pure Poverty," in Puzzles and Epiphanies. London, Routledge, 1962, pp. 155–63.
Leavis, F. R. "The Significance of C. P. Snow," *Spectator*, CCVIII (March 16, 1962), 297–303. Reprinted in Two Cultures? The Significance of C. P. Snow. With a preface by F. R. Leavis, and "Sir Charles Snow's Rede Lecture" by Michael Yudkin. New York, Pantheon Books, 1963.
Muggeridge, Malcolm, and C. P. Snow. "Appointment with C. P. Snow" (excerpt from a television dialogue between Muggeridge and Snow), *Encounter*, XVIII (February, 1962), 90–93.
Nott, Kathleen. "The Type to Which the Whole Creation Moves?" *Encounter*, XVIII (February, 1962), 87–88, 94–97.
Thale, Jerome. C. P. Snow. Edinburgh and London, Oliver & Boyd, 1964. (Contains bibliography of writings by and about Snow.)
"The Two Cultures: A Discussion of C. P. Snow's Views," *Encounter*, XIII (August, 1959), 67–73; XIII (September, 1959), 61–64; XIV (January, 1960), 72–73.
Trilling, Lionel. "The Novel Alive or Dead," in A Gathering of Fugitives. Boston, Beacon Press, 1956.
—— "Science, Literature and Culture: A Comment on the Leavis-Snow Controversy," *Commentary* (June, 1962), 461–77.

MALCOLM LOWRY

Principal Works

Dark as the Grave Wherein My Friend Is Laid. New York, New American Library, 1968.
"Garden of Etla," *United Nations World*, IV (June, 1950), 45–47.
Hear Us O Lord from Heaven Thy Dwelling Place. Philadelphia and New York, J. B. Lippincott, 1961.
"Hotel Room in Chartres," *Story*, V (September, 1934), 53–58.
Lunar Caustic. *Paris Review*, VIII (Winter–Spring, 1963), 12–72; London, Jonathan Cape, 1968.

October Ferry to Gabriola. New York and Cleveland, World Publishing Company, 1970.
"On Board the 'West Hardaway,'" Story, III (October, 1933), 12–22.
The Selected Letters of Malcolm Lowry. Eds. Harvey Breit and Margerie Lowry. Philadelphia and New York, J. B. Lippincott, 1965.
Selected Poems of Malcolm Lowry. San Francisco, City Lights Books, 1962.
Ultramarine. London, Jonathan Cape, 1933; New York, McGraw-Hill, 1964.
Under the Volcano. New York, Reynal and Hitchcock, 1947; London, Jonathan Cape, 1947; New York, Vintage Books, 1958; Philadelphia and New York, J. B. Lippincott, 1965.

Critical Works and Commentary

Aiken, Conrad. Times Literary Supplement (February 16, 1967), p. 127.
Bradbrook, M. C. Malcolm Lowry, His Art and Early Life. London, Cambridge University Press, 1974.
Breit, Harvey. "Introductory Note, Lowry's Through the Panama," Paris Review, XXIII (Spring, 1960), p. 84.
Canadian Literature, Vol. VIII, 1961 (an entire issue devoted to Lowry).
Costa, Richard H. "Ulysses, Lowry's Volcano, and the Voyage Between: A Study of an Unacknowledged Literary Kinship," University of Toronto Quarterly, XXXVI, 335–52.
—— Malcolm Lowry. New York, Twayne, 1972.
Day, Douglas. "Of Tragic Joy," Prairie Schooner, XXXVII (Winter, 1963–64), 354–62.
—— Malcolm Lowry: A Biography. New York, Oxford University Press, 1973.
Edmonds, Dale. "The Short Fiction of Malcolm Lowry," Tulane Studies in English, XV, 59–80.
—— "Under the Volcano: A Reading of the 'Immediate Level,'" Tulane Studies in English, XVI, 63–105.
Epstein, Perle. The Private Labyrinth of Malcolm Lowry. New York, Holt, Rinehart, and Winston, 1969.
Kim, Suzanne. "Les oeuvres de jeunesse de Malcolm Lowry," Etudes Anglaises, XVIII (1965), 383–94.
—— "Par l'eau et feu: Deux oeuvres de Malcolm Lowry," Etudes Anglaises, XVIII (1965), 395–97.
Knickerbocker, Conrad. "Lowry à vingt ans," Lettres Nouvelles (March–April, 1964), pp. 68–94.

—— "Malcolm Lowry in England," *Paris Review*, X (Summer, 1966), 13–38.
—— "The Voyage of Malcolm Lowry," *Prairie Schooner*, XXXVII (Winter, 1963–64), 301–14.
Markson, David. "Malcolm Lowry: A Reminiscence," *Nation* (February 7, 1966), 164–67.
Spender, Stephen. "Introduction" to *Under the Volcano*. Philadelphia and New York, J. B. Lippincott, 1965.
Stern, James. "Malcolm Lowry—a First Impression," *Encounter*, XXIX, No. 3, 58–68.
Woodcock, George, ed. Malcolm Lowry: The Man and His Works. Vancouver, Vancouver University Press, 1971.

WILLIAM GOLDING

Principal Works

Poems. London, Macmillan, 1934; New York, Macmillan, 1935.
Lord of the Flies. London, Faber & Faber, 1954; New York, Coward-McCann, 1955.
The Inheritors. London, Faber & Faber, 1955; New York, Harcourt, Brace & World, 1962.
Pincher Martin. London, Faber & Faber, 1956; New York, Harcourt, Brace, 1957 (titled The Two Deaths of Christopher Martin).
The Brass Butterfly. London, Faber & Faber, 1958.
Free Fall. London, Faber & Faber, 1960; New York, Harcourt, Brace, 1960.
The Spire. London, Faber & Faber, 1964; New York, Harcourt, Brace & World, 1964.
The Hot Gates. London, Faber & Faber, 1965; New York, Harcourt, Brace & World, 1966.
The Pyramid. London, Faber & Faber, 1967; New York, Harcourt, Brace & World, 1967.
The Scorpion God. London, Faber & Faber, 1971; New York, Harcourt Brace Jovanovich, 1971.

Critical Works and Commentary

Babb, Howard S. The Novels of William Golding. Columbus, Ohio State University Press, 1970.

Baker, James R. William Golding: A Critical Study. New York, St. Martin's, 1965.

Biles, Jack I. Talk: Conversations with William Golding. Foreword by William Golding. New York, Harcourt Brace Jovanovich, 1970.

Davis, D. M. "Conversation with Golding," New Republic, CXLVIII (May 4, 1963), 28–30.

Dick, B. F. William Golding. New York, Twayne, 1967.

Elmen, Paul. William Golding. Contemporary Writers in Christian Perspective. Grand Rapids, Mich., William B. Eerdmans, 1967.

Green, Peter. "The World of William Golding," Review of English Literature, I (April, 1960), 62–72.

Hodson, Leighton. William Golding. Writers and Critics Series. Edinburgh, Oliver & Boyd, 1969.

Kermode, Frank. "William Golding," in Puzzles and Epiphanies. London, Routledge, 1962, pp. 198–213.

Kinkead-Weekes, Mark, and Ian Gregor. William Golding: A Critical Study. London, Faber & Faber, 1967; New York, Harcourt, Brace & World, 1968.

Moody, Philippa. A Critical Commentary on William Golding's "Lord of the Flies." Macmillan's Critical Commentaries. London, Macmillan, 1966.

Nelson, William, ed. William Golding's Lord of the Flies: A Source Book. New York, Odyssey Press, 1963.

Oldsey, B. S., and Stanley Weintraub. The Art of William Golding. New York, Harcourt, Brace & World, 1965.

Peter, John. "Fables of William Golding," Kenyon Review, XIX (Fall, 1957), 577–92.

Whitley, John S. Golding: Lord of the Flies. Studies in English Literature, No. 42. London, Edward Arnold, 1970.

LAWRENCE DURRELL

NOTE: The best bibliography of Durrell's work is that assembled by Robert A. Potter and Brooke Whiting in Lawrence Durrell: A Checklist (Los Angeles, 1961), which not only lists 311 Durrell items but frequently includes Durrell's own comments on them. It is supplemented by extensive additional material in Fraser and Friedman (see below). The following list is intended primarily to suggest the range of Durrell's work and the range of critical reaction. Most works by Durrell are available in a *variety of paperback editions. Unless indicated otherwise, Durrell's work is published by Faber & Faber in London and by E. P. Dutton in New York.*

Principal Works

"Acte," *Show*, I (December, 1961), 45–55, 95–105.

The Alexandria Quartet (one-volume edition). New York, 1962.

Art and Outrage: A Correspondence about Henry Miller (with Alfred Perlès). London, Putnam, 1959; New York, 1960.

Balthazar. London, 1958; New York, 1958.

Bitter Lemons. London, 1957; New York, 1958.

The Black Book. Paris, Obelisk Press, 1938. Second edition, Paris, Olympia Press, 1959; New York, 1960.

Blue Thirst. Berkeley, 1975.

Brassai. New York, Museum of Modern Art, 1968.

Cities, Plains, and People. London, 1946.

Clea. London, 1960; New York, 1960.

Collected Poems. London, 1960; New York, 1960.

The Dark Labyrinth (originally titled *Cefalu;* London, 1947). London, 1958; New York, 1962.

Esprit de Corps. London, 1957; New York, 1958.

The Ikons, and Other Poems. London, 1966; New York, 1967.

An Irish Faustus. London, 1963; New York, 1964.

Justine. London, 1957; New York, 1957.

A Key to Modern Poetry. London, P. Nevill, 1952; Norman, University of Oklahoma Press, 1952 (retitled A Key to Modern British Poetry).

Lawrence Durrell and Henry Miller: A Private Correspondence. Ed. George Wickes. New York, 1963.

Love Poems. Read by Lawrence Durrell. Spoken Arts Recording No. 818.

Monsieur. London, 1974; New York, Viking, 1975.

Mountolive. London, 1958; New York, 1959.

Nunquam. London, 1970; New York, 1971.

On Seeming to Presume. London, 1948.

Panic Spring. London, 1937; New York, Covici-Friede, 1937. (Published as "A Romance by Charles Norden.")

Pied Piper of Lovers. London, Cassell, 1935.

Plant-Magic Man. Berkeley, 1973.

Pope Joan. Translated from the Greek of Emmanuel Royidis. London, D. Verschoyle, 1954. Revised edition, London, A. Deutsch, 1960; New York, 1961.

A Private Country. London, 1943.

Prospero's Cell. London, 1945; New York, 1960 (issued with *Reflections on a Marine Venus*).
The Red Limbo Lingo: A Poetry Notebook. London, 1971; New York, 1971.
Reflections on a Marine Venus. London, 1953; New York, 1960 (issued with *Prospero's Cell*).
Sappho. London, 1950; New York, 1958.
Spirit of Place (with Alan G. Thomas). London, 1969; New York, 1969.
Stiff Upper Lip. London, 1958; New York, 1959.
The Tree of Idleness. London, 1955.
Tunc. London, 1968; New York, 1968.
Vega and Other Poems. London, 1973; Woodstock, N.Y., Overlook Press, 1973.
White Eagles over Serbia. London, 1957; New York, Criterion, 1957. (An abridgment, edited by G. A. Verdin, was published in London, 1961.)

Critical Works and Commentary

Aldington, Richard. "Lawrence Durrell," in Selected Writings, 1928–1960. Carbondale, Southern Illinois University Press, 1970, pp. 121–29.
Baldanza, F. "Lawrence Durrell's 'Word Continuum,'" *Critique*, IV (Spring-Summer, 1961), 3–17.
Beja, Morris. "Afterword: Contemporaries," in Epiphany in the Modern Novel. Seattle, University of Washington Press, 1971, pp. 211–33.
Cate, C. "Lawrence Durrell," *Atlantic*, CCVIII (December, 1961), 63–69.
Chapman, R. T. "Dead or Just Pretending? Reality in *The Alexandria Quartet*," *Centennial Review*, XVI, 408–18.
Creed, Walter G. "Pieces of the Puzzle: The Multiple-Narrative Structure of *The Alexandria Quartet*," *Mosaic*, VI, No. 2, 19–35.
Edel, Leon. The Modern Psychological Novel, pp. 185–91. New York, Grosset and Dunlap, 1964.
Flint, R. W. "A Major Novelist," *Commentary*, XXVIII (April, 1959), 353–56.
Fraser, G. S. Lawrence Durrell: A Critical Study. New York, Dutton, 1968; revised edition, London, Faber & Faber, 1973.
Freiberg, L. B. "Durrell's Dissonant Quartet," in Contemporary British Novelists. Ed. Charles Shapiro. Carbondale, Southern Illinois University Press, 1965, pp. 16–35.
Friedman, Alan W. Lawrence Durrell and the Alexandria Quartet: Art for Love's Sake. Norman, University of Oklahoma Press, 1970.

Gindin, J. J. "Some Current Fads," in Postwar British Fiction: New Accents and Attitudes. Berkeley, University of California Press, 1962, pp. 207–25.

Gordon, A. "Time, Space, and Eros: The Alexandria Quartet Rehearsed," in Six Contemporary Novels. Austin, University of Texas Press, 1962, pp. 6–21.

Highet, G. "The Alexandrians of Lawrence Durrell," Horizon, II (March, 1960), 113–18.

Karl, Frederick. "Lawrence Durrell: Physical and Metaphysical Love," in The Contemporary English Novel. New York, Farrar, Straus, and Cudahy, 1962, pp. 40–61.

Kermode, Frank. "Durrell and Others," in Puzzles and Epiphanies. New York, Chilmark Press, 1962, pp. 214–27.

Littlejohn, David. Interruptions. New York, Grossman, 1970, pp. 73–90.

Maclay, Joanna H. "The Interpreter and Modern Fiction: Problems of Point of View and Structural Tentativeness," in Studies in Interpretation. Eds. E. Doyle and V. Floyd. Amsterdam, Rodopi, 1972, pp. 115–69.

Miller, Henry. The Colossus of Maroussi. New York, New Directions, 1941.

Mitchell, Julian, and Gene Andrewski. "Lawrence Durrell" (interview), in Writers at Work: The Paris Review Interviews, Second Series. New York, Viking, 1963, pp. 257–82.

Perlès, Alfred. My Friend Lawrence Durrell. Northwood, Scorpion Press, 1961.

Proser, M. "Darley's Dilemma," Critique, IV (Spring-Summer, 1961), 18–28.

Rexroth, Kenneth. "Lawrence Durrell," in Assays. New York, New Directions, 1962, pp. 118–30.

Scholes, Robert. The Fabulators. New York, Oxford University Press, 1967, pp. 17–28.

Wedin, Warren. "The Artist as Narrator in The Alexandria Quartet," Twentieth Century Literature, XVIII, 175–80.

Weigel, John A. Lawrence Durrell. New York, Twayne, 1965.

The World of Lawrence Durrell. Ed. Harry T. Moore. Carbondale, Southern Illinois University Press, 1962. Includes, among others, the following items: "A Note on Lawrence Durrell," by Richard Aldington; "Lawrence Durrell: The Baroque Novel," by George Steiner; "The Quartet: Two Reviews," by Lionel Trilling; "The Durrell of The Black Book Days," by Henry Miller; "Nougat for the Old Bitch," by Hayden Carruth; "Lawrence Durrell Answers a Few Questions" (interview); "The Kneller Tape (Hamburg)" (interview); "Durrell's

Alexandrian Series," by Bonamy Dobrée; and "Letters from Lawrence Durrell" (to Jean Fanchette).
Young, Kenneth. "A Dialogue with Durrell" (interview), *Encounter*, XIII (December, 1959), 61–68.

IRIS MURDOCH

NOTE: *The novels of Iris Murdoch have all been published by Chatto and Windus in London and by the Viking Press in New York. For a more comprehensive bibliography, see Peter Wolfe's* The Disciplined Heart.

Principal Works

"Thinking and Language," *Proceedings of the Aristotelian Society*, Supplement XXV (1951), 25.
"Nostalgia for the Particular," *Proceedings of the Aristotelian Society*, LII (1951–52), 243.
"The Existentialist Political Myth," *Socratic*, V (1952), 52.
Sartre, Romantic Rationalist. Cambridge, Bowes and Bowes; New Haven, Yale University Press, 1953.
Under the Net. 1954.
The Flight from the Enchanter. 1956.
"Vision and Choice in Morality," *Proceedings of the Aristotelian Society*, Supplement XXX (1956), 32.
"Knowing the Void" [on Simone Weil], *Spectator*, CXCVII (Nov. 2, 1956), 613.
The Sandcastle. 1957.
The Nature of Metaphysics. Ed. D. F. Pears. London, Macmillan, 1957. Contains Iris Murdoch's essay "Metaphysics and Ethics."
The Bell. 1958.
"The Sublime and the Good," *Chicago Review*, XIII (Autumn, 1959), 42.
"A House of Theory," *Partisan Review*, XXVI (Winter, 1959), 17.
"The Sublime and the Beautiful Revisited," *Yale Review*, XLIX (December, 1959), 247.
"Against Dryness: A Polemical Sketch," *Encounter*, XVI (January, 1961), 16.
A Severed Head. 1961.
An Unofficial Rose. 1962.
The Unicorn. 1963.

The Italian Girl. 1964.
"The Idea of Perfection," *Yale Review*, LIII (March, 1964), 342.
The Red and the Green. 1965.
The Time of the Angels. 1966.
Study Group on Foundations of Cultural Unity, Meeting at Bowdoin College, Maine, August, 1966. Paper delivered by Iris Murdoch, "On 'God' and 'Good.'"
The Nice and the Good. 1968.
Bruno's Dream. 1969.
A Fairly Honourable Defeat. 1970.
The Sovereignty of Good. London, Routledge and Kegan Paul, 1970.
An Accidental Man. 1971.
The Black Prince. 1973.
The Three Arrows and The Servant in the Snow. 1973.
The Sacred and Profane Love Machine. 1974.

Critical Works and Commentary

Barrows, John. "Living Writers—7, Iris Murdoch," *John O'London's*, IV (May 4, 1961), 498.
Bradbury, Malcolm. "Iris Murdoch's *Under the Net*," *Critical Quarterly*, IV (Spring, 1962), 47.
Byatt, A. S. Degrees of Freedom. London, Chatto and Windus; New York, Barnes and Noble, 1965.
German, Howard. "The Range of Allusions in the Novels of Iris Murdoch," *Journal of Modern Literature*, II (1971), 57–85.
Gindin, James. Postwar British Fiction. Berkeley, University of California Press, 1961.
Haverwas, Stanley. "The Significance of Vision: Toward an Aesthetic Ethic," *Studies in Religion*, II (1972), 36–49.
Hobson, Harold. "Lunch with Iris Murdoch," *Sunday Times* [London], March 11, 1962, p. 28.
Hoffman, F. J. "Iris Murdoch: The Reality of Persons," *Critique*, VII (1964), 48.
—— "The Miracle of Contingency: The Novels of Iris Murdoch," *Shenandoah*, XVII (1965), No. 1, 49–56.
Kauffman, R. J. "The Progress of Iris Murdoch," *Nation*, CLXXXVIII (March 21, 1959), 255.
Kermode, Frank. "The House of Fiction," *Partisan Review*, XXX (Spring, 1963), 62.
Kogan, Pauline. "Beyond Solipsism to Irrationalism: A Study of Iris Murdoch's Novels," *Literature and Ideology*, II (1969), 47–69.

Kriegel, Leonard. "Everybody Through the Looking Glass," in Contemporary British Novelists. Ed. Charles Shapiro. Carbondale, Southern Illinois University Press, 1965.

McCabe, Bernard. "The Guises of Love," *Commonweal*, LXXXIII (Dec. 3, 1965), 270.

Maes-Jelinek, Hena. "A House for Free Characters," *Revue des langues vivantes*, XXIX (1963), 45.

Majdiak, Daniel. "Romanticism in the Aesthetics of Iris Murdoch," *Texas Studies in Literature and Language*, IV (1972), 359-75.

Martz, Louis L. "Iris Murdoch: The London Novels," in Twentieth Century Literature in Retrospect. Ed. Reuben Brower. Cambridge, Mass., Harvard University Press, 1971.

Modern Fiction Studies, XV (1969), No. 3. (Iris Murdoch special number. Contains essays on Murdoch by Ann Culley, Linda Kuehl, Howard German, Raymond T. Porter, Alice P. Kenney, Peter Kemp, Frank Baldanza, William F. Hall, William M. Murray, and a checklist of Murdoch criticism by Ann Culley and John Feaster.)

Morrel, Ray. "Iris Murdoch: The Early Novels," *Critical Quarterly*, IX (1967), 272-82.

"Observer Profile: Iris Murdoch," *Observer*, June 17, 1962, p. 23.

O'Connor, William Van. The New University Wits. Carbondale, Southern Illinois University Press, 1963.

Rose, W. K. "An Interview with Iris Murdoch," *Shenandoah*, XIX (1968), No. 2, 3-22.

Souvage, Jacques. "The Novels of Iris Murdoch," *Studia Germanica Gandensia*, IV (1962), 225.

—— "Symbol as Narrative Device," *English Studies* [Netherlands], XLIII (April, 1962), 81.

Vickery, John B. "The Dilemmas of Language: Sartre's *La nausée* and Iris Murdoch's *Under the Net*," *Journal of Narrative Technique*, I (1971), 69-76.

Wall, Stephen. "The Bell in *The Bell*," *Essays in Criticism*, XIII (July 1963), 265.

Weatherhead, A. Kingsley. "Backgrounds with Figures in Iris Murdoch," *Texas Studies in Literature and Language*, X (1969), 635-48.

Whiteside, George. "The Novels of Iris Murdoch," *Critique*, VII (1964), 27.

Widmann, R. L. "Murdoch's *Under the Net*: Theory and Practice of Fiction," *Critique*, X (1968), No. 1, 5-16.

Wolfe, Peter. The Disciplined Heart. Columbia, University of Missouri Press, 1966.

The Contributors

David Lodge is Reader in English Literature at the University of Birmingham. He is the author of *Language of Fiction, The Novelist at the Crossroads,* and several novels.

Robert Gorham Davis is Professor of English at Columbia University. He is the author of *John Dos Passos* (in the University of Minnesota series on American writers) and is the editor of *Ten Modern Masters* and *Ten Masters of the Modern Essay.* He is also widely known for his book reviews, which appear in the nation's leading media.

Daniel B. Dodson is Professor of English at Columbia University. He is the author of *The Man Who Ran Away.*

Samuel Hynes is Professor of English at Northwestern University. He is the author of *The Pattern of Hardy's Poetry, The Edwardian Turn of Mind,* and *Edwardian Occasions.*

John Unterecker is Professor of English at the University of Hawaii. He is the author of *A Reader's Guide to William*

Butler Yeats and *Voyager: A Life of Hart Crane* and the editor of *Approaches to the Twentieth-Century Novel* and *Yeats: A Collection of Critical Essays.*

Rubin Rabinovitz is Associate Professor of English at the University of Colorado. He is the author of *The Reaction Against Experiment in the English Novel, 1950–1960.*

Index

Adler, Alfred, 246
Aesop, 168, 169
Aiken, Conrad, 116, 119, 120; *Blue Voyage*, 119, 120
Amis, Kingsley, 53, 59, 199, 282
Aragon, Louis, 61
Atkins, John, 8
Augustine, Saint, 225
Austen, J. L., 330
Austen, Jane, 291; *Northanger Abbey*, 308

Ballantyne, R. M.: *Coral Island*, 169-71, 172, 179, 180
Balzac, Honoré de, 65, 108; *The Human Comedy*, 65
Barbusse, Henri, 61
Baudelaire, Charles, 237; T. S. Eliot on, 13, 20, 30
Bayley, John, 272, 289, 292; *The Character of Love*, 292
Beauvoir, Simone de: *The Mandarins*, 292
Beckett, Samuel, 113; *Murphy*, 282-83
Bede, Saint, 225
Bennett, Arnold, ix

Bergson, Henri, 110, 241-42
Bernanos, Georges, 33, 61
Birney, Earle, 121, 149
Blake, William, 225
Bloy, Léon, 33
Bohr, Niels, 57
Bowen, Elizabeth, 4
Bowen, Marjorie: *The Viper of Milan*, 7, 53
Breit, Harvey, 150
Brontë, Charlotte, ix
Brontë, Emily: *Wuthering Heights*, 308
Brontës, the, 225, 308
Browne, Sir Thomas, 10
Buber, Martin, 275, 329
Buchan, John: *The Power House*, 13
Bunyan, John: *Grace Abounding to the Chief of Sinners*, 137
Burnett, Whit, 121
Burroughs, William, 113
Byatt, A. S.: *Degrees of Freedom*, 279, 297

Cabbala, the, 123–24, 141
Cambridge University, 57, 59, 116, 272, 281

Camus, Albert, 61, 169; *La Chute,* 163; *The Stranger,* 292
Cary, Joyce, 199
Cavafy, Constantine, 220, 265
Chardin, Teilhard de, 44, 55; *The Phenomenon of Man,* 44
City Lights Books, 149
Claudel, Paul, 265
Cocteau, Jean, 130
Coleridge, Samuel Taylor, 151, 152
Conrad, Joseph, viii, 15, 18, 119, 143; *Chance,* 152; *Lord Jim,* 139; *The Nigger of the Narcissus,* 151; "Typhoon," 151; *Under Western Eyes,* 15
Crane, Hart, 149

Dante Alighieri, 125, 130, 143, 225; *Divine Comedy,* 116, 151, 156, 157-58, 286
Darwin, Charles, 241
Day, Douglas, 115, 118, 158-59
Descartes, René, 194, 195, 225, 273-76
Dirac, Paul, 57
Disraeli, Benjamin, 59
Dos Passos, John, 61; *U.S.A.,* 111
Dostoevsky, Feodor, 164, 294, 331; *The Possessed,* 106
Dreiser, Theodore, 61
Du Maurier, Daphne, ix
Durrell, Gerald, 226, 232
Durrell, Lawrence, viii, 219-69; and Henry Miller, 220, 221-22, 226, 227, 228, 230-32, 233, 234, 242, 258, 266, 267; modern physical theory in, 221, 237-43, 246, 258, 268; life of, 222-36; "heraldic universe" in, 222-25, 234-36, 243, 246-50, 252-57, 266-69; literary technique of, 228, 229, 233-34,
235, 238-43, 252-53, 258-69; authorial voice of, 229, 259, 265-69; image of reality in, 237-43, 245-50, 258, 261, 268-69
——"Alexandria," 224; *The Alexandria Quartet,* ix, 220, 221, 234, 235, 236, 237, 238, 240, 242, 244, 248, 251, 254, 257-69; "A Ballad of the Good Lord Nelson," 220; *Balthazar,* 240, 260, 262, 264; *Bitter Lemons,* 220, 234, 236; *The Black Book,* 220, 225, 227, 229, 230-31, 235, 238, 239, 242-48, 249, 250, 251, 252, 263; "Cities, Plains and People," 222, 225, 243; *Clea,* 235, 240, 251, 260, 262-64; *Cleopatra* (film script), 220; *The Dark Labyrinth,* 220, 223, 248, 263; *Esprit de Corps,* 220; *An Irish Faustus,* 223, 253-57, 266; *Justine,* 236, 240, 259, 260, 262, 265, 266; *A Key to Modern British Poetry,* 220, 237-38, 241-42, 246, 249; *Monsieur,* 221, 238, 244, 248, 250, 261; *Mountolive,* 240, 261, 262; *Nunquam,* 221, 224, 244, 251, 252; *Panic Spring,* 228, 230; *Pied Piper of Lovers,* 228; *Prospero's Cell,* 220, 233-34; "The Reckoning," 269; *Reflections on a Marine Venus,* 220, 234; *Sappho,* 224; "A Soliloquy of Hamlet," 220, 252-53; *Spirit of Place,* 220; *Stiff Upper Lip,* 220; *Tunc,* 221, 244, 251; *White Eagles over Serbia,* 220, 223, 248

Eddington, Sir Arthur Stanley, 237
Einstein, Albert, 57, 237, 240-42
Eliot, George, 291

Eliot, T. S., 13, 20, 30, 62, 83, 119, 120; *Four Quartets,* 241; "Geron-tion," 238; "The Love Song of J. Alfred Prufrock," 152; *The Waste Land,* 152, 250
English analytical philosophy, 275-77, 279, 280, 301
Epstein, Perle: *The Private Lab-yrinth of Malcolm Lowry,* 123-24
Erskine, Albert, 162
Esprit, L', 121
Existential thought, 45, 273-75, 276-77, 278, 280, 305, 314; German, 314-15

Faber and Faber, 228, 230-31
Faulkner, William: *Absalom, Absalom!,* 261
Fitzgerald, F. Scott: *Tender Is the Night,* 118
Fleming, Ian: *To Russia with Love,* 53
Forster, E. M., viii; *The Art of the Novel,* 106
Freud, Sigmund, 227, 245-46, 300, 302-3, 310; "The Infantile Genital Organization," 302; "Medusa's Head," 302

Gabrial, Jan (Mrs. Malcolm Lowry), 116-17
Genet, Jean, 113
Gide, André, 151, 238; *The Counterfeiters,* 261
Gilbert, Stuart, 117
Goethe, Johann Wolfgang von, 137; *Faust,* 142
Golding, William, viii, ix, 165-218; stated purpose of his writings, 165-69, 171, 181-82, 188, 197-98, 201, 216-18; form and meaning in, 166-71, 175-76, 177, 180, 187-89, 198-99, 201, 206-7, 208, 210-11, 212-13; moral issues in, 166, 168-69, 170-71, 175, 179-80, 181-82, 184, 186-87, 197-98, 200, 202-6, 211, 212, 214-18; use of literary conventions in, 169-71, 180, 184, 188-89, 191-92; critical interpretations of, 171-72, 176-77, 179-80, 193, 207; symbolic action in, 172-78, 189, 191, 192-93, 195-98, 208-11, 213-14
——"The Brass Butterfly," 216, 217; "Clonk Clonk," 217; "The Crest of the Wave," 218; "Egypt from My Inside," 216; "Envoy Extra-ordinary," 216, 217; *Free Fall,* 199-207, 211, 212; *The Inheritors,* 180-88, 189, 191, 198, 217; *Lord of the Flies,* 166, 169-80, 186, 188-89, 191, 192, 198, 205, 215; *Pincher Martin,* 166, 188-98, 200, 204, 205, 209, 211, 215; *The Pyramid,* 214-16; *The Scorpion God,* 216-17; *The Spire,* 207-14
Greene, C. H., 5
Greene, Graham, vii, viii, ix, 1-56; common themes in, ix, 2, 7-9, 11, 12, 13-15, 25, 26, 46-47, 49-51; Catholic doctrine in, 1-5, 17, 19, 21, 29, 32-37, 40-41, 44-45, 47, 55-56; literary reputation of, 1-5, 19, 41, 48; style of, 3, 15-16, 17, 22-24, 25, 33-34, 39, 40, 50-51, 53, 55-56; authorial voice in, 3, 24, 30, 42, 56; life of, 5-7, 28, 39, 49-50; irony in, 9-10, 11, 16, 26-27, 36, 42-43, 46-47; usage of "key words" in, 15-16, 18, 27, 29, 36, 49
——*Babbling April,* 5; *Brighton*

Greene, Graham (*Continued*)
Rock, 13, 20-23, 25; *A Burnt-Out Case*, 2, 41-45, 55; *Collected Essays*, 48; *Collected Short Stories*, 48; *The Comedians*, 45-48, 52; *The Complaisant Lover*, 40, 41; *The Confidential Agent*, 15-17; *The End of the Affair*, 28, 33-37, 40, 51; *England Made Me*, 18-19; *A Gun for Sale*, 13-15, 22; *The Heart of the Matter*, 28-34, 40, 52; *The Honorary Consul*, 48, 50-51, 54-56; *In Search of a Character*, 42; *It's a Battlefield*, 8, 18; *Journey Without Maps*, 9, 17, 19-20, 46; *The Lawless Roads*, 6, 17, 24, 26-27; *The Living Room*, 40; *Lord Rochester's Monkey*, 49; *Loser Takes All*, 41; *The Lost Childhood*, 7; *The Man Within*, 5, 10-11, 12; *The Ministry of Fear*, 10, 28; *The Name of Action*, 11; *Our Man in Havana*, 41, 45; *The Potting Shed*, 40, 41; *The Power and the Glory*, 4, 6, 23, 24-28; *The Quiet American*, 8, 37-40, 45; "The Revolver in the Corner Cupboard," 7; *Rumour at Nightfall*, 11; *A Sort of Life*, 49-50; *Stamboul Train*, 11-13, 50; *The Third Man*, 2; *Travels with My Aunt*, 48, 51-54; *Why Do I Write?*, 4
Groddeck, Georg: *The Book of the It*, 248-49
Gustaffson, Ralph, 162

Hampshire, Stuart, 301, 302, 330
Hardy, Thomas, 56, 308
Hegel, Georg, 273, 329; *Phenomenology of Mind*, 274

Heidegger, Martin, 314-15; *Sein und Zeit*, 314
Hemingway, Ernest, 61
Hesse, Hermann, 164
Homer, 225, 292; *Iliad*, 285
Huxley, Aldous, 60
Huysmans, Joris Karl, 33

Isherwood, Christopher: *Mr. Norris Changes Trains*, 82

Jackson, Charles: *The Lost Weekend*, 161-62
James, Henry, 3, 8, 62, 64, 79, 228
Jerome, Saint, 225
Johnson, Pamela Hansford, 101-2; *On Iniquity*, 102
Jonathan Cape, 117, 118, 121, 122, 123, 144, 161
Joyce, James, viii, 117, 123, 152, 228, 238, 294; *A Portrait of the Artist as a Young Man*, 229; *Ulysses*, viii, 117, 123-25, 148, 241
Jung, Carl Gustav, 246, 247

Kafka, Franz, 119, 152, 169, 189
Kahane, Jack, 231
Kant, Immanuel, 292-93, 300, 305, 329
Kapitza, Peter, 57
Keats, John, 225
Kermode, Frank, 2, 35, 304
Kierkegaard, Sören, 329
Koestler, Arthur, 89, 97

La Fontaine, Jean de, 168
Lawrence, D. H., viii, 63, 83, 109, 166, 225, 265
Leavis, F. R., 63-64, 293
Le Fanu, Sheridan: "Carmilla," 308
León, Moses de: *Zohar*, 115

Lewis, Wyndham, 58, 62; *Time and Western Man*, 242
Lowry, Malcolm, viii, ix, 115-64; life of, 115-19, 147, 151, 156-57, 162; use of *Divine Comedy*, 116, 125, 130, 143, 151, 156-58; short stories of, 118, 139, 150-58; unfinished works of, 118, 158-61; fictional world of, 119, 120-21, 146, 149, 163; narrative technique of, 119, 121, 122, 124-25, 148-49, 152, 160-62; author's *persona* in works of, 119, 146, 150, 151, 159, 160-61; symbolism in, 123-24, 129-30, 131-32, 135, 140-48; poetry of, 149-50
——"The Bravest Boat," 152-53; *Dark as the Grave Wherein My Friend Is Laid*, 144, 158-60; "Elephant and Colosseum," 154-55; "Epitaph," 150; *Eridanus*, 158; "The Forest Path to the Spring," 151, 156-58; "Gin and Goldenrod," 155-56; *Hear Us O Lord from Heaven Thy Dwelling Place*, 118, 139, 150-58; *In Ballast to the White Sea*, 116, 117; *La Mordida*, 158; *Lunar Caustic*, 121-23; *October Ferry to Gabriola*, 118, 158, 162-63; "The Present Estate of Pompeii," 155; *Selected Poems of Malcolm Lowry*, 149-50; "Strange Comfort Afforded by the Profession," 153-54; "Through the Panama," 151-52; *Ultramarine*, 119-21, 122, 147; *Under the Volcano*, viii, 116, 117, 118, 120, 121, 123-49, 150, 151, 156, 158, 159, 160, 161, 163-64
Lowry, Margerie, 115, 116-18, 151, 156-57, 160, 161, 162; editor of

Malcolm Lowry's works, 121, 150, 159
Luxemburg, Rosa, 287

Mann, Thomas, 61
Marcel, Gabriel, 275, 329; *The Mystery of Being*, 329-30
Marlowe, Christopher: *Dr. Faustus*, 22, 125, 143, 147, 253-55
Matson, Harold, 117, 162
Maugham, Somerset: *Of Human Bondage*, 74
Mauriac, François, 21, 23, 33
Melville, Herman, 122, 152
Miller, Henry, 109, 113; and Lawrence Durrell, 220, 221-22, 226, 227, 228, 230-32, 233, 234, 242, 258, 266-67; *Max and the White Phagocytes*, 231; *Tropic of Cancer*, 228-29
Modernism, literary, viii-x
Muggeridge, Malcolm, 108
Murdoch, Iris, viii, ix, 271-332; ethical concerns of, 271, 274-76, 287-88, 292-93, 296-97, 301-2, 316, 322; life of, 272, 277-78, 289, 295; and the existentialists, 273-75, 277, 278-79, 280, 297, 314-15; and solipsism, 274-76, 278, 289, 297, 301, 306, 310-11, 318, 330-31; philosophical position of, 274-75, 328-31; and the linguistic analysts, 275-76, 279-80, 297, 314, 316, 317, 329-30; political views of, 276-77, 313; common themes in, 283, 285-86, 289, 296-97, 300-301, 304-7, 308-10, 320; aesthetic theory of, 291-94, 299, 300; treatment of religion in, 294-95, 299, 313-16, 320-21
——*An Accidental Man*, 321-22;

Murdoch, Iris (*Continued*)
  The Bell, 295-300, 313; *The Black
  Prince*, 322-24; *Bruno's Dream*,
  318-19; *A Fairly Honourable
  Defeat*, 319-21; *The Flight from
  the Enchanter*, 283-90, 294, 297,
  310, 320, 325; *The Italian Girl*,
  310-11; *The Nice and the Good*,
  316-18; *The Red and the Green*,
  272, 311-13; *The Sacred and Pro-
  fane Love Machine*, 326-28; *The
  Sandcastle*, 289-94, 304, 307, 316,
  326, 327, 331; *Sartre, Romantic
  Rationalist*, 273, 277, 278; *The
  Servants and the Snow*, 324-26; *A
  Severed Head*, 300-304, 310, 331;
  The Sovereignty of Good, 276;
  "The Sublime and the Beautiful
  Revisited," 291-93; "The Sub-
  lime and the Good," 305; *The
  Three Arrows*, 324, 326; *The Time
  of the Angels*, 313-16; *Under the
  Net*, 277-83, 288, 293, 294, 331-32;
  The Unicorn, 307-10; *An Unoffi-
  cial Rose*, 304-7, 310, 316
Myers, Nancy, 227, 231, 236

Nature, 60
New Statesman, 48
Nietzsche, Friedrich Wilhelm, 314
Nin, Anaïs: *Winter of Artifice*, 231
Norden, Charles (pseud. Lawrence
  Durrell), 228, 230

Obelisk Press, 231
O'Casey, Sean, 61
O'Neill, Eugene, 119, 121, 152;
  "The Hairy Ape," 121
Orwell, George, 4, 89, 97; *Inside the
  Whale*, 4

Osborne, John, 59
Oxford University, 5, 272, 275, 277

Paris Review, 121
Pears, D. F., 279
Péguy, Charles, 21, 33
Perlès, Alfred, 220, 231
Plato, 242, 293, 295, 315, 320, 329
Poe, Edgar Allan, 152, 189
Pound, Ezra, 58, 83
Pritchett, V. S., 4, 172
Proust, Marcel, 79, 110-11, 241, 242,
  294

Queneau, Raymond: *Le Chiendent*,
  282; *Pierrot mon ami*, 282-83

Rabi, I. I., 67, 95
Reynal and Hitchcock, 118
Rilke, Rainer Maria, 149; *Duinese
  Elegies*, 241
Roman fleuve, 65, 240
Royidis, Emmanuel: *Pope Joan*, 220
Rutherford, Ernest, 57

Sartre, Jean-Paul, 61, 89; and Iris
  Murdoch, 273-75, 277, 278-79,
  280, 307, 329; *The Age of Reason*,
  278; *Huis-Clos*, 275; *Nausea*,
  278-79
Scientific American, 60
Shakespeare, William, 22, 119, 120,
  225, 285, 292; *Hamlet*, 252-53
Silone, Ignazio, 61
Sinclair, Upton, 98
Snow, C. P., ix-x, 57-114; formal
  conservatism of, ix-x, 113; on science, 57-59, 60, 67, 70, 71, 78,
  86-87, 109; political issues in,
  57-59, 60-61, 83, 88-89, 90-91, 97,
  108-9, 113-14; life of, 59, 66, 71,

99-100; authorial voice in, 62-63, 65, 81, 88-89, 99, 105, 112-13; narrative technique of, 63-65, 73, 79, 85, 101-2, 106-7, 109-14; early fiction of, 71-72
——*The Affair*, 66, 69, 92-94; *The Conscience of the Rich*, 66, 74, 87-89; *Corridors of Power*, 66, 90, 94-100, 109; *Death under Sail*, 71-72; *Homecoming*, 66, 76-79; *In Their Wisdom*, 67, 104-5, 106-8; *Last Things*, 65, 66-67, 101, 103-4, 105, 106; *The Light and the Dark*, 66, 81-84, 89; *The Malcontents*, 67, 104-6; *The Masters*, 61-62, 66, 69, 90-92, 94, 95, 111, 112; *New Lives for Old*, 71; *The New Men*, 66, 84-87, 89, 94; *Science and Government*, 58; *The Search*, 60, 62, 64-71, 72; *The Sleep of Reason*, 66-67, 100-103, 105; "Strangers and Brothers" series, 61-62, 64-67, 101-2, 104-5; *Strangers and Brothers*, 65, 66, 72, 79-81, 89; *Time of Hope*, 66, 72-76, 84; "The Two Cultures," 57, 59, 60, 61, 62, 63, 67
Sophocles: *Antigone*, 137
Souvage, Jacques, 302
Spender, Stephen, 61
Steinbeck, John, 61
Story, 121
Stratford, Philip: "Unlocking the Potting Shed," 9
Sunday Telegraph, 102

Thomas, Alan, 229
Thomas, Dylan, 220
Thompson, Francis, 21

Times (London), 5, 110
Tolstoy, Leo, 110, 292, 294, 327, 331
Trollope, Anthony, 64-65, 214; his Barsetshire novels, 64, 65; *The Last Chronicle of Barset*, 94; *The Warden*, 64

"Upstairs, Downstairs," 107

Villa Suerat Library, 231

Wain, John, 282
Waugh, Evelyn, vii
Weil, Simone, 275, 283-85, 287-88, 295, 305, 309, 329; *Gravity and Grace*, 284, 288, 309; *The Need for Roots*, 284; *Oppression and Liberty*, 287
Wells, H. G., 59, 62, 214, 217-18; and William Golding, 180-82, 185, 188; *The New Machiavelli*, 62; *Outline of History*, 180-82; *Tono Bungay*, 62
Whitehead, Alfred North, 237
Wittgenstein, Ludwig, 280-82; *Tractatus Logico-philosophicus*, 280-81
Wolfe, Thomas, 152
Woolf, Virginia, viii, 238; *To the Lighthouse*, 162
Wordsworth, William, 156-57; *The Prelude*, 157

Yeats, William Butler, 58, 83, 149, 206, 243
Young, Kenneth, 242

Zarin, Eve, 250
Zola, Émile: *Germinal*, 111